Great Railroad Tunnels
of North America

Great Railroad Tunnels of North America

William Lowell Putnam

McFarland & Company, Inc., Publishers
Jefferson, North Carolina, and London

ALSO BY WILLIAM LOWELL PUTNAM
AND FROM MCFARLAND

Percival Lowell's Big Red Car: The Tale of an Astronomer and a 1911 Stevens-Duryea (2002)

The Kaiser's Merchant Ships in World War I (2001)

John Peter Zenger and the Fundamental Freedom (1997)

***Frontispiece:* The author (seen here outside the Johnson Canyon tunnel) visited many railroad tunnels in the course of researching and writing this book (Graham A.B. Vickowski).**

LIBRARY OF CONGRESS CATALOGUING-IN-PUBLICATION DATA

Putnam, William Lowell.
Great railroad tunnels of North America /
William Lowell Putnam
p. cm.
Includes bibliographical references and index.

ISBN 978-0-7864-5951-3
softcover : 50# alkaline paper ♾

1. Railroad tunnels — North America.
2. Railroads — Design and construction — History. I. Title.
TF230.P96 2011 385.3'12 — dc23 2011013573

BRITISH LIBRARY CATALOGUING DATA ARE AVAILABLE

Front cover image: The first locomotive to pass through the Hoosac Tunnel emerges at the west end of the tunnel (Graham A.B. Vickowski)

Manufactured in the United States of America

McFarland & Company, Inc., Publishers
Box 611, Jefferson, North Carolina 28640
www.mcfarlandpub.com

Fondly to the late **Carl Fiebelkorn**
of the United States Forest Service
and Company L of the 87th Mountain Infantry,
who advised me not to go into that railroad tunnel,
but had the grace to let me run out of it ahead of him

Contents

Preface

THIS WORK WAS STARTED AS A report and update on the (in)famous Hoosac Tunnel, which is not far from where this aging wordsmith grew up in Springfield, Massachusetts. Along the way, it became clear to the publisher that "A Great Bore" (which was what I had titled my offering relative to the Hoosac Tunnel) was insufficient for their purposes, but that my research might more profitably be broadened to include other tunnels. However, the surface layers of planet Earth are now laced with all sorts of tunnels, and there has to be some limit on everything. So, after a pleasant debate, we settled on including histories of the major standard-gauge railroad bores under North America's mountains.

That soon led us to a debate as to what constituted North America — was Hispanic Mexico in Central America, NAFTA notwithstanding? So we undertook to ignore the local drug wars and learn what we could about Mexican railroad *tunéls* and particularly some of the 86 such under the Tumahumara Range between Topolobambo Bay and Chihuahua.

Discussing any such hole in the earth tends to lead the curious mind down a variety of literal and figurative sidetracks, as will be noted in chapter 3, where we include a divergence to the predecessor and contemporary tunnels to the Blue Ridge in the eastern United States. Because the Hoosac was such a landmark venture and was bored in two sufficiently distinct phases, we dwell on it at greater length. This then led us into a further diversion in chapter 5 back to the Frejus (Mont Cenis) Tunnel in the Graian Alps. In chapter 6 we break our own rule about standard-gauge to include a brief discussion of the historic Alpine Tunnel that was used by two of the formerly ubiquitous narrow-gauge rail lines of Colorado. Happily, there are no further diversions to be found thereafter. The Great Northern Railroad had only one main line, but it ultimately utilized two major bores, and since 1988 the Canadian Pacific Railway (CPR) has had four notable tunnels on its main line. Though some century and a quarter after naming it, the CPR's proprietors have yet to get around to boring anything through the minor natural edifice east of Banff that they dubbed, and everyone still calls, "Tunnel Mountain."

A reader might also wonder why someone who has been so deeply associated with mountaineering and its literature should wander off in his dotage to a discussion of the holes that railroads have bored through mountains, but the explanation of how I got there is simple. The early literature of mountaineering is in many ways and places intimately connected with that of exploration; and railroad (rail*way* in Canada) exploration many times was responsible for the accurate filling of significant gaps in geographic lore — most often in mountainous terrain. Following from an acceptance of that obvious fact, it is clear that railroads, and particularly reports on their location and construction, have thus often become primary sources for the study of early North American mountaineering and exploratory ventures. One such venture was the lengthy *tour de force* by dogsled undertaken by the redoubtable surveyors Edward Jarvis and Charles Hanington through the northern Canadian Rockies in the winter of 1874, all the gruesome details of which were duly enumerated in Sir Sandford Fleming's 1876 *Report to the Canadian Parliament*.

So here we are — B-o-o-o-a-r-d!

* * *

In the course of my career in alpinism, I have visited all of the major sites mentioned herein — climbed on the peaks above Kicking Horse and Rogers Passes, skied on the slopes near Stevens and Hagerman Passes, and even been in the cab of a CPR Royal Hudson 4-6-4 (#2816) going through the Connaught Tunnel — but I cannot claim an intimate personal acquaintance with the interiors of all the bores that are mentioned below. Most of them are presently closed to human visitation by continued usage, external rock slides, responsibility-fearing bureaucrats and/or serious cave-ins. Indeed, though brought up in relative proximity, I have never been deep inside the one tunnel that started this all off, for its present owners are not particularly inviting.

However, I can claim considerable familiarity with a certain lesser tunnel on the Denver & Rio Grande Western's then main line near Minturn, Colorado. When using the tracks as a shortcut on an overnight walk (mostly along U.S. 24) from Pando to Glenwood Springs one evening in the early spring of 1944, the light we noticed at its west end suddenly roared into being the headlamp of an approaching 4-6-6-4 upbound with freight, and we GI hikers had to run for our lives back to our point of entry. We had almost developed a closer acquaintance than we needed with one of that railroad's famed, articulated, freight engines with their 70-inch driving wheels and rigid rear unit of a mere 12 feet 2 inches in length, so eloquently described by Selwyn Kip Farrington, Jr. (1905–1983) on page 157 of his then recently-published opus, *Railroading from the Head End*:

> These haughty-plumed, husky-voiced prima donnas of the rail occupy the center of the railroad stage today, here among the cathedral spires of the Continental Divide, and we cannot help but look on them with awe and solemn wonder, and yet never let it be said that their regal presence will dim the memory of those first little narrow-gauge engines that showed them the way.

* * *

CPR Royal Hudson exiting Connaught Tunnel at Glacier with the author in its cab (Graham A.B. Vickowski).

We have included a glossary of argot terms frequently used in mining and geology with which some persons may not be familiar. Where first used in the text, we have marked these terms with an asterisk.* Also, where first mentioned, railroads will generally have their names in full, and thereafter may be referred to by their initials or most familiar name, i.e., Pennsylvania Railroad as Pennsy or Denver & Rio Grande Western Railroad as D&RGW or simply Rio Grande.

Selecting the major tunnels for this endeavor was the easiest part of this project. The Virginia Central's Blue Ridge was the longest tunnel in North America that was constructed solely by human labor, enhanced only with gunpowder — shades of John Henry — but it had a few shorter though significant predecessors, which shall be duly noted. The Hoosac was so notorious for the slow progress and the "excessive" cost of its construction that we have compared it herein to Boston's "Big Dig" of more than a century later. A dozen years after the "completion" of that modern "landmark" — just as in the case of the Hoosac — the Commonwealth of Massachusetts was still working off its mortgage (this time of federal highway support) by delaying and eliminating most other rehabilitation and construction projects elsewhere in the state, while Bostonians got to use the multibillion dollar result without any bother or toll. This is a politico/financial result somewhat akin to the ultimate financing of the Hoosac, and a prime example of the dichotomy that exists between the denizens of Beacon Hill and those who live in the rest of that Commonwealth. Besides, the Hoosac remains a global landmark for its ultimate combination of innovations in tunnel technology, though its constructors could surely have used the cryotechnology developed more than a century later for handling the muck of Boston Harbor, whereas the Big Dig is a modern monument to something.

The Moffat was very much a Denver-oriented concept from day one, but was preceded in its passage under the Continental Divide of the Centennial State by the Denver & South Park's Alpine Tunnel and the Colorado Midland's Hagerman Tunnel. It was also preceded, of course, by several narrow-gauge lines that went over Colorado's high passes and the Rio Grande's standard-gauge line at Tennessee Pass.

The Great Northern's Cascade Tunnel #2 was the second of its name and place and was bored in fulfillment of its principal owner's insistence on a quality railroad. It was initiated because of the notoriety associated with the deaths of nearly a hundred patrons of that railroad when a late winter climax* avalanche piled into a whole train that was parked on a siding just outside the western portal of its much shorter and higher predecessor. The Great Northern, always a pioneer in railroad managerial efficiency, also constructed — in more recent times — the 11.3 km. Flathead Tunnel to, *inter alia,* help reduce a major kink in its line through the Rocky Mountains of northwestern Montana. Construction of this late-coming tunnel was precipitated by virtue of the 1961 treaty with Canada on upstream dams in the Columbia basin. The treaty envisaged the construction of three major dams for water retention and power generation in British Columbia (Mica, Keenleyside or Revelstoke and Duncan) and one (Libby) in Montana, plus a stabilizing dam for the Upper Arrow Lake in British Columbia. In filling up Lake

Koocanusa behind the Libby Dam, many miles of the original Great Northern line were flooded and had to be relocated.

A similar cause lay behind the relocation of a short stretch of the Canadian Pacific's main stem at the upper end of the much expanded Kinbaskit Lake behind Mica Dam. That much larger lake was once officially named for Andrew George Latta McNaughton (1887–1966), a prominent Canadian soldier and diplomat of the 20th century. Soon, however, a number of persons complained that this had resulted in a gratuitous disservice to a prior Canadian soldier and diplomat of regional fame, "Paul Ignatius" Kinbaskit, an early 19th century chief of the Kootenay tribe.

The Canadian Pacific's two shorter main line tunnels in the Rockies, the Spirals — the lower of which is seen in operation by thousands every year — were made necessary by the ongoing operating difficulties and expense associated with the CPR's original paucity of construction funds; whereas the two in the Selkirks, Connaught and Macdonald, have different origins as well as very different ages.

Thus, after the first two, most of the tunnels we dwell on were bored for different particular reasons after the original lines had been built and found lacking. They are all landmarks of North American engineering, but only about half of the them — the 86 of the tunéls on El Chepe (which collectively equal less than half of one Hoosac), the several at Donner Summit, the Moffat, Cascade and Flathead — are still regularly used for passenger train travel.

We have established a home for our source citations; they are to be found in the endnotes. But some folk may recognize that the numerous parenthetical notes serve also as an outlet for the author's love of trivia.

* * *

Our thanks are vast; starting with Almyra LaBerge, legal secretary to my distant cousin William Amory Lowell Esq. of Boston, who helped immensely in unearthing various elusive personal data, along with a copy of the 1866 *Report of the Joint Standing Committee of the Massachusetts Legislature*— a veritable bonanza of data on the Hoosac project, including much trivia from which we have extracted a number of pertinent tidbits. We also owe thanks to Margaret Humberston, curator of Springfield's Connecticut Valley Historical Museum; to Cecelia Mullen of the University of Massachusetts; to Antoinette Beiser, Drs. Giorgi Manduschev and David Schleicher of Lowell Observatory; and to Richard Mangum Esq., historian of Northern Arizona, all of whom "turned over rocks" for my inspection and pointed me at various other reliable sources. A dear friend of old climbing days, James Peter McCarthy Esq., suggested we reorder the segments on the Hoosac to help in comprehension of the narrative. Much good criticism came from other loyal acquaintances in world mountaineering: Michael Kenneth Mortimer, the current president of the world organization of Alpine Associations (UIAA); Silvio Calvi, engineer and architect of Bergamo, Italy; and Professor Emeritus T. C. Price Zimmermann of Davidson, North Carolina.

We also owe thanks to Payton Hayes, Jr., chief engineer of the Chattanooga Choo Choo (whose office is just over track 29), for sharing his insights into the railroad history of the Cumberland plateau. The nice ladies at the Albemarle County (Virginia) Historical Society provided generous access to biographical and other data, as did Eugene Carlson, treasurer of the North Adams Historical Society (NAHS), and Curt Johnson for the Burlington Northern Santa Fe Railway (BNSF). Our secretary and maid-of-all-work, Annie Bennett, convinced her husband, Glenn, to present us with an image of Sir Matthew Bailey Begbie (one of my heroes); and Arnoldo Pedroza graciously enlightened me on several matters regarding El Chepe.

The attentive reader may notice a photographic credit for Howard Palmer (1883–1945), a man I never met but whose footsteps I have followed in the world's mountains, one of the author's more distinguished predecessors as president of the American Alpine Club and a pioneer bushwhacker of "wrong valleys" in much of British Columbia. For the CPR pictures, we are grateful for the skills of Peter Rosenthal, one of the most intellectually useful persons I have ever known, who performed wonders with some of the ancient prints I provided him. Those prints were first given me by my late and beloved friend, Omer Lavalee, archivist of the Canadian Pacific Railway, and used to enhance the American Alpine Club's *Great Glacier and Its House*, 1882. Before he died, Omer also saved for me the Seth Thomas clock that once hung in the Glacier House station.

My competent and enjoyable grandson, Graham Vickowski (GABV), not only "surfed the web" for me, as only someone of his vintage can do, but aided with some of the picture taking as did my one-time and honored business competitor, David Starr, president of the Springfield *Republican* newspaper. Throughout it all, my dear wife, Kitty, put up lovingly with my frequent long bouts of silence as I whaled away at the innocent word processor.

Along the way, our old college friend from sixty plus years ago, Robert Bruce Rutherford, suggested that we go look into the aqueduct/tunnel on the Aegean island of Samos. We didn't actually do so, since we could learn of no nearby railroad, though we did learn that such visitation is often done by modern tourists. Our knowledge of the bedrock geology pertinent to some of our subject railroad bores was vastly enhanced through the courtesy of Darlene Ryan of the U.S. Geological Survey (who also helped us in her mother's native language while researching El Chepe) and Dr. John Oliver Wheeler, sometime chief of field work for the Geological Survey of Canada and scion of a family notable in mountaineering.

Introduction

IN EVERY MODERN WORK DEALING with engineering matters, there arises the question of which form of measurement to use — English or metric. We have opted for the latter, perhaps prematurely, but with a hopeful eye toward eventual wider acceptance by Americans of that system which is in use by every modern nation except ours. So, for the benefit of those who do not wish to be left behind, we offer the following.

One of our antiquated miles is equivalent to 1.61 kilometers, or — read the other way — one kilometer is equivalent to 0.6 of a mile. One inch is equal to 2.54 centimeters (the studs in the walls of your house thus might well be called 5 × 10s rather than 2 × 4s); one foot is equivalent to 30.5 centimeters, and one meter is 39.37 of those ancient inches, one of which apparently was standardized (according to the Oxford English Dictionary) to "three grains of barley, dry and round, placed end to end lengthwise," not to the knuckle length of some Medieval English king, although in 1150 King David I of Scotland is alleged to have decreed that "ye ynche" was the breadth of a man's thumb at the base of the nail. Anyhow, Stevens Pass — under which presently runs the Great Northern Railroad — with an English altitude of 4,061 feet above sea level, will appear below in metric as 1,238 m. ASL. The length of the present Cascade Tunnel is given in English as 7.8 miles but will appear below as 12.56 km., representing a savings in altitude for the Great Northern of 359.7 m. over its earliest, but frequently snow-bound, route across the top of the pass. The multiplication (division) factor is .3048 — use it wisely, or just go metric cold turkey. To paraphrase *Star Trek*'s Mr. Spock, "It's very logical." And every modern nation except America has long ago seen that wisdom.

However, since this opus deals with railroads of a gauge* called "standard," which comes down to us from the axle width of ancient Roman chariots and became formalized two centuries ago at 4 feet 8 inches (a dimension which, more than coincidentally, turns out to be, of necessity, the width of two horses' hindquarters — a point that might not be wasted on the irreverent), I will spare those brave enough to have read this far from referring to it more consistently as 133.5 cm. But, for the benefit of some of my traditionalist friends, the "magic" English altitude of 10,000 feet has unfortunately been reduced to a more humble-sounding 3,048 meters.

* * *

The art of tunneling has changed a great deal from its earliest historic applications, largely due to drilling and blasting innovations that were initiated and perfected in the course of boring the Frejus and Hoosac. However, a major challenge in all tunneling has always been to ensure that any opposing tunnel headings actually meet, not pass each other, in the bowels of some mountain. This is a process requiring very accurate surveying, much of it done over steep and difficult terrain and often under extremely trying conditions. Since medieval times this has generally been accomplished by clear-cutting a direct line, often through scrub and timber, across the tops of the target mountain(s) to each end of the proposed bore; then placing bolts to verify the way; and finally erecting fixed transit — or alidade* — stations beyond the ends of the tunnel that can actually sight into the portals.* In the end, the alignment and gradient issues of the 7.6 km. Hoosac Tunnel, which utilized two intermediate shafts* and three pairs of headings,* were overcome with sufficient accuracy. When the various headings finally met, the worst discovery was a difference in alignment of slightly more than 1 cm. and a minutely larger amount in level.

The epitome of accuracy in such tunnel surveying came about in 1907 because of 25 fatalities that occurred during the boring of the original 14.6 km. Lötschberg Tunnel between Kandersteg and Goppenstein under the Bernese Alps (not to be confused with the more ambitious and contemporary project, the Lötschberg Basis Tunnel). Misgauging the thickness of the bedrock overhead and consequently the depth of glacial outwash* gravel filling a streambed under which the tunnel was passing, when a round was fired in the limestone under the Kander Torrent, the mining crew was crushed by the water and alluvium from above the unexpectedly thin bedrock roof of the tunnel. After appropriate obsequies, the Berner Oberland Bahnen then opted to close off much of the now silt-filled north heading and divert both headings eastward, toward the 4,166 m. Jungfrau, to ensure there was adequate solid rock overhead. As a result of revived Swiss accuracy in surveying, when the two headings finally met, after each had curved far around the dangerously thin area, they were in disagreement by a mere 10 cm. (four inches) in level and only 25 cm. in alignment over the entire distance.

Another issue, which was particularly virulent in the case of steam-powered locomotives, is the matter of ensuring proper ventilation. Most of the subject tunnels were, therefore, built on an ascending grade so the bore could act somewhat like a chimney — a condition also made necessary so that water, which is usually met with in large quantities, may be easily drained off. In some cases, however, like the Hoosac and the Moffat, where there is no significant difference in elevation of the portals, the only method of securing proper drainage was to have a summit at the midpoint, from which the grade descends to either portal. In the cases of lengthy bores, chimney effect or not as we shall note, drainage and ventilation became topics of great concern — greater in some instances than merely holding the roof up.

* * *

But this is meant to be about railroad tunnels and railroads mostly using maple, oak, chestnut or fir stringers (this is the opposite of corduroy roads which are made by placing logs transverse to the direction of travel) and sometimes shod with iron straps which had been around for some time in North America. Inclined planes, less generally abetted by iron straps but often with a cable and pulley arrangement at the top, supplemented the wooden rails on projects where the grades were steep. In Boston, for instance, rails of this nature were used in the 19th century for the carts that transported the hard pan* material from the glacial drumlin* called Mount Vernon, next to Beacon Hill, into filling part of the Back Bay, so that both areas could become real estate developments. The principal contractor for this urban enhancement project was Vermont-born Norman Carmine Munson (1822–1885), who was compensated mostly by retaining ownership of some of the real estate thus created, and who later did another "final" alignment and grading for the east approach to the Hoosac Tunnel.

This author's grandparents lived at 49 Beacon Street, two blocks down from the golden-domed statehouse on the east side, his great-uncle Lawrence had his home a half-mile to the west in the increasingly fashionable Back Bay, and his great-uncle Percival maintained a home on the southwest flank of a much smaller Mount Vernon.

> Historically the first tracks to be used were constructed of wooden rails upon which thin straps of iron were fastened to provide a running surface for the wheels. Later, iron rails, many of them imported from England, gradually replaced the iron-surfaced ones. It was 1870 before the steel rail came into extensive use. By the late 1890s steel had taken the place of iron along railroad highways. Both weight and length of the single rails increased as time went on. The earliest strap rail was 8 or 10 feet long. By 1850 rails reached 18 or 20 feet, and in time, rails grew to even greater lengths. The first iron rails weighed about 55 pounds to the yard. As traffic and the weight of the traffic on the rails increased, the rail that bore that weight had to be made both stronger and heavier.[1]

Also, and widely regarded as the first commercial railroad in North America, was the horse-powered Granite Railway of Quincy on Boston's South Shore, which utilized a short tunnel in delivering the blocks of stone cut from the Swingle and Wigwam Quarries of West Quincy down to tidewater at Neponsett. As any proper Bostonian knows, there are only two shores for all the Earth's oceans, the more fashionable of which lies to the north of the "Hub of the Universe," and that which abuts the ocean on the south. There they could be floated to a landing site at Charlestown for construction of the Bunker Hill Monument.

The Baltimore & Ohio Railroad, which enters into this narrative peripherally, was North America's first steam-powered line. Its ground breaking was attended on July 4, 1828, by Maryland's "Grand Old Man," Charles Carroll "of Carrollton" (1737–1832), the last surviving signer of America's fifty-two-year-old Declaration of Independence. But there ultimately totaled less than three miles of tunnel (Kingwood, Doe Gully and Sand Patch) along its main line from tidewater at Baltimore to Chicago. However, the first schedule of steam-powered service appears to have been provided, starting on Christmas Day of 1830, behind the vertical boiler of the "Best Friend of Charleston" on the South Carolina Canal & Railroad Company's line inland from the Atlantic Ocean. This was also the first American-made steam engine, a product of the West Point Foundry in New York, and was also the first to explode when the fireman got tired of listening to the pressure excess valve and tied it closed.

Though there are presently numerous railroad tunnels, many built by "cut and cover"* methods under various urban areas with their traffic mostly powered by electric engines, we will avoid going down that primrose path except to mention our awareness of the lengthy Howard Street Tunnel under two kilometers of Baltimore, Maryland, and the 50-year piecemeal collapsing of the Church Hill Tunnel that once went under much of Richmond, Virginia. As part of the Chesapeake & Ohio expansion instigated under the leadership of Collis Huntington, a rail passage was necessary to extend the Virginia Central trackage to reach the company's new coal pier in Newport News. Completed in 1875, this tunnel was not in hard rock, but rather in surficial deposits mostly of marl and clay, so it was more subject to periodic cave-ins. The final and most notable of these collapses occurred on October 2, 1925, resulting in the burial of an entire 4-4-0 steam locomotive, 10 flat cars and most of a construction crew engaged in rehabilitating the tunnel to a larger dimension. Rescue operations were ineffectual, resulting only in further collapses. Eventually the state Corporation Commission ordered the portals sealed and the tunnel backfilled with sand.

We have also managed to ignore the often-rumored system of tunnels that allegedly served a variety of questionable purposes under the streets of Tacoma, Washington, on the other side of the continent. However, we have not included a discussion of all railroad tunnels, only the major bores; for every project has to have some limitations, and almost every railroad in the world has used some form of tunnel somewhere along the line. A great many such minor bores were enhancements to eliminate curves or annoying upgrades after the line had been in use; other minor bores were completely eliminated, becoming open cuts when ongoing tunnel maintenance became an expensive nuisance.

In 1943 one railroad tunnel of about 4 km. was bored in Alaska to connect the Port of Whittier with Anchorage. This was done as a wartime emergency measure, somewhat like the Alcan Highway, and had the approval of Ernest Gruening (1887–1974), the governor, a man we knew and admired. It stemmed from concern that Japanese submarines might cause grief to seaborne traffic from Seattle. However, we suspect the Anton Anderson Tunnel (revised for automobile and rail traffic in 2000) to have been somewhat of a boondoggle; for this author's ragtag troopship sailed from Kiska in the outer Aleutian Islands, with most of the 87th Mountain Infantry, via Adak to Seattle in mid–December of that year, unaccompanied.

Coincidentally, we noted one interesting regional difference in railroad construction and operation: there were far more serious train wrecks on Southern railroads than on those in the North or in Canada. In one pre–Civil War decade (1850s) there were more fatal train wrecks in Virginia and Kentucky than in all the rest of the continent combined. The Southern economy was mostly agricultural, so Southern railroads were more lightly constructed; and with major cities farther apart, trains like that pulled by "Old 97" were often run at higher, and more often fatally unwise, speeds.

* * *

In the course of preparing this opus, we found it desirable to delve into the formality of numerous political boundaries and some of the origins thereof. As a result of several duplicative royal charters, the royal colony of Virginia was once decreed to encompass everything north to the "Dominion of New England" (which later was decreed in 1686 to include all of modern Pennsylvania, New Jersey, New York and New England; and of which the governor, Sir Edmund Andros (1637–1714), became so unpopular that in 1689 he was shipped home from Boston in irons, though returned in 1692 for a six-year stint as governor of Virginia), west beyond the Mississippi River to the Pacific, east to include Bermuda and south to a line "200 miles south of Point Comfort," which is now guarded by Fortress Monroe, at the extreme tip of the Virginia Peninsula to the north of Hampton Roads.[2]

Such legal complexities got so confused as a result of numerous conflicting and overlapping royal grants made in the 16th and 17th centuries — and almost always based on geographical ignorance — that at one point in 1836 in preparing to argue a boundary case before the U.S. Supreme Court, noted Massachusetts lawyer and sometime senator Rufus Choate (1799–1859) proclaimed:

> The commissioners might as well have stated that the line between the states was bounded on the north by a bramble bush, on the south by a blue jay, on the west by a hive of bees in swarming time, and on the east by five hundred foxes with fire brands tied to their tails.[3]

Choate had specific reference to the then indistinct northern boundary line of Rhode Island with Massachusetts, but his point was illustrative of many other contested North American boundaries that were subsequently settled, mostly by arbitration. Of greater relevance to one of the rail lines mentioned below, the Chesapeake & Ohio, in 1784 when Virginia ceded to the nascent United States, many of her pretentions to land beyond her present boundaries (which in this case included all of Delaware, Maryland, Pennsylvania, Ohio, Indiana and Illinois), she retained the Ohio River, which was even then regarded as the prime route to the West. Thus, when the 15th state (Kentucky) was carved out of far western Virginia in 1792, her northern boundary was defined as the low watermark on the north side of that river.

According to Virginia's "second" charter of 1609, King James I assigned to the territory named in honor of his predecessor ruler all the lands

> situate, lying and being in that part of America, called *Virginia,* from the point of Land, called Cape or Point Comfort, all along the Sea Coast to the Northward, two

> hundred miles, and from the said point of Cape Comfort, all along the Sea Coast to the Southward, two hundred miles, and all that space and Circuit of Land, lying from the Sea Coast of the Precinct aforesaid, up into the land, throughout from Sea to Sea, West and Northwest; And also all the islands lying within one hundred miles along the Coast of both Seas of the Precinct aforesaid.[4]

A "third" charter issued in 1611-12 was even more generous and included "all and singular those islands whatsoever, situate and being in any part of the Ocean Seas bordering upon the Coast of our said first colony in Virginia, and being within three hundred leagues of any of the Parts heretofore granted."[5]

In all this, no one ever bothered to consult with Chief Powhatan (d. 1618) (though he was crowned in 1609 by direct order of King James II's agent, Christopher Newport) as to how he or his people felt about this broad-brushed expropriation of their homeland. A similarly cavalier attitude was displayed toward Chief Massassoit and his people by Kings Charles I and II in regard to the northern colonies in New England. However, Church of England-leaning Virginia was at least clearly given lands all across North America to the "South" Sea, whereas the various Puritan colonies to the north (New Haven, Connecticut, Rhode Island and the Providence Plantations, Plymouth — the "Old" Colony, Massachusetts Bay and even the late-coming New Hampshire) were left to fend for themselves for territorial claims to the west, versus the previously Dutch colony of New York.

1

Canals versus Tunnels

IN 1810 DEWITT CLINTON (1769–1828), a prominent New York State politician and man of many other meritorious pursuits, began his long (14 years) tenure as his state's canal commissioner and started pushing the idea of a "water-level" route for commerce between the vicinity of Albany and Lake Erie. This project was the culminating North American example of a mania that swept the Western world prior to the advent of steam-powered railroads. The Erie Canal also became the training ground for numerous engineers, surveyors and future contractors who went on from their first employment in upstate New York to other comparable projects across North America. Among the more notable of these "graduates," was Major Albert Bowman Rogers, a native of Orleans, Massachusetts, and a "hero" of our penultimate chapter. In 1883 he discovered the pass that enabled the Canadian Pacific Railway to be completed across the Selkirk Range of British Columbia.

In 1825, the year that Clinton was finally elected governor, his canal was opened to traffic. By this time canals were being dug almost everywhere, and in 1819 one was proposed to connect Greenfield, Massachusetts, with "the West" by paralleling and utilizing the Deerfield and Hoosic Rivers, though requiring a tunnel under the very prominent barrier of Hoosac Mountain. But the Erie Canal, with its corollary of the Hudson River (which is delightfully navigable, as first reported by Henry Hudson in 1609, and affected by oceanic tides as far north as Albany), was the making of the Port of New York to the disadvantage of Boston, which had no comparable "water level" route to the interior. They had instead to contend with the series of "hills" in central Massachusetts and then with the more rugged terrain formed by the Berkshire and Taconic Ranges between the south-flowing Connecticut and Hudson Rivers.

Canals became so omnipresent that in 1845 John Augustus Roebling (1806–1869), a native of Mühlhausen, Thuringia, in Prussian Germany, built his first steel-wire–supported suspension bridge to carry a canal across the Allegheny River. However, there soon developed a line of thinking that reasoned "steam could go uphill faster than water could run down." This belief came totally a cropper when recurrent problems with the Troy & Greenfield's roadbed frequently washing out along the tortuous valley of the Deerfield River demonstrated that sufficient water going downhill did indeed pose serious problems for steam heading up. Nevertheless, it became increasingly clear to all dispassionate observers that steam power — with steel wheels rolling on steel rails — embodied both speed and efficiency and was the wave of the future, as investor Warren Buffett has more recently reminded us. Such considerations, though, did not bother the parochial members of the New York State Legislature. For many years after completion of the Erie Canal, railroads in upstate New York were forbidden to carry freight in competition with the state-owned, but mule-powered, canal — except when it was frozen over.

Due to the obvious success of the Erie Canal, in 1829 the lower house of the Massachusetts Legislature (known quaintly, but legally, in Massachusetts as the "General Court" — a heritage of Puritan times, which its members alone sometimes refer to as "Great" and "General") launched a further study of how best to open canal routes between Boston and the western portion of the Commonwealth. They engaged the noted civil engineer Loammi Baldwin, Jr. (1780–1834) to look into the situation. Loammi's father was a Revolutionary War hero, who enjoyed good political connections but is probably best remembered for the strain of apples he bred. In due course the younger Baldwin, who also did comparable work for the Commonwealth of Virginia, reported that, because of more amenable water conditions, a canal route from Boston through Fitchburg and Greenfield paralleling (and utilizing) the Miller and Deerfield Rivers was preferable to one through Worcester and Springfield following the line of the Quabaug (Chicopee) and Westfield Rivers. He did report that the 782 m. (2,566-foot) Hoosac Mountain would be a serious obstacle, though perhaps a five-mile tunnel would obviate that issue. After formally receiving Baldwin's report, the General Court, in the finest traditions of American politics, did nothing.

It is interesting to note the longevity of "canal thinking" in transportation planning. In 1861 the U.S. Army's Corps of Engineers — as it was preparing to help in General Ulysses Grant's first major blows to the Confederacy — used shallow-draft, ironclad gunboats, the product of America's foremost civil engineer and inventor of the diving bell, James Buchanan Eads (1820–1887), on the Tennessee River and its tributaries. This lead to the capture of Vicksburg by establishing the existence of reliable minimal depths for the Ohio River as follows: Cairo to Louisville — six feet; Louisville to Wheeling — five feet; Wheeling to Pittsburgh — four feet.

* * *

Tunnels have been part of mankind's activities for a long time. In the 6th century B.C.E., the Aegean Sea island of Samos was ruled by a famous pirate/tyrant named Polycrates, who, for understandable reasons, was not all that popular with his neighbors. During his reign, two groups working under the direction of an engineer/mathematician named Eupalinos from Megara, bored a tunnel through 1,440 m. Mount Kastro for an aqueduct to supply his capital city (today called Pythagoreion) with fresh water, despite any unfriendly landings on his island. The Eupalinian aqueduct is cited by the contemporary historian and traveler Herodotus:

> I have dwelt longer upon the history of the Samians than I should otherwise have done, because they are responsible for three of the greatest building and engineering feats in the Greek world: the first is a tunnel nearly a mile long, eight feet wide and eight feet high, driven clean through the base of a hill nine hundred feet in height. The whole length of it carries a second cutting thirty feet deep and three broad, along which water from an abundant spring is led through pipes into the town. This was the work of a Megarian named Eupalinus, son of Naustrophus. Secondly there is the artificial harbor enclosed by a breakwater, which runs out into twenty fathoms of water and has a total length of over a quarter of a mile.[1]

A buried channel with periodic inspection shafts winds eastward along the steep hillside to the northern portal. A similar hidden channel buried just below the surface of the ground leads from the southern exit eastward to the town of Pythagoreion. Within the mountain itself, water still flows in a channel several meters below the human access channel and connects up to it by shafts or by a trench.

This tunnel was bored with hammer and chisel through the soft, native limestone — the northern portion, being in less competent rock, is barely wide enough for one person to squeeze through and has a tapered ceiling; the southern portion has a more traditional square-cut cross section because it is bored through stabler rock. In planning the project, Eupalinos used what are now well-known principles of geometry, which were codified by Euclid, another Megarian, several centuries later.

Eupalinos was aware that any mistakes in his measurements could make his working crews miss their expected meeting point, either horizontally or vertically. Since parallel lines never meet, he recognized that an error of more than two meters horizontally or vertically would make them miss. Having calculated the expected position of that point so that an intersection would be guaranteed even if the two headings were previously parallel and far away, he directed his crews to make a slight turn, one to the right and the other to the left. Since there was also a possibility of deviations in the vertical, even though his measurements were quite accurate, Eupalinos increased the likelihood of the two headings meeting by increasing the height of both tunnels. In the north heading he kept the floor horizontal and increased the height of the roof, while in the south, he kept the roof line horizontal and deepened the floor. As noted below, more modern engineers using vastly more sophisticated equipment have not done nearly as well. With a cross section of less that two meters and a total length of 1,036 meters, the Eupalinian subterranean aqueduct is justly famous as one of the masterpieces of ancient engineering.

The Mesopotamians used *qanaats* to distribute the waters of the Euphrates for irrigation; the Egyptians built astronomical versions of them into their pyramids; the Romans, who were the first to appreciate the strength of the arch in building, ran their famous roads straight through some of the softer rock formations they encountered. And in the Middle Ages, Austrian miners hollowed out great dome-shaped underground cavities in the development of their highly profitable *salzmineralwerke*. Short tunnels became almost commonplace in more recent Western civilization, even in the wild expanses of North America. But the increasing pace of life, after modern man learned to burn the cadavers of his most-distant ancestors in his competitive haste to "get somewhere" on this Earth, meant that major obstacles to travel and transport, such as wide rivers and snow-clad mountains had to be crossed, circumvented or otherwise overcome.

During the time when the Blue Ridge and the Hoosac were being bored, the English, as befits the pioneers of railway development, already possessed the longest tunnel in the world — the three-mile (with five shafts for ventilation) Woodhead Tunnel through the Millstone Grit in the southern Pennines and in use by the Manchester, Sheffield & Lincolnshire Railway from 1845 to 1981. Nowadays, the Woodhead is actually a combination of tunnels ventilated by several shafts. It consists of two single-track railroad bores (1845 and 1852) and a third of two tracks completed in 1954. In addition, the three-mile Huddersfield Canal was in use under a corner of the mountain from 1794 to 1811.

As noted above, most tunnels are bored with an ascending grade, necessary in order that subterranean water, which is usually met with in large quantities, may be drained away. In case the portals are at about the same height above sea level, the only method of securing proper drainage is to have a summit at the center from which the grade descends to either portal. But this manner of constructing a tunnel increases the difficulties of ventilation. If built on a continuous grade, an upward current of air might be expected; and when this fails to secure ventilation, the rapid driving of a train through the tunnel often creates a current by which it might be cleared of exhaust or smoke. But if built with a summit in the center, neither of these methods could be depended on. The use of compressed air for the drills at the headings solved the ventilation issue during the second phase of the Hoosac construction and for many subsequent such ventures. Therefore, it is often necessary to sink a shaft from high on the mountain to the summit level of such a tunnel. By such a shaft it is possible not only to secure ventilation, but also to expedite the work when the shaft is sunk to grade by affording four faces of rock instead of two to work upon. The central shaft of the Hoosac was, however, a belated afterthought, not having even been thought of until the work had been in desultory progress for several years.

In the *Encyclopedia of North American Railroads* by Middleton, Smerk, and Diehl (Indiana University Press, 2007) cited further below, on page 269, the topic is concisely analyzed:

> The art of tunneling has been practiced since ancient times. Early civilizations built a variety of underground shafts, temples, tombs, aqueducts and the like, with some early Egyptian subterranean tombs dating as far back as 1500 B.C. The Romans were the greatest early tunnelers of all. One tunnel completed by Emperor Claudius in 52 A.D. to drain a lake east of Rome was 3 miles long and took 11 years to build.
>
> These early tunnels were built without machinery or explosives. Rock was most

> often removed by hammer and chisel. The Egyptians used channeling and wedging, a method whereby wooden wedges were driven into channels cut in the rock, which was broken out by the swelling action of the wedges when soaked with water. Still another method was to heat the rock to a very high temperature with fires and then quench it with water, causing the rock to shatter from the sudden change in temperature...
>
> By 1850, some 48 railroad tunnels had been completed in the United States. These early tunnels were typically driven through hard rock by laboriously drilling holes with hammer and chisel and then blasting with black powder. Removal of excavated material, or mucking,* was usually accomplished by means of horses and wagons or small railcars. Sometimes the surrounding rock was firm and stable enough that no additional support was required, but more often some form of timber or masonry lining was required.

Tunneling done this way, even when much of it was done by slave labor, was expensive and very time consuming. In drilling the Virginia Central's Blue Ridge Tunnel at Rockfish Gap, only three-quarters of a mile in length but the longest ever bored in North America by hand drilling and black powder blasting, the tunnelers averaged just 5 m. per month at a cost of $300 per meter. Tunnelers using the same primitive methods struggled ineffectively for some 15 years to bore less than half of the 7.8 km. Hoosac Tunnel in Massachusetts before the Shanly Brothers' introduction of improved tunneling methods and nitroglycerine finally brought that project to completion.

* * *

The major mountains of Western Europe, the Alpine chain which circles northern Italy, were the site of the first major tunneling endeavor — notably the Frejus, or, as it is sometimes known, the Mont Cenis (see Appendix). The motivation for this notable project was well described in the opening passages of chapter 6 of Gösta Sandström's 1963 book, *Tunnels*:

> Between the embryonic northern and southern [railroad] systems lay the impenetrable barrier of the Alps. It was not only a physical barrier, it was a cultural, religious and psychological one that from the beginning of time had divided Europe in two. To the south of the inaccessible peaks and deadly glaciers were the lands of the sun, the heirs of Paradise gained and lost, of culture and sophistication. To the north were the impenetrable forests, and in the bone-chilling mists rising from the bogs, men vied with the aurochs, bear and wolf for ascendancy. To the south were Christ, Augustus, Franciscus and Machiavelli; to the north were Valhalla, Odin, Goths, long-haired Merovingians, Calvin and Luther. It was a formidable barrier indeed that had to be crossed in order to link the two railway systems.
>
> Nevertheless, the challenge had to be accepted. In the early 1850s Stephenson and Swinburne were called to Switzerland to lend their advice on a tunnel through the Alps. They took one look at the country and declared that it could not be done. No locomotive could climb the gradients necessary for a railway across the mountains. They left it to the natives to muddle through as best they could.
>
> Behind these outstanding English railway engineers was ranged a phalanx of sup-

porting scientific opinion. The geologists maintained that the temperature under the mountains would reach such heights that men would be scorched to death. The mathematicians backed them up with beautiful fireworks of calculus suggesting that a tunnel through the Alps was vulgar nonsense. On the other hand, there were leading technical authorities who maintained that it was feasible to cross the Alps with summit railways at elevations of from 6,000 to 9,000 ft., using, if necessary, short tunnels under the passes. But these proposals bore the marks of desk work: they seemed to ignore the climate prevailing in the Alps at such altitudes. At the heights suggested the snow lasts for up to nine months of the year and covers the ground to 13 ft. or more.

* * *

In a dramatic contrast to the contemporary Frejus tunnel project in the Graian Alps, the Hoosac Mountain bedrock geology was scientifically analyzed after the fact rather than in preparation for the work. While the field labors of Professor Angelo Sismonda, a distinguished member of the University of Turin faculty, aided the tunnelers in northwestern Italy by determining where and what they would likely encounter, American geologists came to Hoosac Mountain after 1870 to learn more about the complex nature of New England's bedrock geology, as it had been experienced by those actually laboring a quarter mile under the crest of the mountain.

The list of American scientists who became more educated as the Hoosac Tunnel was being bored, but mostly after it was completed, is long and noteworthy. It starts with Edward Hitchcock (1794–1861), one of the pioneers of geological science in North America, who became the president of Amherst College and was the first "authority" on the geology of Vermont. In his capacity as state geologist of Massachusetts, Hitchcock assured the Troy & Greenfield Railroad promoters that Hoosac Mountain was composed of "sound rock" and that they would "encounter little water" once fairly into the bedrock.

Next in chronological noteworthiness came Charles Doolittle Walcott (1830–1927), North America's leading paleontologist, patron of the geologically noteworthy Burgess Shale of Alberta, and Secretary of the Smithsonian Institute. The area was soon thereafter studied by Raphael Pumpelly (1837–1937), the leading light of Harvard's geologists and principal author of the United States Geological Survey's Monograph XXIII, *Geology of the Green Mountains in Massachusetts*. Finally, this grateful alumnus is pleased to give a belated plug for his distinguished professor of orogeny and structural geology at Harvard, Marland Pratt Billings (1902–1996), the lead author of the Geological Society of America's *Geology of the Appalachian Highlands of East-central New York and Southern New Hampshire*.

Altogether there have been fifteen other learned studies (interspersed around those cited above) that contributed to the 1961 USGS Map CQ 139, Bedrock Geology of the North Adams Quadrangle, besides its noteworthy compiler, Dr. Norman Herz, of the University of Georgia. These authorities all agree that this bedrock is enormously ancient and very complex, much of it dating from the pre–Cambrian — at least a billion years ago — perhaps when there was no Atlantic Ocean and North America was still attached to the continental mass of Eurasia or Pangaea.

It is now permissible to believe in continental drift—flat earth and intelligent design devotees, as well as devout followers of the Rev. James Ussher (1581–1656) and some of his contemporaries notwithstanding. When this author was much younger and a student of geology, if one endorsed the concepts of the heroic German geomorphologist Alfred Lothar Wegener (1880–1930), one was labeled as "some kind of a nut who doesn't belong in geology." Now, however, and thanks to the persuasiveness of the late Canadian geophysicist John Tuzo Wilson (1908–1993), if one does not give credence to the same preachments, one is soon labeled "some kind of a nut who doesn't belong in geology." The major problem that humans have in understanding the geologic processes by which our Earth has been created to today's form lies not merely in the hangover of literal interpreters of the rambling and contradictory accumulation we call Holy Scripture, but in the fact that our life-spans are so relatively short that we are thereby forced to see some of these processes — earthquakes, landslides, volcanic eruptions, etc. — as catastrophic events, not the routine humdrum of Mother Earth.

The first recorded use of drilling and blasting — as a means of creating a tunnel — appears to have been in 1617 at the direction of Martin Weigel (1555–1618), *oberbergmeister* in the east German silver mining city of Freiberg on the Mulde River. However, much of what we know about early tunnels is owed to the historical research of the lesser-known Renaissance scholar Georgius Agricola (1494–1555), who, like many of his literate contemporaries, Latinized his name from its original Georg Bauer. He was a Saxony-born contemporary of da Vinci (1452–1519), Erasmus (1469–1536), Copernicus (1473–1543) and Luther (1483–1546), whose 1530 book, *De Re Metallica*, discusses much of the methodology of mining as it was known at the time. Agricola placed much store by the traditional means of heating the rocks to be weakened with fire, then dousing the appointed area with water, thereby, as many campers have learned, causing the target rocks to spall* and fracture apart. Then do it all again, and again, and again — an obviously tedious process. Some accounts have Hannibal using vinegar for the same purpose in removing obstacles to his passage over the Alps, but the mild acidity does little — as has been learned by anyone with a granite kitchen countertop. The shock of sudden differential temperature change is the working force; the different minerals making up most rocks all having different coefficients of expansion.

* * *

The iron horse works best where its gradient* is less than 2 percent. Thus, its tracks reached easily into the valleys of the Alps, but it was left to charabancs, marrones, porters and sleighs to handle the steep and difficult terrain between the major valleys where friction* railroads had been successfully established. There were several potential crossings of these mountains, of which the lowest, the 1,475 m. (4,496 foot) Brenner

(Brennero in Italia) at the head of the south-flowing Fiume Adige, was actually traversed by a standard gauge railroad in 1867.

Another important gap was on the popular pilgrimage and commercial route over the Alps between Lyon in south-central France, and Turin in northwest Italy. Napoleon, in his campaigns against the Austrians who had occupied much of Italy for generations, finally (in 1806) ordered the construction of a military highway across the easier grades of the 2,281 m. (6,827 foot) Mont Cenis Pass (Moncenisio in Italia). But the impetus for a tunnel came after his exile and death during the era of the "Pax Britannica," when standard-gauge railways were in operation across much of Europe and Imperial communications mandated an ever-swifter passage between London and Bombay (Mumbai).

The Italian State Railroads reached to Susa on a headwaters tributary of the Po, whence steam trains ran down the Po valley and along the east side of the Apennine Mountains to Brindisi, with steamships thence to Suez; and French *chemins de fer* reached from Calais well up in the valley of the Isère on the west. Though elephants could surmount the high ground between (as had been demonstrated at this pass by Hannibal two millennia earlier), and after the completion of Napoleon's road, horse- and mule-drawn vehicles could make the crossing between Modane and Susa seem easy in good weather; by mid-century the move for a railroad tunnel had become sufficiently strong that the rulers of Savoy and Italy announced in 1855 that they would jointly commence such a project. But drilling and boring methods were famously slow in those days, and it was predicted likely to take longer than twenty years for this railroad to become operative. However, the project was well-financed, with the national credit of both Italy and Savoy (later France) fully behind it.

Imperial communications could not wait; so while the 13.7 km. Frejus Tunnel was being drilled and blasted and despite the dour advice of Stephenson, John Barraclough Fell (1815–1902) with the financial patronage of the British railway tycoon and Liberal politician George Granville William Leveson-Gower (1815–1891), the 3rd Duke of Sutherland, designed and built an uniquely powered, non-cog railway. It had a gradient of up to 8 percent and was largely covered over but mostly paralleled Napoleon's road. The nonuse of cogs was necessary to avoid infringing on the various patents on rack* railroads held by the American Sylvester Marsh (1803–1884) and the Swiss Nicholas Riggenbach (1817–1899). In operation from 1868 to 1871, it climbed up from 1,057 m. ASL at St. Michel in the valley of the Isère on the west, passed the ancient monastic hospice at 1,930 m., and descended more than 1,525 m. to reach Susa on the Dora Riparia. When the tunnel, under construction from 1857 to 1871, was opened for traffic (very gently uphill by more than 100 m. into Italy), the "Fell Railway" was quietly removed after three years of accident-free and generally reliable operation.

Various parties combined to make the Frejus Tunnel project come to reality. Belgian engineer Heinrich Mauss, retained in 1845 to study potential routes, dusted off a seven-year-old plan by Giuseppe Francesco Medail (1784–1844), a native of Bardonnecchia and former shepherd for whom the town's main street is now named, which showed the practical valley routes to both ends of a potential tunnel. Meanwhile the eminent Torinese geologist Angelo Sismonda, director of the Museum of Mineralogy and a trusted scientific confidant of the Sardinian king, studied the bedrock formations of the region and determined that the 2,935 m. Monte Frejus was composed of various partially metamorphosed rocks of Mesozoic Age (folded and crunched up into mountains by the northward movement of the "African" plate). Sismonda (1807–1878) was a native of the village of Corneliano d'Alba, southwest of Asti and almost equidistant southeast of Turin. An eminent stratigraphic geologist, his brother, Eugenio, was almost as distinguished in paleontology.

In America Jonathan J. Couch (1789–1870) of Philadelphia, with the occasional assistance of Joseph W. Fowle, had been designing steam-powered drills since 1849, but became unhappily aware of the severe limitations of steam lines in lengthy tunnels. (In England Thomas Bartlett (1789–1864) had been working on the same issues for coal mining.) But it was Germain Sommeiller (1815–1871), a University of Turin educated Savoyard, who, in 1861, successfully adapted the use of compressed air to such drills with his *marteau-piqueur pneumatique*, driven by air compressors from the water-power of streams pouring down off the Frejus massif.

Impressed with the topographic layout by Medail and a tunneling plan by Sommeiller, in 1857 the Sardinian prime minister, Count Camillo Bensodi Cavour (1810–1861), threw his considerable support behind the idea and soon the Italian government agreed to put up 40,000,000 francs to bore the tunnel through. The Kingdom of Sardinia had been greatly enlarged by the 1815 Council of Vienna after the Napoleonic Wars, which added the mainland territory of Savoy to that of the large Mediterranean islands, after which the titular rulers of Italy (until 1946) were known as the "House of Savoy."

Overseen throughout by Severino Grattoni (1816–1876) of San Gaudenzio as general superintendent, work was commenced at Modane, the north portal, by firing the first round on August 18, 1858, with king Victor Emanuel and prince Louis Napoleon on hand to observe. Work at the south (Bardonnecchia) end commenced on the following November 4. The Frejus drilling was done entirely with hand-held tools until Sommellier's machines were installed in 1861. And perhaps due to some of the hangups of Ascanio Sobrero, an Italian who had invented nitroglycerine in 1845, black gun powder rather than "blasting oil" was used throughout most of the period of construction. The Englishman Roger Bacon (1214–1279) appears to have mastered the formula for the Chinese invention of gunpowder; but his work, like that of Galileo some time later, was subject to papal restriction. But Berthold Schwartz, a sometime Franciscan monk (which order — with its emphasis on poverty — was frequently at odds with the more luxurious lifestyle of numerous popes), seems to have actually perfected gunpowder in 1320.

The mid–19th century War of Italian Unification (Risorgimento) was no hindrance

Moncenisio Road and Fell Railway, as it was in 1866. The modern highway closely follows Napoleon's road (E. Whymper).

to the project, the French military help having been essential to evict the undesired Austrians. And after it was concluded, the territory of Savoy—including Garibaldi's hometown of Nizza (Nice)—was ceded to France. But the French government then took over one-half of all succeeding costs, including the promise of a bonus for swifter completion, which happened eleven years ahead of the earlier predictions. (One of Mussolini's stated reasons for his "stab-in-the-back" declaration of war against France in 1940 was to recover the littoral of Garibaldi's Nizza.) After initially curving near both the portals, the Frejus headings ran on a lengthy tangent* to meet 1,600 meters beneath the mountain's crest on Christmas Day 1870, when they were found to disagree on alignment by 40 cm. vertically and 60 cm. in the horizontal, over the 13,636 m. in total length (almost three times as long as anything previous). Its first traffic was on September 17, 1871, three years before anything passed through the much longer-awaited and much shorter Hoosac. The Frejus Tunnel remains the stuff of Italian history; as recently as 1997, Edoardo Altara wrote a book entitled *Frejus 1871. Primo traforo alpino.*

* * *

One of the most important of the non-political players in modern tunnel driving was the Maine-born, Fitchburg-based, mechanic-inventor Charles Rogers Burleigh

(1824–1883), whose rail carriage-mounted, compressed air-powered array of several more than two hundred pound drills was modeled after a number of steam-powered drill rigs that had been tried by Couch and Fowle, and adapted to the use of compressed air by Sommeiller for the Frejus. Famed alpinist engraver/author Edward Whymper (1840–1911) visited the French heading of the Frejus tunnel in 1869 and produced a fine engraving of Sommeiller's system, which is reproduced herein. Once Burleigh's second generation of such rigs were put into action in 1869 under the management of a competent contractor, progress continued through Hoosac Mountain at a fairly regular pace, punctuated mostly by the unfortunately variable quality of steel used in the star-bit heads. In the days before the development of tungsten carbide alloys, some of them were good for only a few feet, while others were durable enough to hammer a hole through up to a mile of rock. In 1872, with patent litigation looming, Burleigh sold his patents and business to Simon Ingersoll (1818–1894), a fellow inventor from Stanwich, Connecticut, whose name is still on the masthead of the world's biggest maker of such equipment.

In 1866 the Hoosac Tunnel Commission reported to the Massachusetts legislature that the Burleigh Machine

> has a solid piston (so-called) which has a hole in its back end to allow the feed-screw to pass in without touching; the drill is secured to this piston. On the back end of the piston is a section of a ball used as a cam, which works the valve and feed-motion. The valve is rotated by a rod lying on the band of the cylinder; upon this rod are two cams which perforate the band of the cylinder. The action of the piston brings the ball on its end in contact with these cams, rocking them up and down; the rod to which they are secured being connected with the valve, imparts to that its motion. The machine is fed altogether on ways, or a bed-piece, upon which is the feed-screw; the feed nut is upon the end of the cylinder-band. To this feed-nut is attached a feed-ratchet, which is held between two collars, allowing it to turn round. Upon the cylinder-band is a lever, one end of which passes through the band; upon the other end is a pall. The motion of the piston raises the lever up, pressing the end containing the pall against the ratchet which turns the nut on the feed-screw, thus moving the machine forward. The rotating ratchet is in the band of the cylinder and has a spline in it, and a pall on its outside. The piston having a spiral groove is turned by this ratchet as it moves down. On the return of the piston, the pall drops into the ratchet and the piston is turned. The piston is not encumbered with any machinery, and moves alone; its area of air is greater on the forward than on the backward stroke; the alternation of the valve admits the air. The machine, like the last one described, contains eighty pieces; it has the same number of screws and pins, and weighs 372 pounds including the ways or bed-piece; without the weighs its weight is 212 pounds. Its number of strokes is about 800 per minute, and its blow is somewhat lighter than that of the other...
>
> These machines stand the work much better than those first made at Fitchburg. Their average time in the tunnel without repairs in the interval, is about five days; they have needed repairs in two days; one remaining at work fourteen days. They

Sommeiller drill carriage and crew at work in the French (north) heading of Frejus tunnel, 1866 (E. Whymper).

> accomplish double the work without repairs than those do which were made after the previous pattern. There is a further advantage is using the Burleigh machines; their breaking, when it occurs, is not very serious, the injured parts consisting mainly of cams, can generally be replaced at the tunnel; whereas for the repairs on the Brooks, Burleigh and Gates machine, the dependence to a very great extent has been upon the machine shop at Fitchburg.[2]

Many subsequent miners used "burleys" in the course of their endeavors; but in 1897, John George Leyner (1860–1920), who also later sold his invention to Ingersoll-Rand, seized on the idea of having a hole though the core of the drill shaft and bit so that a periodic blast of air or water could cool the drill bits and drive out the accumulated rock dust as a slurry, and holes were drilled even faster.

2

South of the Border

THE OCEAN TO OCEAN CROSSING of Mexico does not lend itself to easy transit, certainly as compared with the generally gentler terrain of the American Southwest. The country is ribbed with dry and rugged terrain in the north and with damp and rugged terrain in the south. Even to reach that nation's capital city requires the crossing of major mountain ridges from any direction. As if to emphasize this difficulty, the highest volcanic peaks of North America — Pico de Orizaba, 5,700 m., Ixtaccihuatl (the White Lady), 5,286 m. and Popocatepetl (the Smoking Mountain), 5,426 m. — dominate and surround the route from the coast. The first recorded ascent of Popo (which was then in vigorous eruption) was made by a party sent out by Hernan Cortez (1485–1547) to obtain sulfur to help replenish his dwindling supply of gunpowder. This endeavor also served to impress on the locals that the Spaniards were capable of great accomplishment, for the smoking mountain was a source of fear and malefic prophecy. The party was headed by Captain Diego de Ordaz (1485–1533), who caused his second-in-command, Lt. Francisco Montaño, to be lowered into the smoking crater in a basket to find and retrieve some of the elusive sulfur. For this accomplishment, Ordaz was later given a coat of arms by the king of Spain, but the smoke-filled Montaño who had no such pull, remained unhonored. The relatively minuscule (700 men) army of Cortez was able to conquer the much larger country, however, by virtue of a secret and heretofore unknown weapon for which the natives were totally unprepared — small pox. Periodic outbreaks of this plague almost completely eliminated the native Mexican population over the next two decades.

On the modern rail line between (La Villa Rico de la) Vera Cruz and Mexico City, which was originally laid out in the mid–19th century, one traverses the longest railroad tunnel — the 2,972 m. El Mexicano — in all of Latin America. This bore was completed in the 1980s to eliminate the original, and very circuitous, route over the high pass at 2,700 m. near the great volcano of Orizaba, the third highest mountain in all of North America after Mt. McKinley (Denali) and Mount Logan. This is the same pass that was used in 1519 by the invading army of Spaniards under Cortez. The present route has a maximum gradient of 2.7 percent, whereas the original railroad required the operationally expensive and unacceptably steep gradient of 4.7 percent.

The original line was franchised in 1837; but, as in many things Mexican, timeliness was not of the essence, so very little construction occurred until after 1857. During the time of the American Civil War, the ambitious French ruler Napoleon III saw the Americans as too busy with internal issues to enforce it; and thus it was a good opportunity to get around the Monroe Doctrine. He landed another army at Vera Cruz, which soon resulted in the enthronement of a transplanted Austrian Archduke as Emperor Maximilian (1832–1867) and his much longer-lived Belgian consort, Carlotta (who managed to flee home to her father in Bruxelles and beg for papal help in restoring her husband to his unpopular throne). In 1873 the permit for a railroad was finally completed by the prominent Mexican business and political figure Antonio Escandon (1825–1882) six years after the execution by Benito Juarez's revived republic of the very much unwanted Austrian.

At the close of the American Civil War in early 1865, a number of die-hard anti–Unionists led by C.S.A. General Sterling Price (1809–1867), a native of Virginia who had become elected governor of Missouri, decamped to south of the Rio Grande rather than accede to the victorious North. They found a form of refuge in Mexico, though the populist revolution led by Pablo Benito Juarez (1806–1872) made them equally uncomfortable, so much so that many of them soon returned quietly to their homeland. However, a few stayed on and took root, giving rise to such prominent Mexicans as Enrico Clay Creel (1854–1931), a sometime ambassador to the United States whose name is commemorated both in a city among the Tarahumara Mountains and a courthouse plaque in Greensburg, Kentucky.

* * *

In 1872 a civil engineer, Albert Kimsey Owen (1847–1916), who had been born of Quaker parentage in Chester, Pennsylvania, and was an integral part of the Utopian colony of New Harmony, Indiana, was hired by General Palmer (see chapter 6) of D&RGW fame. He was to explore down the west coast of Mexico to a good harbor location, known as Ohuira Bay, that had recently been visited by a small flotilla under the future admiral George Dewey (1827–1917). Dewey knew the harbor as Topolobambo Bay, but Owen saw it as the port that might well serve as an outlet for grain shipments from and exotic Asiatic imports to the American Midwest. Owen spent four years after 1875 figuring out how to get a railroad from the American Midwest to this place, which was calculated to be 400 miles closer to China than any other similar facility in North America.

Owen, whose papers are to be found in the C.P. Huntington Library at San Marino, California, was finally granted a franchise to build a portion of the resulting through line, but was unable to obtain sufficient financing before his seven-year franchise ran out. Then came a New York financier, Andrew Foster Higgins (1831–1916), who had interests in several Mexican mining companies. In 1897 he picked up a permit for a similar line, renamed it the Rio Grande, Sierra Madre & Pacifico and built a rail line from Juarez south to serve his mining properties near Covialitos. When it became obvious that Higgins was not serious about getting his franchise through to the Pacific, Enrico Creel, a sometime governor of the State of Chihuahua, obtained a permit in partnership with Alfredo Spendlove, a transplanted New Jerseyite, to build a line called the Chihuahua al Pacifico from Chihuahua to the coast. But these men were only able to get a line built as far as Miñaca, at 2,100 m. ASL, just shy of the Continental Divide.

* * *

Next to see something beautiful in this striking terrain was Arthur Edward Stilwell (1839–1928), a banker of Kansas City who had numerous allied railroad interests. He enlisted help from Ulysses S. Grant, Jr. (1852–1929), a lawyer, sometime army general and son of the former president, and Levi Parsons Morton (1824–1920), a prominent financier and soon to be vice-president of the United States on the Republican ticket with Benjamin Harrison. In 1881 this combine formed the Texas, Topolobambo & Pacifico Railroad & Telegraph Company, which morphed into the Kansas City, Mexico & Orient in 1902 having only been able to build a line eastward from sea level at Topolobambo to the old inland stronghold of El Fuerte. However, these entrepreneurs also managed to extend Enrico Creel's line westward from Chihuahua to the city of

Entering one of El Chepe's 84 short tunéls with a second such tunél in the right distance (D. Starr).

Creel (ca. 1,600 m. ASL) utilizing three switchbacks to cross the Divide at Ojitos (2,450 m. ASL).

This effort, in time, was acquired (almost accidentally and surely incidentally) by the Santa Fe Railroad in 1928, which quickly spun off the Mexican trackage to the Ferrocarril Mexicano, while retaining the lines serving the oil-producing areas of west Texas. Through all this history, the remaining 258 km. of route proposed by these various redundant franchises — through the Tarahumara Mountains and down the Barranca del Cobre (Copper Canyon), far and away the most difficult part — remained isolated and even unsurveyed.

Then, in 1940 when World War II was breaking out, the Government of Mexico, where many of the foremost business figures were of German ancestry, nationalized the entire project along with a number of other American-owned properties. The federales then took another decade to ponder the matter before actually getting to work on what has been described as the greatest Latin American work of engineering. The track — mostly along the right side of the Rio Septentrion — followed by today's El Chepe was finally opened through the very scenic Copper Canyon on November 24, 1961, with a maximum grade of 2.5 percent. Along the completed line, the newest "transcontinental" in North America, there are 86 scenic bridges and 34 minor tunnels. There are two

El Chepe's Temeris Bridge is long, high, pre-stressed, and curves. This picture was taken from a train window (D. Starr).

bores of major significance: the 1,260 m. Continental Tunél at the crest of the Sierra Charamuscas (which eliminated the three switchbacks built by the Stilwell group to reach Ojitos); and the more than mile-long El Descanso at the lower, west end of the canyon, which got its name because the miners were finally able to take a rest.

* * *

In reporting on railroad tunéls in Mexico, it would be improper to leave out the San Diego & Arizona Eastern Railroad (SD&AE), which was chartered on December 14, 1906, the fourth attempt to build a line directly east from the southernmost port of California and thus connect more directly with the Imperial Valley and eastward via Tucson. The most vigorous of the three earlier attempts got only as far as Otay before running out of financial steam.

Differing from its bankrupt predecessors, the SD&AE started from the intersection of San Diego's Main and 26th Streets by going south toward Tijuana and thence looping eastward, so as to circumvent the 1,867 m. mass of Mount Palomar and its lesser neighbors that lie just east of San Diego. Though an American line, it thus had to deal with Mexican authorities (and revolutionaries) for its right-of-way. It came as no surprise when the SD&AE had frequent delays in construction, for not only did it have very difficult terrain to cross, but construction difficulties were exacerbated by numerous adherents to the anti–Carranza cause of Francisco "Pancho" Villa (aka Doroteo Arango). Making completion of the line even more onerous, after the United States entered the Great War in 1917, the United States Rail Road Administration (for more on which, see chapter 6) stuck its bureaucratic oar into the process, which resulted in delaying completion until November 15, 1919, when a "golden" spike was finally driven by the line's major investor, the Carolina-born sugar and shipping magnate John Diedrich Spreckels (1853–1921).

The total construction cost of the 236 km. (146.5 miles) of track was approximately $18 million, or some $123,000 per mile, thus matching experience in comparable terrain elsewhere, because the original estimate was a mere $6 million. The bulk of this underestimate was accounted for in the 18-km. segment through the Carrizo Canyon area where the line reentered the United States. This included one segment of four km. with 17 tunnels that cost more than $4 million to hole through, while all five of the tunnels along the rest of the line ran to but another $1.8 million. Carrizo Canyon also included nearly four km. (2.5 miles) of bridges, embankments and wooden trestles,* one of which was the highest in the world.

To construct and maintain the 72 km. segment that ran through the state of Baja California Norte, the SD&AE formed the subsidiary operating company, Ferroccarril Tijuana y Tecate. Though its internationally vulnerable lines officially ended back in the United States at Seeley, trackage privileges over lines of the Southern Pacific gave the SD&AE the ability to run trains as far as El Centro and south to Calexico. Unfortunately, damage to the line was frequent, the causes ranging from flash floods and landslides to fires. Intermittent disputes with Mexican authorities also resulted in irregular service along with clashes and vandalism inspired by union organizers. By 1932 the Spreckel heirs had had enough and sold their shares in the SD&AE to the Southern Pacific (SP) for a measly $2.8 million. The SP promptly gave up on the line, and today the costly tunnels are mostly caved in and the once-magnificent trestles have collapsed into the desert.

3

Unto the Blue Ridge Mountains of Virginia

THE COMMONWEALTH OF VIRGINIA, by far the geographically largest of the original thirteen states, has always been a leader in transportation, particularly since the dawn of the railroad age. (Only four of the United States use the term "commonwealth"—indicating a descent from the English Revolution of John Hampden and Oliver Cromwell—to designate their form of government: Pennsylvania #2, Massachusetts #6, Virginia #10, and Kentucky #15. All the rest are "states.") The Old Dominion's collective dream included a commercial connection of its Atlantic tidewater area to the Gulf of Mexico. Thus, the Commonwealth actually came to own the Virginia Central Railroad through an investment made in 1849 by the Virginia Board of Public Works in the earlier Louisa Railroad. In fulfillment of the Old Dominion's desire to enhance communications with the state's western segment—to the wide Shenandoah valley, to the Ohio, the Mississippi and beyond—an easy crossing of the lengthy Blue Ridge was important.

An interesting aspect of early railroad construction in the United States was the assignment—under provisions of the General Survey Act of 1824—of West Point trained (and federally paid) engineers, who were mostly of Northern origin and ultimate loyalty, to supervision of the layout and grading of privately-owned railway projects throughout the growing nation. Thus, U.S. Military Academy instructors, like the French-born Colonel Crozet as well as New Hampshire–born Major Stephen Harriman Long (1784–1864), a Dartmouth graduate, came to be among the more sought after among North American railroad layout and bridge designers.

While a professor of military engineering at West Point, Long had published two pamphlets on bridging technology, one in 1830 and a second in 1836. A native of Hopkinton, east of Worcester, Massachusetts, and latterly famous as the starting point of the Boston Marathon, Long had previously been on several exploring ventures to the West and had been assigned by the War Department as a consultant on the initial layout of the Baltimore & Ohio, as well as chief layout engineer for the Western & Atlantic. Longs Peak (4,345 m., 14,225 feet) in Colorado was named in his honor, as he had been the first surveyor to sight it. Long's truss, however, was itself the forerunner of that more advanced concept of truss which was developed by William Howe (1803–1852) and subsequently used on dozens of railway bridges (mostly in the Northeast) by his brother-in-law, Amasa Stone (1818–1883), whose death occurred by suicide after the tragic, midwinter collapse of one of his later iron railroad bridges near Ashtabula.

Howe's design entailed the use of sturdy wooden diagonals, held in alignment to the bottom chord by threaded vertical iron rods as tension members. Though admittedly modeled to some extent on earlier designs by Long, Howe was subsequently granted two patents on his formula; one on July 10, 1840, and a second on August 3. All of these wood-dependent bridges — and the northeastern states still have a number in use including one over the Connecticut — came to be "covered," either in their totality or at least over their structural members. Their life expectancy in rural use was thereby extended immensely, because they did not need routine detailed inspection and maintenance. In railroad use, however, the danger of fire from exhaust sparks soon led to reconsideration of the need for complete roof coverings, while red-hot clinkers falling from passing engines' fireboxes caused their builders to search for base-level structural materials that

Town Truss Bridge over the Ware River at Gilbertville, Massachusetts. In 1930 there were railroads (B&A and Central MA) on each bank of the Ware River at this bridge.

Town Truss Bridge in detail with Kathryn Putnam. Lattice members are spruce timbers 8 cm. × 20 cm. and pinned at each joint with oak dowels.

were not quite so flammable. In this author's youth, the forested slopes of Tekoa Mountain, just where the Boston & Albany tracks begin their climb up and over the Berkshire Mountains, were routinely set afire by engines as they built up more steam for the hard work ahead.

In the *Encyclopedia of North American Railroads* by Middleton, Smerk, and Diehl (Indiana University Press, 2007), page 254, one can read of the historic place of the Howe truss:

> One early design favored by railroad builders was a wood lattice truss patented by Ithiel Town in 1820. This was built with principal horizontal top and bottom sections, or chords, of two or more timber members with a latticework web of planks between them. Most were built as covered bridges, contributing to a remarkable longevity. The design was popular in New England, where more than 100 survived into the twentieth century on Boston & Maine branches.
>
> A much more successful early timber truss design was developed in 1838 by Elias [sic] Howe of Spencer, Massachusetts. The Howe truss was not, strictly speaking, an all-timber design, since it contained heavy top and bottom chords and diagonal members of wood with vertical tension members of wrought iron. Later simplified, the Howe design soon became the most widely used wooden truss for railroad bridges.

The first major work of Town (1784–1844), an architect and engineer of Connecticut, was a truss supporting the roof of a church in New Haven.

* * *

Benoit Claudius Crozet (1789–1864) was born in the east-central France city of Villefranche-sur-Saone, some dozen or more kilometers upstream from the larger metropolis of Lyon, made historically notorious by the onset of the disturbing social chaos of the French Revolution. He graduated from the École Polytechnique and entered the Army as a sub-lieutenant where he was assigned to the Artillery School, of which the great Napoleon Bonaparte had also been a graduate. After only three years on active duty, he was involved in the Emperor's disastrous invasion of Russia and was captured 70 versts (an obsolete Russian measurement of distance — 3,500 feet or 1.07 km.) outside Moscow during the September 7, 1812, battle of Borodino, when Marshal Mikhail Kutuzov lost the day, shortly before the Russian winter won the campaign.

Held prisoner for two years before his release during a period of detente, Crozet was befriended by a well-placed Russian nobleman (whose name seems to have escaped all three of Crozet's biographers) and actually learned the Cyrillic language so well that he compiled a textbook for his countrymen on the Russian language. Like one of Napoleon's more famous subordinates, Marshal Michel Ney, Crozet was dispatched on a side errand just prior to the climactic battle of Waterloo, and got bogged down (literally) en route to the place where his ammunition train was desperately needed. Crozet was not shot for his failure, as was Ney, but married Agathe DeCamp in June of 1816 and rapidly exited the country.

Just prior to the battle of Waterloo, Ney (1769–1815), who had been one of Napoleon's favorite and most competent subordinates, was dispatched with several divisions to head off a Prussian detachment under Field Marshall Gebhard Blücher (1742–1819), known to be hastening to assist Wellington's army. He failed completely to even find this approaching force, for which the Chamber of Deputies (six months later) ordered him to be shot for treason. Despite this harsh treatment, three of his sons and two of his grandsons all served in the French Army. When Napoleon saw the successfully arriving blue-coated reinforcements for the British army, he is reported to have uttered one word: "*Merde*!"

Arriving in the United States, reputedly armed with an introduction by the Marquis de la Fayette, Crozet found employment as an instructor at West Point until 1823, during which period he introduced blackboards to American education and pioneered in the use of descriptive geometry. Then he made his wife much happier by leaving the northern winters to become the official cartographer and state engineer of Virginia. Crozet was later among the three founders of the Virginia Military Institute, one of whose early instructors in artillery tactics and natural philosophy was a local boy from Clarksburg (and West Point graduate) known in American history as "Stonewall" Jackson. The most brilliant of General Lee's subordinates, many historians believe that the death of Jackson (1824–1863) from "friendly fire" at the Battle of Chancellorsville deprived Lee of the one person who could have made a real difference in the subsequent three-day battle of Gettysburg.

Crozet's work as state engineer brought him to the task of laying out the Blue Ridge Railroad, which was absorbed into the Virginia Central after completion of the Blue Ridge Tunnel brought rail access from the James River drainage to the Shenandoah Valley (which drains northeastward to meet the Potomac at Harpers Ferry). Though a number of political reasons urged use of the more roundabout and slightly higher Swift Run Gap for a railroad, Crozet disliked its lengthy approach, as curving the line too far north for a sensible connection between Virginia's larger cities and "the West." He opted for the next major crossing to the south, Rockfish (striped bass) Gap, which was vastly closer to Charlottesville and Staunton, as well as some hundred meters lower.

This project, as completed, actually required the use of three lesser tunnels in working up the east slope of Bear Den Mountain, before culminating in the 1,299 m. major work, which took eight years to hole through. Crozet — who (unlike many contemporary Americans) managed to shift his thinking from the metric system, devised by the vicar of l'eglise de St. Paul in Lyon, Gabriel Mouton (1618–1694), and mandated by Napoleon in 1799, to the uncoordinated English measures used in his new country — personally aligned his surveys, and his workmen used only hand-held drills (driven to a depth of only some 30 cm.) and black gun powder. Some of these workmen were recent immigrants, mostly from Ireland, but a good many were Negro slaves supplied under contract. But the accuracy of Crozet's surveying was such that the two headings of the major tunnel met (on Christmas Day 1856) with only 15 cm. (6 inches) disagreement on alignment. Due to overlapping political pressures in Richmond, temporary tracks had earlier been laid over the top of the pass, requiring two switchbacks, grades of 5 percent and curves with a radius* of 500 feet — the occasion for several wrecks and runaways — but regular service through the tunnel was begun in April of 1858.

The smaller tunnels, piercing subsidiary ridges on the east approach from the James River drainage up to the crest of the Blue Ridge, were named as follows: Greenwood, at 164 m.; Brooksville, at 246 m.; and the highest but shortest, Little Rock, at only 30 m. These were easily driven, but only the longest, at the summit, required especial effort. With its western portal some 19 m. higher than the east, The Blue Ridge Tunnel was designed with the possibility of a "chimney effect" for future ventilation. But this had a drawback in construction, for some 300 m. (1,000 feet) into the tunnel, the workmen on the west heading encountered one of the almost routine nuisances that faced such endeavors — a 60 gallons per minute flow of water. Unfortunately, with the heading now being measurably below the adit,* this amount of water could have put a prompt end to driving the tunnel from the west. However, Crozet was able to obtain a sufficient supply of three-inch pipe and start a siphon to drain the face of the heading. The siphon worked so well that it became necessary, from time to time, to divert water from a small stream near the portal to flow into the tunnel and thus keep the siphon occupied with adequate water so that it would not lose its prime through the admission of air.

Unlike the Hoosac (as discussed in the following chapters) there was no steady drumbeat of political opposition and few disruptions to the orderly construction of the Virginia Central. From the start it was a more or less enthusiastically state-financed project, intended to link the main core of the Old Dominion waterways with the potential riches of the West and provide expeditious passage to the Mississippi, the Gulf of Mexico and whatever prosperity might be generated from beyond. However, during the Civil War, much of the fighting took place in the rural area between Richmond and Washington, thus disrupting a lot of agriculture and, thanks to Crozet's tunnel, the valley of the Shenandoah thus became the breadbasket for the capital of the Confederacy.

This is not to imply there were no problems or arguments during construction, for Crozet had a number of difficulties with contractors and a running disagreement with the Commonwealth's legislature which (agreeably enough) authorized the entire project, but then kept him on a tight fiscal leash by limiting his actual appropriations to $100,000 per year. However, the bedrock through which the Blue Ridge Tunnel was bored is only mildly metamorphosed, somewhat fossiliferous, blessed with an easily predictable subsurface projection (dip* and strike*), and often of a regular, blocky nature; which is a considerable advantage in drilling, boring and mucking over the tougher, more homogeneous and largely unseamed schistose bedrock of Hoosac Mountain.

Crozet could have used some of Ascanio Sobrero's nearly contemporary invention, which might have been available to him, for Alfred Nobel's first North American agent was a native of Tidewater, Virginia, but came by his military title of colonel thanks to the Commonwealth of Kentucky. This substance had been invented in 1845 by Sobrero (1812–1880), a Piedmontese who was so frightened by the power of his discovery that he kept it a secret for a year. Though eclipsed by Alfred Nobel (who was a fellow student in Paris, but had no such inhibitions and went on to develop safe methods of handling the substance) Sobrero became another leading light of Turin University.

Talliaferro Preston Shaffner (1818–1881) was also a most intriguing, if questionable, character. Born in Smithfield, he died in Troy, New York. In 1864 he was in the service of Denmark during that nation's self-inflicted and humiliating war with Prussia. Self-educated, an author and admitted to the bar, he was an associate of Samuel Morse in the introduction of the telegraph and also wrote *History of the United States of America*, in two volumes, published in London in the 1860s, and *The Telegraph Manual, A Complete History and Description of the Semaphoric, Electric and Magnetic Telegraphs of Europe, Asia, Africa, and America*, published in New York by Pudney & Russell in 1859. For some spicy details see "Adventures of a Pacifist" in the March 15, 1958, issue of *The New Yorker* by Robert Preston. That article includes an account of some of Nobel's most galling experiences in the world of business — a patent war and other skulduggery allegedly practiced by Shaffner.

When it was completed, the Blue Ridge Tunnel was far and away the longest in the New World, but failed to exceed the length of England's much older Woodhead by almost two miles. Ventilation was more of an issue in construction than in operation, for with its west portal at 580 m. ASL, some 19 meters higher than the east, when holed through, this did perform like as a chimney, so forced air movement was never necessary. However, during construction Crozet managed the ventilation issue on the working headings by the use of a mule-powered bellows arrangement, patterned after a design by the British general Sir John Fox Burgoyne (1782–1871), the leading figure of Queen Victoria's sappers and son of the "Gentleman Johnny" whose loss at the battle of Saratoga was critical to the American Revolution. But though longer than any North American bore heretofore, it was far from the first railroad tunnel in North America.

* * *

The honor of being North America's first railroad tunnel comes close to being claimed in northwestern Georgia, where in 1850 the Western & Atlantic Railroad, which ran for 216 km. (137 miles) from Atlanta to Chattanooga, taking 13 years to complete and was engineered throughout by Major Long, completed a 350 m. bore under Chetoogeta Mountain (later known as Tunnel Hill) north of Dalton in Whitfield County. This stayed in use until 1928, when a considerably larger diameter replacement

Second Chetoogeta Tunnel from north in 2009. The older tunnel is some distance to the left.

was bored nearby by the successor rail line, the Nashville, Chattanooga & St. Louis, at a cost of just less than $300,000, and which is currently large enough to handle the ubiquitous "double-stacks" of modern railroading. This second bore is still in use by the same CSX that now operates the one-time Virginia Central.

The Chetoogeta Tunnel also featured peripherally in one of the more bizarre Civil War encounters between soldiers of the North and South. In preparing to assault the city of Chattanooga, soldiers from the forces of the noted astronomer and Union general Ormsby MacKnight Mitchel (1809–1862) undertook to dress as civilians and make their way through the lines to blockade and paralyze traffic on the Western & Atlantic (W&A). Led by 33-year-old James J. Andrews, a civilian, the 21 volunteers (among whom were two locomotive engineers) made their way south and assembled at Marietta. There, on the morning of April 12, 1862, they boarded the northbound express to Chattanooga. When the train stopped so everyone could have breakfast at the four-room Lacey Hotel (later burned by Sherman's army) in Big Shanty, Georgia, the raiders took over the engine — fortuitously named General — and several box cars, disconnected everything else and took off up the line, planning to tear up some track and burn a few bridges, so the W&A could not be used to aid in the defense of Chattanooga.

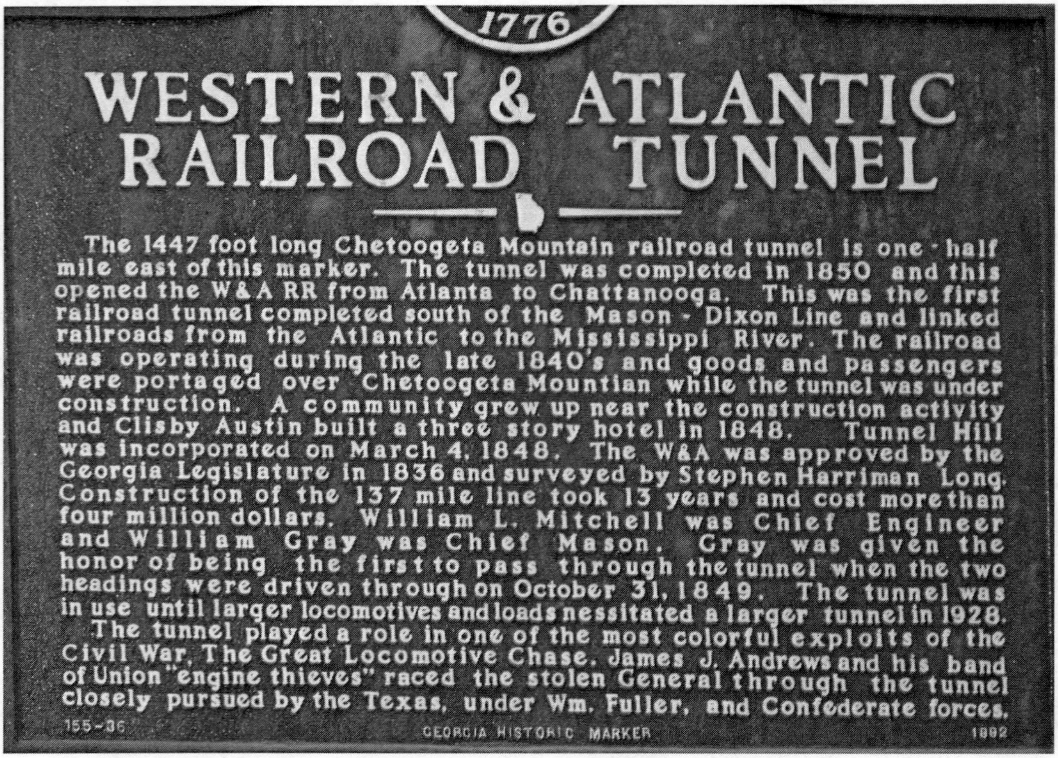

Modern sign for Western & Atlantic Railroad Tunnel.

Unfortunately, the weather was against them and rain made it difficult to get anything to burn. Also against the raiders was the irate conductor, William Allen Fuller (1836–1905), much of whose train had been stolen. When he realized what was happening, he left his meal uneaten and took off running in hot pursuit. He found a hand car and eventually commandeered the Yonah, a yard engine, while the raiders would periodically pull a few spikes, cut the telegraph wires and try to tear up rails or unhook one of their stolen cars to stall pursuit. At Kingston, Fuller and Anthony Murphy, chief engineer of the W&A's Atlanta shops, were able to get a faster engine, the Texas, from another passenger train and gain on the raiders, though traveling in reverse. The chase went on for dozens of miles and through the tunnel before the General ran out of fuel and was placed in reverse, while Andrews and his men jumped clear and took off into the woods. The Texas, however, had enough fuel to keep its steam pressure up and was able to nudge the dying General to a halt. All of Andrews' men were eventually captured, and several, including the civilian leader, were hanged as spies — but were also the first American soldiers to be awarded the Congressional Medal of Honor. Both Buster Keaton and Fess Parker starred in movies featuring this remarkable chase. The General was a typical 4-4-0 of the period made in Paterson, New Jersey, in 1855.

Not far up the line from Tunnel Hill toward Nashville is another bore constructed so that Chattanooga could be linked to the rest of Tennessee. The kilometer-long Cowan Tunnel was bored through the flat-lying softer sediments of the Cumberland Plateau during the four years after 1848 and was distinguished in that over its south portal ran the tracks of the now abandoned Tracy City branch of the Tennessee Central, which brought coal mined on the plateau to the east down to the major rail lines and cities of the state.

* * *

Even earlier, however, was Pennsylvania's Staple Bend Tunnel, near the Conemaugh River, which was completed in 1834 after three years of boring. At 275 m. it is shorter than the Chetoogeta but there is little dispute that it was the first significant railroad tunnel in North America, though its primary purpose at the start was to enhance the operation of canal traffic. However, the Black Rock Tunnel on the Philadelphia & Reading Railroad was opened soon thereafter, in 1837. Close behind these was the 320 m. Bundy Hill Tunnel, which was driven on a curve (no less) through gneissic rock for the Norwich & Worcester Railroad in northeastern Connecticut, and which was laid out and supervised by James Laurie (1811–1875), the Scots-born organizer in 1852 of the American Society of Civil Engineers. Laurie later jeopardized his luster somewhat by virtue of a consultative affiliation with the never-ending Hoosac bore (see chapter 4). Unfortunately, he did not comprehend the intense qualitative difference between the layered gneiss of northeastern Connecticut and the even more ancient schists of Hoosac Mountain. However, he was farsighted enough to insist that his line not use the easily available "snake rails"* but hold off tracklaying for two years to become the first in North America to make use of the modern style of all-iron "T" rail.

Early in its corporate life, the Pennsylvania Railroad also commissioned a pair of tunnels, followed by frequent improvements on those tunnels, in close proximity to each other in the rugged area between Altoona and Johnstown which are now collectively known as the Gallitzin Tunnels. They were bored starting in 1851 and formed the Pennsylvania's passage through the main barrier of the Allegheny Mountains en route from Philadelphia to Pittsburgh. It was in this effort that Herman Haupt gained his familiarity with the tunneling process; though he, too, obviously failed to appreciate the qualitative difference between the folded and layered sediments of western Pennsylvania and the much tougher and homogeneous schist of northwestern Massachusetts.

The first tunnel, which is the middle of the three bores through the sedimentary rocks of Allegheny Mountain, was constructed by the Pennsylvania beginning in 1851 and was opened for traffic in 1854. Originally named Summit Tunnel, it is 1,100 m. long at an elevation of 660 m. ASL and is known today as the Allegheny Tunnel. The second tunnel, the southernmost of the three bores, was constructed by the Commonwealth of Pennsylvania from 1852 to 1855 as part of the New Portage Railroad. In 1857 the NPRR was purchased from the Commonwealth by the Pennsy, which then applied the name "Allegheny" to its Summit Tunnel. The New Portage Tunnel was taken out of service shortly after its purchase by NPRR until the 1890s when it was expanded to two tracks and utilized as the primary route for eastbound traffic. The third tunnel, which is the northernmost of the three bores and is located immediately to the north of the Allegheny Tunnel, was begun in 1902, opened in 1904 and is actually in the township of Gallitzin, a locality which derived its name from Demetrius (1770–1840), the son of a Russian prince who became a Catholic missionary and founded the town. From 1993 to 1995 Conrail (with financial support from the Commonwealth of Pennsylvania) made significant revisions to the Allegheny and New Portage Tunnels to permit double-stack container trains to fit through these bores. The New Portage Tunnel was revised in 1993 for eastbound traffic, and the Allegheny Tunnel was substantially widened from its original 1854 dimensions to contain two tracks for double-stack traffic which could be used in either direction.

* * *

In an undated report compiled by Harvey Hicks, one can learn about one of the folklore-famed men often involuntarily employed (pre–Emancipation Proclamation) on other projects of this nature.

> John Henry was a steeldriver and was famous in the beginning of the building of the Chesapeake & Ohio Railroad. He was also a steeldriver in the extension of the Norfolk & Western. It was about 1872 that he was in this section. This was before the day of the steam drills and drill work was done by two powerful men who were special steel drillers. They struck the steel from each side and as they struck the steel they sang a song which they improvised as they worked. John Henry was the most famous steeldriver ever known in southern West Virginia. He was a magnificent specimen of

> genus homo, was reported to be six feet two [188 cm.], and weighed two hundred and twenty-five or thirty pounds [100 kg.], was a straight as an arrow and was one of the handsomest men in the country—and, as one informant told me, was "as black as a kittle in hell."
>
> Whenever there was a spectacular performance along the line of drilling, John Henry was put on the job, and it was said he could drill more steel than any two men of his day. He was a great gambler and was notorious all through the country for his luck at gambling. To the dusky sex all through the country he was "the greatest ever," and he was admired and beloved by all the negro women from the southern West Virginia line to the C&O. In addition to this he could drink more whiskey, sit up all night and drive steel all day to a greater extent than any man at that time. A man of kind heart, very strong, pleasant address, yet a gambler, a roue, a drunkard and a fierce fighter.[1]

Near Talcott, West Virginia, one can find more on John Henry. The famous ballad of John Henry, who allegedly swung a ten-pound hammer in each hand, while his assistant rotated the drill shaft, was derived from work done for the C&O:

> The man who owned the steam drill,
> Thought it mighty fine.
> But John Henry, he drove fourteen feet,
> And the steam drill only nine.

Truly steam-powered drills were a short-lived and ineffective invention of the 1850s. By this time, Burleigh's drills were in place almost everywhere, but using compressed air often acquired thanks to a steam-powered compressor. In association with a very substantial two-ton bronze statue, one can learn that the legend of John Henry is based on real, though nonspecific events involving an African American steeldriver in 1870 during the two-year boring of the Big Bend Tunnel under Great Bend Mountain on the Chesapeake & Ohio Railroad. After the American Civil War, many newly freed blacks, like John Henry, went to work rebuilding the transportation system of the states through which their war of liberation had been fought.

* * *

During the early years of the Civil War, the Blue Ridge Tunnel was integral to C.S.A. General Thomas Jonathan (Stonewall) Jackson's "Foot Cavalry," by means of which this brilliant tactician—a native of the region—was able to move his limited forces rapidly from one side of the range to the other. He thereby confounded better equipped and better manned Union commanders by confronting them with superior forces on very short notice. Because it turned out to be a vital supply line to the Confederate capital at Richmond, this line thus served an important (if in the end unsuccessful) function in the Civil War. It generated communications relative to its use and security such as those cited below between Henry Donald Whitcomb (in volume 26, page 88, of the *Confederate Veteran*, Whitcomb is referred to as "Colonel," a generic title for railroad conductors, and as a "prominent veteran"), the Maine-born, thirty-five-year-old general superintendent of the Virginia Central; James Alexander Seddon (1815–1880), the C.S.A. secretary of war, who had been a member of the 29th and 31st Congresses, but when the chips were down, became an ardent secessionist; and General Robert Edward Lee.

Headquarters Army of Northern Virginia,

June 28, 1864

Hon. Secretary of War,
Richmond:

Sir; The enemy has been engaged to-day apparently in strengthening his lines in front of Petersburg, advancing them at some points. His cavalry, after being repulsed at Staunton River bridge on the afternoon of the 25th, retired in the direction of Christianville, where they encamped for the night. The next morning they continued their march toward Lawrenceville by way of Brentsville, and a part of them encamped last night about eight miles northwest of the former place. They appear to be making their way back to the main body of the army.

Very respectfully, your obedient servant,
R. E. Lee,
General

Virginia Central Railroad,
General Superintendent's Office

Richmond, Va., June 28, 1864

Hon, James A. Seddon,
Secretary of War:

Sir: This road will be opened to within four miles of Staunton on Thursday. Permit me to urge upon you the importance of protecting us at Hanover Court-House. That is really the only point east of Gordonsville where a small raiding party can injure us materially by destroying the trestles and the bridge over South Anna, four miles beyond. Our road is not so important as it has been, but we hope to bring the city a considerable amount of wheat and other supplies. We have now repaired about nine miles of burned track, besides the bridges. We cannot hope, with the materials we have on hand or likely to get, to survive a similar disaster. We have yet about eight miles of track to repair at and west of Staunton, and ten bridges to rebuild. We do not propose to repair west of Staunton at present. I have requested the editors of the city papers [of which there were five] not to notice the re-opening of the road.

Very respectfully, your obedient servant,
H. D. Whitcomb
General Superintendent

To which lugubrious information and, after endorsements by Seddon and Hugh Lawson Clay, the assistant adjutant-general, Lee responded two days later.

Respectfully returned to the Adjutant and Inspector General.

I do not think there was any danger to the road from small raiding parties, at least none that could not be met by the reserve force, which I have previously recommended should be placed at the bridges. I also advised that the cavalry company, under Captain Anderson, in Hanover, should be used for the same purpose. They could give information of the approach of the enemy. Now that the enemy's cavalry is in force on the north side of James River the roads are exposed to attack. That can only be met by our cavalry, which has been ordered to that side of the James. **A permanent guard for the bridges cannot be furnished from this army** [emphasis added].[2]

Barely nine months later, the Confederacy's remaining rail system having been largely destroyed by the Union forces under Generals Grant and Sherman, and its governance a shambles, General Lee was forced to surrender the pitiful remnants of his army and sue for such clemency as he could get at another Court House location on a southerly tributary of the James River.

Many of the subsequent logistical problems of the Confederacy were explained in a letter of September 23, 1861, from Whitcomb to C.S.A. quartermaster Major W. S. Ashe:

There are three causes why the Government freight has been deterred to some extent, as follows

1st. The want of rolling stock. This road was provided with barely enough stock for the transportation of produce etc., in ordinary times, and even then we had delays from want of cars at certain seasons. Now we have the armies of the West, the Northwest, and of the Potomac, the population of a considerable city to supply. I think I am reasonable in saying that 77 percent of the supplies for this army is taken over some portion of our road.

2nd. The Government freight is irregular. Two weeks since (I write from memory) I applied to you, as you may recollect, for freight to transport, for I feared the very state of affairs which has since occurred, and for want of government freight we were transporting goods and merchandise for private parties. Then came this rush upon us, to be followed by another leisure spell.

3rd. Want of storage room at several points where goods are sent from by wagons to the army at Manassas, Fairfax and Millborough. At these points goods have remained in their cars, because they could not be unloaded for want of storage. It is not long since one of my employees, one who is considered a reliable man, saw thirteen trains at Manassas; eleven of which were loaded. Some of the trains probably came from Lynchburg. But as we have never sent more than two freight trains from Richmond to Manassas, you must see that there has been detention at one tiptoe, to say the least. I have no doubt there was good cause for it. I know that the cars have been detained at Millborough. There were probably fifty loaded cars there on Friday last. You have been obliged to issue orders to have them unloaded without a shelter for the goods. In future I suppose this cause of delay will not trouble us.

But with all the delays I can assure you that the detention at Richmond has not been serious. My impression has been that it has not exceeded forty-eight hours, except in the case of the flour mentioned. The order for that came on the 18th, we sent seventy barrels that day, and the last of the lot was loaded the 21st and went off this morning.

We are taking no private freights without permission from the quartermaster's office.

Very respectfully.
H. D. Whitcomb[3]

"State's Rights" thinking, rather than of the Confederacy as a whole, continued to afflict the South throughout the entire war. Until the very end, many states kept members (whole units) of their armed forces and other useful resources within their own boundaries, not allowing them to be used elsewhere, even in the common cause.

* * *

After the American Civil War — during which Virginia lost its 55 northwestern counties to their largely non-slaveholder population who seceded from the seceders, and in 1863 were admitted as a separate entity forming the 35th state — the Virginia Central was merged with the Covington & Ohio. It reappeared in 1869 as the Chesapeake & Ohio under the leadership of a "carpetbag" Connecticut Yankee, Collis Potter Huntington (1821–1900), earlier one of California's notorious "Big Four" of Central Pacific fame. Today the CSX Corporation, having swallowed up a lot of its competition (most notably America's first steam-powered line, the Baltimore & Ohio), has bypassed the venerable Blue Ridge Tunnel for an easier grade, a bit to the south under Afton Mountain, which was put into service in 1944. This is now officially known as the Blue Ridge Tunnel, with the name of Crozet being applied to the original, but now abandoned older. It is intriguing to note that the two headings of the replacement tunnel, though of comparable length and engineered and bored with vastly more efficient and modern means, were off alignment by the relatively massive amount of 1.2 m. when they met.

The sufferings of the B&O during the Civil War were complicated and enhanced by the actions of a sometime counsel for the competing Pennsylvania, who was Lincoln's secretary of war, and later largely responsible for the impeachment proceeding against President Andrew Johnson. Edwin McMasters Stanton (1814–1869) ordered cannibalization of parts of the B&O to repair other nearby lines.

All this subsequent consolidation was memorialized in a statement to both houses of the 40th Congress (1867–1869), in which Virginia was not represented (being still under reconstruction and not fully readmitted to the Union until January 26, 1870) and of which Schuyler Colfax (1823–1885) of South Bend, Indiana, was the Speaker. Later vice-president during Grant's first term, Colfax was unindicted but integral to the Crédit Mobilier Scandal relative to the Union Pacific Railroad. The C&O memorial was ordered to be printed on June 29, 1868, and reads, in pertinent part:

> The memorial of the Virginia Central Railroad Company respectfully represents, that by virtue of acts of the legislatures of the States of West Virginia and Virginia, copies of which are herewith presented, they are about to close a contract with the commissioners named in those acts, to complete the Covington & Ohio railroad. That when

> the contract is closed, the said Virginia Central Railroad Company becomes the Chesapeake & Ohio Railroad Company, and acquires all the rights and privileges conferred by those acts; that those rights and privileges are very valuable, among which is, becoming entitled, without charge, to an amount of work already done in graduation and masonry on the Covington & Ohio railroad, to the value of three million two hundred fifty thousand dollars ($3,250,000;) that it will require now about ten millions of dollars ($10,000,000) to complete the road; that the Chesapeake & Ohio Company is authorized to mortgage the whole property of the company from Richmond to the Ohio river; that its basis of credit, independent of the franchises of the Covington & Ohio road, cannot be estimated at less than fourteen millions of dollars ($14,000,000) after retiring the present debts of the Virginia Central Railroad Company; all of which will more fully appear by reference to a pamphlet which is herewith presented. That the road when completed will be worth upwards of twenty millions of dollars ($20,000,000) and will connect with the whole net-work of railroads in Kentucky and Ohio. This road lies on a direct line between Fortress Monroe and Norfolk and the mouth of the Ohio river, commencing at Richmond, passing by Charlottesville, Staunton and Covington, to which point it is now in operation 205 miles, crossing the Alleghany mountain in the county of Greenbrier, West Virginia, by a tunnel now finished, with a grade of only 29½ feet to the mile, then following the valleys of Greenbrier and Kanawha [one of the names initially proposed for the 35th state] rivers, and terminating on the Ohio river, by two branches, one at Point Pleasant, mouth of the Kanawha, the other at Catlettsburg, the mouth of Big Sandy, there being no grade eastward from the mouth of the Kanawha to the Alleghany exceeding twenty (20) feet to the mile.[4]

* * *

The CSX Corporation was formed in 1980 for the purpose of completing the merger of the Seaboard Air Line, the Baltimore & Ohio and the Chesapeake & Ohio Railway, among other railroads. (Somewhat at variance with our earlier semantic distinction between a railroad and a railway, the two terms have often been used in the United States to create a legal distinction between corporate entities in cases of bankruptcy or major reorganization — which happened to the Chesapeake & Ohio in 1873.) The Richmond, Fredericksburg & Potomac (on, around, and over which, much of the Civil War was fought) was acquired by CSX in 1991. An interesting sign of our times is that CSX presently runs four daily unit trains from New York City toward Florida; every train consists of 50 cars, each with four twenty-foot containers of trash bound for cogeneration plants or landfills from Virginia to Florida.

The litany of once independent lines that now form CSX is one of great nostalgia. It includes those already named above and the following, that were all to be found on the almost unanimously maroon-colored freight cars (This color of paint was alleged to have a longer life-span in its resistance to the sun's ultraviolet rays. A very few maverick lines, recognizing the advertising value of their freight cars, used other colors) of North America until after World War II: Atlantic Coast Line; Carolina, Clinchfield & Ohio;

Central of Georgia; Charleston & Southern; Louisville & Nashville; Monon (while its four main lines met at the small Indiana town of Monon, this "streak of rust" was formally known as the Chicago, Indianapolis & Louisville Railroad); Nashville, Chattanooga & St. Louis; Pere Marquette, Piedmont & Northern; Pittsburgh & Lake Erie; and Western Maryland; plus two one-time Vanderbilt lines, the New York Central and the New York, New Haven & Hartford. Much of this consolidation occurred in 1997, when the Norfolk & Southern acquired 58 percent of the assets of Conrail (which itself was the recipient of numerous bankruptcies, starting with that of the Penn-Central) and CSX acquired the remaining 42 percent.

Today, the CSX runs unit coal trains under Rockfish Gap; not as "purebred" or specifically operated as those of the CPR (see chapter 8), but serving the same purpose, from "captive" mines in West Virginia through to Norfolk for export to Europe. These trains are "mongrels," partially made up of cars gleaned from a number of no-longer extant lines; but they travel on rails that have been substantially upgraded, in many places consisting of 120 lb. continuous welded rail.

However, to actually enter the venerable tunnel of Colonel Crozet takes some special doing as the terrain of Rockfish Gap has been monumentally modified by the deep cut made through the ridge for Interstate Highway 64.

4

Politics Meets Geology Under Hoosac Mountain

PROMPTED, IN DUE COURSE, by the report of Loammi Baldwin, Jr., a special commission of the Massachusetts Legislature reported in 1825:

> There is no hesitation ... in deciding in favor of a tunnel; but even if its expense should exceed the other mode of passing the mountain, a tunnel is preferable.... And this formidable barrier once overcome, the remainder of this route from the Connecticut to the Hudson presents no unusual difficulties in the construction of a canal, but in fact the reverse; being remarkably feasible.

Because this was a landmark undertaking and in the end the actual dollars involved became so large in both relative and absolute terms—$22,000,000 (in 1870) vs. $22,000,000,000 (in 2000)—it is ineffective to enter into any comparisons as to the percentage of the body politic that benefitted from this first "dig" as opposed to those who benefitted from the more recent one, which was exclusively Bostonian. This process is even more difficult due to the declining real value of the dollar over the century and more between the 1860s and '70s and the 1990s and 2000s when the second great mortgaging of the Commonwealth of Massachusetts' credit took place. Nevertheless, this and the following chapter represent an apolitical undertaking based firmly on the hard rock of Hoosac Mountain, and only slightly on the muck of Boston Harbor and that of its nearby statehouse. Both ventures involved transportation; both cost many times more than the optimistic preliminary estimates; both ran into unforeseen obstacles, political and engineering; and both were finally completed after much controversy and loss of life.

Massachusetts has a long history of benign concern about its northwestern corner. After having finally cleared its title to the area by virtue of extensive negotiations with the Colony (and then State) of New York, in 1797 the Commonwealth chartered its second turnpike, to build a toll road "from the west line of Charlemont in the county of Hampshire, to the west foot of Hoosuck Mountain in Adams, in the county of Berkshire" (presently known as the North County Road), leaving New York State's eastern boundary controversies to be continued thereafter with the newly constituted 14th state,

Vermont. Hampshire County originally included the three other present Massachusetts counties of Berkshire, Hampden and Franklin. Berkshire was set off in colonial days, 1761, leaving Hampshire as what is today called the Pioneer Valley. The northern part of this smaller Hampshire was set off as Franklin in 1811. The southern part, Hampden, named for the roundhead catalyst of England's 17th century Civil War, was set off in 1812. Even later, 117 years to be precise, the Commonwealth constructed a highway (State Route #2 — AKA, The Mohawk Trail) largely following the line of a competing turnpike and going nearly across the top of the mountain, descending by one long switchback on the steeper west side.

* * *

In 1773, a year that ended with the dumping of 342 chests of unwanted bohea tea from the holds of the *Dartmouth*, the *Eleanor*, and the *Beaver* into Boston Harbor, Joseph Hawley (1723–1788), a prominent lawyer, politician and colonial patriot of Northampton, worked with representatives of neighboring New York to settle and define the western boundary of Massachusetts. There had been a large number of overlapping and conflicting royal grants made to the various colonies and/or royal favorites over many prior years. Sometimes the same territory was granted four or five times — mostly due to geographical ignorance, but never giving consideration to the rights of prior inhabitants — and none of the previous grantees recognized the validity of subsequent grants. According to one of these documents, Massachusetts extended westward all the way to the "South Sea."

In a gesture that helped to clear up much of the confusion, on Patriot's Day of 1785 (a State holiday in Maine and Massachusetts, April 19, commemorating the battles at Lexington and Concord in 1775), Massachusetts executed a deed transferring to the newly created United States of America, all rights, title and interest in lands west of the present western boundary of New York. Connecticut was a bit slower in so doing; Moses Cleaveland (1754–1806) led the state's first "paleface" settlement into northern Ohio in 1796, and the cession of that state's western reserve claims came in 1800. Western Reserve University, however, was founded in 1826. Incidentally, the truculence of the Bay Staters in regard to boundaries, tea dumping, jurors' strikes and similar manifestations of displeasure with royal authority were due, in some measure, to the fact that the Bay Colony, unique among the surviving thirteen (several colonies, such as those of Plymouth and New Haven, were legally merged into their larger neighbors prior to 1775), initially held a charter that did not require its annual corporators' meeting to be held in old England, where it could be supervised by vigilant royal minions.

Hawley had worked through the previous summer to survey and establish an agreeable boundary line, later described on page 22 of the New York Revised Statutes of 1875:

> Beginning at a monument erected in 1731 by commissioners from Connecticut and New York, distant from the Hudson River 20 miles, and running north 15 percent

> 12'9" east 50 miles 41 chains and 79 links, to a red or black oak tree marked by said commissioners, which said line was run as the magnetic needle pointed in 1787...

This acceptance of the migration of the magnetic north pole was a sophisticated subtlety that escaped many contemporary boundary surveyors, and the absence of which was to cause many controversies in later years. Presumably, with the passage of time, the oak tree proved an insufficient landmark and Hawley's line was resurveyed in 1889, a century later, and remarked (red or black oaks do not have the longevity of white oaks) and further refined in subsequent statutes adopted by the legislatures of both states.

* * *

Hoosac (an Algonkian word meaning "stony place") Mountain lies around the head of Cold River, a steep, westerly branch of the Deerfield River, itself a lengthy tributary to the Connecticut on the west that rises in Vermont and curves east to enter the main stream just south of Greenfield. It was recognized by everyone that reasonable grades for a canal or railroad were to be found along its banks and along those of the Hoosic River down to the Hudson, some miles above Troy on the far (western) side of the mountains. Scraped and sculpted by the repeated passage of continental glaciers during the Pleistocene period, the gneissic and schistose rocks of Hoosac Mountain were sufficiently durable to withstand the powerful erosive action that glaciers possess, leaving this obstacle as a barrier to easy transport between the subsequent towns of Florida, on the east, and North Adams, on the west. Many of the township names in western Massachusetts pertain to heroes of the American Revolution — from Adams, via Hawley, Heath, Lee, Pitt and Prescott to Washington. However, glaciers, when melting away, drop all the material they have in transit, leaving a substantial ground cover of generally difficult and "bony" soil, from which enterprising Yankee farmers fled by the thousands when the much easier farmland of the American Midwest became available in 1790 — leaving behind their stonewalls but taking along many of their place names. For example, Worcester is Wooster in several Midwestern states; but Springfield is harder to misspell and can be found in 43 other states.

According to arithmetic compiled by the Commonwealth of Massachusetts (which typically did not include the carrying costs of interest on the debt) the Hoosac Tunnel cost the taxpayers of the Bay State about $14,000,000 (or $2,917,000 per mile). On the other hand, according to European governmental arithmetic (which may well be equally distorted from financial reality) the Frejus cost $15,000,000 (or $1,829,000 per mile) as reported by the Italian State Railways. Modern French sources put the final cost at 75 million francs; though no one specifies which brand or vintage of franc. Not all this difference in cost can be blamed on Derby, Crocker, Haupt, or any of the other engineers involved, for the pre–Cambrian bedrock of the Berkshires is a lot older and tougher than the Mesozoic formations which make up the much younger Blue Ridge or Graian Alps.

In contrast, Laommi Baldwin's first report of 1825 (the same year that the world's first steam-powered railroad — the Stockton & Darlington — began operation in England) indicated that a five-mile canal through Hoosac Mountain could be bored for less than a million dollars, and included a pitch for funding such an expenditure by means of a state lottery: "If an unabatable evil does exist, let it be converted to the best possible purposes." A further report, three years later, by the Massachusetts Board of Internal Improvements, suggested three trans–Massachusetts routes from Boston, of which two and two-thirds were ultimately constructed: The B&A (to Albany), the Fitchburg (to Troy) and the Central Massachusetts (only to Northampton and later largely abandoned). This report also cited Baldwin relative to the Hoosac line: "It seems as if the finger of Providence had pointed out this route from the East to the West..." to which some irreverent skeptic later appended: "It's a great pity the same finger wasn't thrust through the mountain."

* * *

Washington Gladden (1836–1918) was a congregational clergyman and prolific author who was a pastor in North Adams from 1866 to 1871, and thus had a personal familiarity with the great project going on in his area. He was then called down to Springfield's North Church where he stayed ten years until he went to Columbus, Ohio. Gladden was a progressive in all positive senses of the word; very much opposed to racial segregation and a leader in his line of endeavor, who later served as president of Ohio State University. In *Scribner's Magazine* for December 1870, starting on page 143, he wrote an article including the following geographical analysis:

> The westernmost of the three mountain chains which form the great Appalachian system, stretches without interruption from the western boundary of South Carolina to the northern boundary of Maine. Through the Carolinas, Virginia, Maryland, and Pennsylvania, it is known as the Blue Ridge. In New Jersey it is called Schooley's Mountain. Crossing into New York, it breaks into a magnificent group of craggy peaks, and, parting to let the Hudson pass, is christened the Highlands. Thence it trends to the eastward, and pushes away to the north near the western boundary of Connecticut, till it reaches the southern line of Massachusetts, where it divides into two parallel ranges. The western range serves as a boundary between Massachusetts and New York, and bears the name of the Taghkanics or Taconics. Over the tops of the other range of hills which are known as the Hoosac range, the zig-zag line of Berkshire county runs. Near the Vermont border these parted columns are massed again in the broad bulwark of the Green Mountains, which stretches northward through Vermont, then north-westward along the northern boundary of Maine, terminating in the Canadian [Gaspé] peninsula that separates the Gulf of St. Lawrence from the Bay of Chaleur...
>
> We are only concerned at present, however, with the fact that the western ridge of the Appalachian chain separates New England from the rest of the Union. A narrow belt of country in Vermont is found on the west of this natural boundary, but neither of the other States crosses it. The commercial intercourse of New England with the West has been greatly obstructed by this mountain barrier. It has not served to stem

the tide of emigration westward, neither has it weakened the affection of the people of the new States for their old homes; but it has prevented the emigrants from keeping up the close business relations with their native States that they would, under other circumstances, have maintained. The western merchant, arriving at Albany or Troy by railroad or canal, finds a magnificent river waiting to bear him and his merchandise to New York; while between him and the New England markets, stretches for hundreds of miles up and down an abrupt and difficult mountain wall. It is not surprising, therefore, that he goes to New York with his merchandise. Emigration may follow parallels of latitude, but traffic always follows the easiest and shortest route to market, with no reference at all to parallels or pedigrees...

At the present time freight and passengers from the West are brought to the metropolis of New England by three principal routes: the Grand Trunk Railroad through Canada, which reaches the Atlantic coast at Portland, Maine, and approaches Boston from the East; the Vermont Central Railroad, which draws its traffic from the St. Lawrence river by various connecting lines; and the Boston & Albany Railroad. Of these three roads, the two former pierce the mountain barrier by passes far to the northward without any very difficult engineering, but they follow routes too circuitous to be of much practical advantage to Boston as through lines from the West. The Boston & Albany Railroad is nearly as short as any railroad connecting the Hudson river with Boston can be; but between Springfield and Pittsfield, where it climbs over the Hoosac range, the grades are terrific. For this reason, though the railroad is managed with vigor and enterprise, it is still inadequate for the transaction of the business that ought to be carried on between Boston and the West.

* * *

The Hoosac project, however, had other issues to overcome, not merely those due to its difficult geology and underfinanced promoters. A good many people, among whom was the distinguished medical doctor and essayist Oliver Wendell Holmes (1809–1894), felt it was not worth doing at all and a gigantic waste of resources. His poem "Latter Day Warnings" in *The Autocrat of the Breakfast Table*, self-published in 1858, echoed much popular opinion:

When legislators keep the law, When banks dispense with bolts and locks,—
When berries, whortle-rasp — and straw — Grow bigger downwards through the box,—
When he that selleth house or land — Shows leak in roof or flaw in right,—
When haberdashers choose the stand — Whose window hath the broadest light,—
When preachers tell us all they think — And party leaders all they mean,—
When what we pay for, that we drink — From real grape and coffee-bean,—
When lawyers take what they would give — And doctors give what they would take,—
When city fathers eat to live — Save when they fast for conscience' sake,—
When one that hath a horse on sale — Shall bring his merit to the proof,—
Without a lie for every nail — That holds the iron on the hoof,—
When in the usual place for rips — Our gloves are stitched with special care,—
And guarded well the whalebone tips Where first umbrellas need repair,—
When Cuba's weeds have quite forgot — The power of suction to resist,—

And claret-bottles harbor not — Such dimples as would hold your fist, —
When publishers no longer steal, And pay for what they stole before,
When the first locomotive's wheel rolls — Through the Hoosac tunnel's bore;
Till then let Cummings blaze away — And Miller's saints blow up the globe;
But when you see that blessed day — Then order your ascension robe!
[emphasis added].

Joseph Cummings (1817–1890) was among those who waxed eloquent about the "Great Comet" of 1854 and William Miller (1782–1849) was a fiery second Adventist preacher, then of Pittsfield, Massachusetts.

* * *

In his monumental 1995 work *The North American Railroad*, James Elmon Vance, Jr. (1925–1999), a native of Natick, Massachusetts, and UC Berkeley professor of economic geography, gives a concise analysis of the reasons for Massachusetts — as personified by the leading merchants and businessmen of Boston — to develop efficient railroad access to the West, and how that process was damped and frustrated by competing political and economic interests, notably those of New York City and State.

> The Western Railroad of Massachusetts was the first American line actually to cross the Appalachians [as manifested by the glacially scoured, pre–Cambrian bedrock hills of southern New England], so in its construction the great purpose of the initial stage of national railroad development was first accomplished. That it was only partially successful from an economic viewpoint in gaining an opening for Boston to the West was not the fault of the engineers who accomplished the not inconsiderable feat of crossing two major divides of the Appalachian system [that between Worcester and Springfield, and the considerably more formidable one between Springfield and Albany]; the rub came in the political geography of the eastern United States. In the case of New York State and Pennsylvania, and only in a precise sense less so for Maryland [and Virginia] the trans–Appalachian crossing could be accomplished within the jurisdiction of the state whose metropolis sought through rail-building to gain a line of mercantile advance into the interior. But for Boston and Massachusetts, no such easy course was open. Once across the Appalachians, the engineers still had to face the [political] fact that there is no way out of New England within the United States save through New York State. To gain the development objective of the West there had to be cooperation from the state legislature of New York, and that body showed little inclination to render such aid. It was one thing to authorize the extension of the Massachusetts rail line for the ten miles that intervened between the Commonwealth's western boundary and the Hudson River, another to encourage the extension of Boston interests all the way across the Empire State.
>
> If New York City had sat idly by while such an undertaking was entered into, which was unlikely and did not happen, the interests of the state would have obviated such a course. The state, having invested millions in the building of the Erie Canal, sought to guard that facility, and its tolls, against railroad competition.[1]

In 1828, another special commission of the Massachusetts legislature reported that westward communications could get over the mountain with a railroad more quickly and cheaply than they could get through it; thus dampening enthusiasm for the idea of a Hoosac Mountain Canal and giving legislative endorsement to the use of a more southerly line, which was very soon followed by the Western Railroad of Massachusetts. Vance noted:

> The hills determined the road's character. The Boston & Worcester had seventeen miles of level track, the Western only seven; the maximum [grade] was 83 feet [per mile] and there were one hundred and seven miles that had grades in excess of any on the Boston & Worcester. The Western was a road of deep cuts, great embankments, sharp curves and great costs. The summit section at Washington [Massachusetts], 1456 feet [444 m.] above sea level, was 1.8 miles [2.9 km.] long and cost $241,311. As late as the mid–1860s the most powerful engines were carrying over the road trains of only eight to ten cars averaging ten tons to a car fully loaded.
>
> The grades were in fact slightly steeper — eighty-seven feet per mile, or 1.5 percent — because at the time of construction it was found necessary to carry the grade somewhat higher above the turbulent streams [Quabaug and Westfield Rivers] than had been anticipated. In crossing the eastern summit the company had to choose between directness and gentle grades. Many routes were examined in the "highlands which divide the waters of the Blackstone River, upon which the village of Worcester stands, and those of the Chickopee [and Quabaug, flowing into the Connecticut], extending from north to south across the state. They are broken into numerous ridges and ravines; and to surmount these at any reasonable grades, resort must be had to a succession of cuttings and embankments, or a constant series of curves...."[2]

In the widespread flooding associated with a 1955 hurricane, many segments of these embankments were washed out; in one case near the Chicopee River in Wilbraham, leaving almost a quarter-mile of track, complete with attached ties, hanging unsupported. However, there has always been a sense of economic frustration afflicting the thought processes of Massachusetts' (mostly Bostonian) political decision-makers, who were urged on and supported by the merchants and shippers of Boston, in their natural desire to overcome any drawback to good western access. Bostonians knew that their port was closer to all points in Europe (if not China) than New York, a geographical advantage of a sort; but their frustration only increased as the economic advantages of New York's superior connection to the interior of North America continued to bring ever greater revenues to that port, while Boston's overseas shipments languished or grew only marginally. In 1811 the foreign trade of Boston and New York were roughly equal; but by 1859 Boston's was sixteen million dollars, whereas New York's had risen to forty-one million. In addition, New England farmers and shippers were very unhappy with "Mr. Madison's War" (that of 1812) because they had waxed prosperous in selling foodstuffs to Wellington's Army in the "Peninsula Campaign" against Napoleon. The otherwise unnotable central Massachusetts hill town of Petersham had become the largest wheat producing locality in the nation and secession was widely bruited in many town meetings.

> The northern line was not, however, abandoned. But for the one formidable obstacle presented by the Hoosac range it was by far the most practicable route between the

> East and the West. Extending west from Fitchburg, it descends the valley of Miller's River to Greenfield; then crossing the Connecticut, it finds a deep though sinuous passage which the Deerfield River, coming from the west, has cut through the hills for thirty miles. Following this stream upward without difficulty, it reaches at length a bend in the river where the Deerfield comes down from the north, and its course is no longer practicable. Up to this point, with a little care in his alignments, the engineer has found an easy passage, but now he is confronted by the steep sides of the Hoosac mountain range, standing directly across his path.
>
> Starting at Troy, the western end of his line, and going eastward, he meets with exactly the same problem. The Hoosic River, which empties into the Hudson a little above Troy, has cut the Taghkanics in twain for him, and a most beautiful route is open to the village of North Adams, where the west side of the Hoosac mountain rises before him more abrupt and lofty than the eastern side. But for this Hoosac mountain, the route, as the Commissioners say, is, considering the nature of the country between the Connecticut and the Hudson, remarkably feasible.[3]

In 1840 a committee of the Western directors journeyed to Albany to negotiate their road's entry into New York State. This group was headed by Elias Hasket Derby III (1803–1880) of Salem, a shipping magnate (mostly in the China trade), capitalist, lawyer, diplomat, confidante of Daniel Webster, and specialist in railroad litigation, who lived in Boston; and, being primarily interested in freight rates to that port, ultimately came to see much merit in completion of the Hoosac Tunnel. Somewhat to their surprise, they returned home with a commitment for a $650,000 construction loan to be used for that portion of their line in New York State.

* * *

The major personality in the forefront, as well as behind the scenes, throughout the development of the Hoosac Tunnel was Alvah Crocker (1801–1874), a fourth generation descendant of the England-born Captain John Crocker (1699–1763). Captain Crocker with his son Benjamin (1732–1777) sailed the coast of New England from Newbury in the brig *Ranges* and later established the first ropewalk in Newburyport. Benjamin's son, the Baptist deacon Samuel Crocker (1774–1856), became a papermaker a generation after the English Parliament had enraged Americans by enacting such regulations as the infamous Stamp Act, and removed from the coast to the Leominster/Fitchburg area. Alvah, John's great-grandson, took over his father's papermaking business, expanded it greatly and passed it on to his siblings (as Crocker-Burbank & Co.) and their descendants, who expanded their operations in Fitchburg and throughout Massachusetts, at Turners Falls (where the dam and hydroelectric development morphed into the Western Massachusetts Electric Company, later a major component of Northeast Utilities) and most notably in Holyoke where there was even greater waterpower available. In the course of developing their paper mills, the Crocker family found themselves deeply immersed in the business, social and philanthropic affairs of Fitchburg.

> No one will ever know the extent of Alvah Crocker's philanthropies, but it is fitting that he will be best remembered by the citizens of his native city for his magnificent gift of Crocker Field, the first and finest schoolboy athletic plant in the state.[4]

Throughout the years, the Crocker family continued as the prime philanthropists of the Fitchburg area; Bigelow ("Big") Crocker, Jr. (1922–2007), Alvah's great-grandson and member of the fifth generation management team, left a million dollars to the Fitchburg Historical Society. Alvah's donation of Crocker Field in Fitchburg is frequently mentioned as equally illustrative of the Olmstead (father-and-son) talent in the development of public parks, along with Yosemite National Park, the Common in Boston and Central Park in New York City. Alvah's nephew, Clifton Alvah Crocker (1858–1939), became a prominent citizen of both Holyoke, where his paper mill was located, and Springfield, where he lived. A leading light of the YMCA movement, he hobnobbed with the likes of William Howard Taft, who even came to address such a group in the Crocker home at 297 Union Street — the front hall and living room of which pre–Revolutionary War structure were specially reinforced with multiple posts in the basement for this "weighty" occasion — when he was serving as unpaid water commissioner of Springfield and the latter was chief justice of the United States.

Alvah Crocker, who attended the nearby and soon-to-be prestigious Groton Academy (when he had the necessary funds), made a good product that was much in demand, and prospered sufficiently that he sought to expand his market into Boston. In time, the mills he operated became the largest in the United States and were the first to use the waste fiber from the cotton mills of Waltham, Lowell and Nashua, to enhance the quality of their paper. The logistic issue of getting various raw materials to his mills and then moving the finished products to the nearby major market of Boston brought him to promoting the idea of a railroad. And in 1842 he became a prime mover in raising $750,000 for the construction of what was soon officially called the Boston & Fitchburg Railroad. Crocker even went to England to purchase its original rails, and the line's first train arrived in Fitchburg on March 5, 1845, with Alvah himself riding the engine.

Alvah became a member of the lower house of the state legislature — serving as a Whig in 1836, '41 and '43 — then led in the westward extension of the Fitchburg, and later served two terms in the state senate, during which he became the driving member of the state's Hoosac Tunnel Commission. After his sojourns in both houses of the Massachusetts Legislature, Crocker was elected (as a member of the dominant Republican party) to the 42nd Congress (1871–1873) to take the seat vacated by William Barrett Washburn (1820–1887) of Greenfield, who had been elected governor of the Commonwealth.

Parenthetical to this narrative (see chapter 7), another member of the wider Crocker family, Charles (1822–1884) — the closeness of whose relationship to Alvah, though traced back to England, is difficult to verify — was born in Troy, but migrated to California with the 49ers and became a merchant and then a banker in Sacramento. With

Mark Hopkins, Collis Huntington and Leland Stanford, he became an owner of the Central Pacific Railroad, ultimately driving it to completion across Donner Pass to Promontory Point, Utah, and into American history books as the master on-site builder of California's not-always-beloved "Big Four."

In the Congress,[5] Alvah Crocker made several presentations and speeches about the evil effects of the tariff on imported iron and steel, pointing out that the value to the United States of improved railroads was worth much more to the nation than whatever might be gained by protecting domestic producers of iron. In one of his speeches he cited statistics published by the Massachusetts Legislature relative to construction of the Western Railroad to indicate the total tonnage (3,878,000 lbs.—including 950,000 lbs. for 29 engines alone) of iron necessary to build railroads. In this line of thinking, he was flying in the face of American history and the tariff policies of Alexander Hamilton that had financed the federal government almost entirely—set at 40 percent in order to help pay for the Civil War. However, Crocker's best speech may well have been that given on June 5, 1874, as shown in the *Congressional Record*, in support of a measure that Virginia would have found dear, when he spoke on the desirability of a federal appropriation to remove the notorious sandbar at the mouth of the Mississippi River that restricted upstream navigation for oceangoing craft:

> ... did Boston, the pride of New England, after the loss of one hundred millions by fire, hold back? [Boston's "Great Fire" of 1872 took out scores of city blocks and 349 buildings.] Are we not ready to share what God in his mercy has given us? Ay, sir, say not South, or West. So long as our glorious inland seas from the cold Superior to Ontario lave our northern shores, or the roar of Niagara's cataract is heard to heaven; or the stormy Atlantic billow roars its requiem upon the rockbound shores of New England; so long as the electric wire from our shores under its bed, three thousand miles away, clicks the business throb of a great country, so throbs the heart of our people from every state in our Union. [The Atlantic cable, promoted by Cyrus West Field (1819–1892) of Stockbridge, Massachusetts, had been successfully completed in 1866.] Touch Louisiana, or California or any other State with distress and suffering, and you touch the East and North.

The South Pass pilings and weirs were completed five years later and remain among the most notable projects of James Buchanan Eads.

* * *

In the other enterprise to which Crocker devoted his great energy, the westward extension of the Fitchburg Railroad, his most formidable foe—second only to the difficult rock of Hoosac Mountain—was another business magnate of the state, Chester Williams Chapin (1798–1883) from Springfield. He had been a member of the Massachusetts Constitutional Convention of 1853—at which the major item of debate was whether the state should be allowed to invest in private enterprises (like railroads)—and was later elected (as a Democrat) to the 44th Congress (1876–1878). When he was not engaged in politics, Chapin was a major ownership and management figure of the Western Railroad Corporation and its successor (after the merger of 1867), the Boston & Albany Railroad that ran west from Boston through Worcester, Springfield and Pittsfield to Albany. This iron-shod line (its original snake rails were spaced 3 feet apart and 3/16 inches thick) was one of the country's earliest, having been initiated in 1831 as the Boston & Worcester Railroad. It was opened for traffic in stages, as were most railroads — as far as Newton in mid–April 1833; to Wellesley in early summer and Ashland in late summer; to Westborough by late 1834; and finally to its initial terminus at Worcester on July 6, 1835. It ran through largely level terrain and encountered few obstacles to tax its construction crew.

Chapin was an important figure in the regional economy, mostly of western Massachusetts; one of the founders of the Massachusetts Mutual Life Insurance Company; and a respected member of one of the major family names of the area, a man with great social, economic and political influence and a strong supporter of the community's railroad. The most visible public statue in the Springfield area, adjacent to the public library on State Street, is an oversize St. Gaudens rendering in bronze of the settlement's first magistrate, Deacon Samuel Chapin (1598–1675).

In 1844 Crocker, who was also an organizer of the Fitchburg Mutual Fire Insurance Company, began to extend his Vermont & Massachusetts Railroad westward through Gardner, Athol and Orange to Greenfield, with a branch from Millers Falls to Brattleboro and an obvious eye toward making a westerly connection beyond the Berkshire Mountains. Chapin and his associates began to worry about the impact such a line might have on the business of their road. Fortunately, there was no legal prohibition in those days (or since) about using political influence to gain an economic advantage.

The principal among Chapin's railroad associates was Daniel Lester Harris (1818–1879), a native of Providence who became an active and prosperous entrepreneur in Springfield and one of the principal owners of the Connecticut River Railroad, which ran north, mostly along the west side of the river from Holyoke and brought much traffic downstream to the Western. Harris was also in politics, a sometime member of the General Court and mayor of Springfield in 1860. The Commonwealth, moreover, had a vested interest in the Western; in 1836 the General Court had authorized a major loan, along with the purchase of a million dollars worth of its stock, and four members of its board of directors were the state's nominees. However, citizens of western Massachusetts have long felt neglected, overlooked and abused by the majority in the state house representative of the more populous east. Thus, when Boston interests worked to promote an easier — but non–Springfield — route for freight to reach their port from the hinterland of America, it was civic — almost patriotic — on the part of residents of the Springfield area to oppose such a proposal. The local voters expected such, bought the newspapers that agreed with their sentiments, and generally cheered their champions on.

Meanwhile, Chapin's coterie, in a ploy meant as an economic deterrent to Crocker's plans for a through railroad across the northern tier of Massachusetts (which they knew — if ever completed — would end up with a far easier grade than the summit elevation of the Western), wasted no time in announcing they would soon have their railroad double-tracked all the way from Boston to Albany. Chapin also welcomed the construction of branch trackage off the Western — several short bits in the Boston area, and two major lines in mid-state. One was the Ware River line from Palmer north to Winchendon, on the New Hampshire state line (Governor Washburn's hometown), which was financed largely with subscriptions from the towns along its route and started in 1868, finally reaching Winchendon in 1873. When its operating lease to the New London & Northern (thence to the Vermont Central) expired upon completion, Chapin personally bought the entire line and resold it to the B&A, a tale that modern muckrakers might find irresistible.

The Athol branch, north from Springfield, was built initially with similar subscriptions, as the Athol & Enfield, starting south in 1870. Burdened with a heavy debt, it collapsed in 1879 and was promptly gobbled up by the B&A. The A&E's biggest financial gain may well have been in 1874, when the it sold one hundred car loads of ties to the Troy & Greenfield for rebuilding after the flood of October 1870. Both these additions to the B&A had long lives; the Athol branch finally falling victim to the creation in the 1930s of Quabbin Reservoir (which also wiped out four whole townships — Dana, Enfield, Greenwich and Prescott), while the Ware River line was partially overwhelmed by increasingly better highways and recurrent contemporary floods. Chapin had taken an equally significant deterrent step in 1849 by extending a 20-mile Western branch north from Pittsfield to North Adams (now a bike trail).

Crocker, however, had the strong support of soon-to-be Governor Washburn, who had varied business interests in Erving and Greenfield; and who, like Crocker, was personally anxious to enhance their economic potential by improving the east-west transportation system as it impacted his community. Washburn had been in the Congress after 1863 until he resigned to become governor at the end of 1871. After two years in that office, he was elected to the United States senate, to fill the vacancy caused by the death of Charles Sumner, but he refused reelection in 1875 and thereafter devoted himself to his various business interests in western Massachusetts. Among those interests was the Connecticut River Railroad, which was ultimately extended on northward to White River Junction, but was leased in 1893 to the Boston & Maine.

The Western Railroad of Massachusetts, the extension of the B&W onward from Worcester, was chartered in 1833, with construction beginning in 1837. Its "Eastern Division" — from Worcester to Springfield — was completed through somewhat more difficult terrain by the fall of 1839; and the promoters then faced the novel challenge of a bridge across the Connecticut River — the major stream of New England, which then had only ferries for crossing most of its four-hundred-mile length. The chief engineer assigned to the Western Railroad in 1840 was a sometime lieutenant of artillery, George Washington Whistler (1800–1849), father of the famed artist, who had also

Whistler/Birnie bridge over the west fork of Westfield River, still in use on the B&A with vastly heavier rolling stock, after more than 170 years.

worked on the B&O and later went to Russia to lay out the Tsar's railroad from St. Petersburg to Moscow. Some of the massive keystone arch bridges Whistler designed for the B&A are still in use 170 years later, though they were actually built under the immediate direction of an immigrant Scotsman from Portobello, William Birnie (1818–1899). Whistler later became a partner with Howe and Stone on railroad bridge projects all over southern New England, while Birnie went into the building supply business in Springfield. The massive masonry structures that the CPR caused to be built at Rogers Pass (see chapter 8) were also done by Scots masons.

* * *

Other pertinent personages who played serial parts in the drama of the Hoosac bore were some of its numerous subsequent engineers and contractors — after the state foreclosed in 1862 on its initial loan of $2,000,000 to the Troy & Greenfield Railroad. This list should be headed by Hermann Haupt (1817–1905) of Philadelphia, "a small, wiry looking man, of great capacity and boundless energy,"[6] who had been appointed to the United States Military Academy at the age of 14 by President Andrew Jackson and graduated in 1835 to be commissioned a second lieutenant in the 3rd U.S. Infantry that July. He resigned his commission three months later to become a civil engineer and work on bridge and tunnel construction for New Jersey's Norristown Railroad. From 1840 to 1847 Haupt was professor of mathematics and engineering at Gettysburg College (then known as Pennsylvania College). He returned to the railroad business in 1847, becoming a construction engineer on the Pennsylvania Railroad, and then its general superintendent from 1849 to 1851. He was detached to serve as chief layout engineer for the Southern Railroad of Mississippi from 1851 to 1853 — extending its tracks to Vicksburg — and then returned as chief engineer of the Pennsylvania until 1856, during which period he completed its mountain division with the Allegheny Tunnel, opening the line to Pittsburgh.

The subsequent personal tribulations of Haupt in dealing with: (1) his own friends and partners, mostly from Philadelphia; (2) a series of inept and/or faithless employees and agents; (3) his own occasionally incomplete accounting; and (4) a seemingly interminable series of nitpicking, obstinate and often spiteful bureaucrats and officials in the Massachusetts State House, all amount to a dismal story of a good and brave engineer brought to despair and financial ruin. This sad tale is well, if not pleasantly, documented in a lengthy article by Edward Rice Ardery (1920–2006) from which we cite further below. Haupt put his heart, soul, family and all he possessed into the Hoosac Tunnel project; having his two teenaged sons working with him in the field, personally soliciting subscriptions from the townships along the route, and even having his wife, née Anna Cecelia Keller (1821–1891), run a smallscale boarding house in Greenfield to help keep the family afloat.

Then there was the trio of civil engineers, one of whom was sent to Europe in 1863 to learn about tunnel techniques from the Frejus project: (1) the Bostonian Charles Storer Storrow (1809–1904), who had worked on layout for the Boston & Lowell Railroad, then designed the Great Stone Dam on the Merrimack River, which furnished reliable water power to the mills of Lowell; (2) the Scots-born James Laurie (1811–1875), chief engineer for the thousand-foot Bundy Hill Tunnel of the Norwich & Worcester Railroad in 1835–37; and (3) William Scollay Whitwell (1809–1899), who had designed some of Boston's pre–Quabbin water supplies and the extensive sewerage system for Jersey City and was the Commonwealth's supervising engineer for the tunnel after 1870.

* * *

On May 10, 1844, Alvah Crocker, then in elective public office, secured a charter in the name of three prominent citizens (George Grennell, Jr. [1786–1877], previously a member of Congress and later a judge; Roger H. Leavitt; and Samuel H. Reed, later clerk of the Superior Court) of Greenfield for the Troy & Greenfield Railroad from the General Court of Massachusetts, which specifically included provisions for a tunnel under Hoosac Mountain. As was commonplace in major railroad projects, all of which required state-issued charters to qualify for the privilege of eminent domain, separate but companion corporations were organized in Vermont and New York, thus forming a regional railroad (on paper) composed of five legal entities — of which Alvah Crocker was directly involved in three. The Troy & Boston Railroad was chartered on November 22, 1849, and completed from Troy to the Vermont state line (35 miles) in 1852.

Getting a line built up along the Deerfield River was relatively simple, though the earliest layouts were so beset with washouts and excessive curvature that the route had to be substantially relocated before any real use could begin. And even unto the present day, several upgrades later, high water occasionally takes out parts of the roadbed. Nevertheless, Crocker felt that with the funds available to the Troy & Greenfield he could get on with the tunnel. In 1848 with the slogan "On to Hoosac, on to the West," the Troy & Greenfield line was activated, taking over from the "three prominent citizens of Greenfield" who had been its legal godfathers. The long-predicted tunnel was now planned to cost under $2,000,000 (it ultimately reached in excess of ten times that amount), and on January 8, 1851, ground was broken on the east side. Parting with $25,000, he arranged with a south Boston firm — Richard Munn & Company — to furnish a 100-ton, rail-mounted, steam-powered machine largely made of cast iron and allegedly capable of grinding a center hole and a thirteen-inch-wide groove around the circumference of the proposed twenty-four-foot diameter of the tunnel, for all of five miles, and do it in 1,556 working days. Assuming that Sundays were to be observed as rest days, this would be just under five years. The idea was that once a segment of this groove had been cut, the 100 horsepower machine could be run back on its rails and the resulting core removed by more traditional quarrying techniques. Munn's "Patented Stone-Cutting Machine" ground away at the mountain for a total of ten feet, then became hopelessly jammed and died in place, whence it was dismantled and sold as scrap. As of 2010 the initial hole can still be seen, and the "false bore" was later to serve as a blacksmith shop. At first on the west (North Adams) side, things seemed to be progressing; the tunnel itself had not been started, but the gutter approach was underway.

Following this disappointing debacle and faced with his own predictions, and hence public expectations, that the entire job of getting an operating railroad from Greenfield to Troy would take no longer than five years, Crocker ordered that work be continued with hand-held drills and gunpowder. When the shaft of such a drill is struck by an up to twenty-pound hammer, it must be spun a few degrees by hand before a second blow can be effective. Once any "double-jack" team had drilled a hole about 75 cm. (2 feet) deep they would fill it with black power and blast, crumbling out a few hundred pounds of scree along with a lot of bad air and mineral dust. Many miners died young from the choking disease of silicosis caused by repeated inhaling of such material.

Crocker took the wise precaution of going back to the legislature and, citing the 1825 report, managed to secure passage of a "Tunnel Aid" bill in 1854 (after being handed rejections in the two prior sessions) that gave his project a further state credit of $2,000,000 (due to inflation, this would amount to something close to $30,000,000 by the early 21st century). But this required *inter alia* that the T&G contract with someone whose reputation in this sort of undertaking was better known than A. F. Edwards, the company's heretofore chief engineer. The aid bill was in the form of a mortgage on all the assets of the Troy & Greenfield, and was executed on July 28, 1855 — all the painful details of which were enumerated in the Massachusetts Legislature's Joint Standing Committee Report of 1866. Edwards was later reported serving under Serrell in the shelling of Charleston, South Carolina, and died during the Civil War. His body is said to be buried in the Mound City National Cemetery of Illinois.

Crocker promptly selected a firm headed by Edward Wellman Serrell (1826–1906), a prominent civil engineer of New York City, who had been the assistant engineer in charge of the Central Railroad of New Jersey. He had supervised the construction of the suspension bridge across the Niagara River at Lewiston and another over the remarkable tidal estuary at St. John, New Brunswick. Serrell, whose financial arrangements turned out to be dubious, if not shady, but who later did very effective work during the Civil War in railroad repair and heavy gun emplacements, began work in 1855. But when complex financing issues arose, he ratted out on the job before the year was out. Crocker then turned to Hermann Haupt, who became the Hoosac's chief engineer from 1856 to 1861; and thereafter achieved greater fame in the Civil War as a quick and reliable constructor of bridges, according to Abraham Lincoln, "from bean poles and corn stalks." But the whole economy of America was afflicted by a financial panic that struck on August 24, 1857.

> To salvage Serrell's company and the tunnel contract, Haupt turned to his Pennsylvania Railroad friends for financial support. Using his personal property as collateral, Haupt arranged a $100,000 loan from George Howell and Christian Spangler, fellow directors of the Pennsylvania Railroad, and Horatio Burroughs, a very successful Philadelphia merchant. Nevertheless, as fast as Haupt solved a problem, another appeared in the tangled mess Galbraith and Serrell had created while trying to build the tunnel on the backs of small subcontractors...
>
> Haupt had bought into the partnership with visions of engineering triumph. Now it was becoming apparent that if he was to succeed in overcoming the engineering challenge of tunneling 5 miles through the mountain, he must first solve Serrell's old financial obligations. To meet those obligations, Haupt had to turn again to his friends in Philadelphia. He persuaded J. Edgar Thomson and Thomas A. Scott, of the Pennsylvania Railroad, together with Pat McAvoy, Horatio Burroughs, who had already participated in one loan, and Andrew Eastwick, a pioneer locomotive builder from Philadelphia, to invest $60,000 in the partnership. This time the money came not as a loan, but as an investment in the Hoosac contract. In effect, acting as investors, these men purchased an 11 percent interest in the contract that the partnership held with the T&G, but as soon as Haupt found money, Galbraith found outstanding obligations.[7]

William Ayres Galbraith (1823–1898) was a shadowy legal figure who arrived with Serrell and contributed no money of his own to the project, but somehow kept finding new obligations for Haupt to pay. An independent Democrat and an 1845 graduate of Harvard's Dane Law School, he later became chief judge of Erie County, Pennsylvania, an office which his father had held previously.

The T&G loan had numerous other strings attached, including tunnel dimension specifications and a $600,000 private stock subscription requirement. However, with this loan on the books, the Troy & Greenfield signed its contract with Edward Serrell. Somewhat later, due to the railroad's inability to meet the stock sale requirements (though, at Haupt's personal urging, many of the towns along the way ultimately chipped in), Serrell used that non fact as an excuse to declare his contract void and then walked off the job in January of 1855, dumping the entire matter back into Crocker's hands.

By the spring of that year — sufficient of the financial issues having been resolved — the Troy & Greenfield was able to sign Hermann Haupt with a contract for $3.9 million. Haupt, however, became responsible not only for the tunnel, but for the entire right-of-way for the railroad west from Greenfield. At this point major problems with the tunneling techniques began to become apparent. Saprolite, a very watery, crumbly "porridge stone," or as tunnel opponents enjoyed calling it "demoralized rock," was discovered to be in great abundance on the west end. Every time a shovelful was removed, it was filled by the another shovelful of the slumping stone. Workers described this process as trying to "shovel eels," with the roof continuously falling in on them. This problem would ultimately require six to eight layers of brick in tube form — bottom as well as sides and top — to support the tunnel overhead. Also of Cambrian age, and now called the Dalton Formation, this semisolid rock is scientifically described most recently as "arkosic quartzite, dark schist and conglomerate."

At this stage of its construction, the tunnel was described in the 1866 Report of the General Court's Joint Standing Committee:

> The tunnel enters the eastern side of Hoosac Mountain, in the town of Florida, a few rods from the right bank of the Deerfield River. The eastern summit of the mountain is 2,210 feet above tidewater [This is the mean between normal high tide and normal low tide. For Massachusetts, the measurement is based at a point on Commonwealth Pier in Boston Harbor] 1,499 feet above the Deerfield River, 1,429 feet above the grade of the railroad, and is distant from the East Portal of the tunnel 6,100 feet. The western summit is 2,510 feet above tidewater, 1,788 feet above the Hoosac River, 1,718 feet above the grade of the railroad, and 6,700 feet distant from the West Portal. Each portal of the tunnel is 766 feet above tidewater. The summits are 2 & 41/100 miles distant from each other, and the valley between them at its lowest depression is 801 feet above the grade of the railroad.
>
> The length of the tunnel, from the East End to the West End, as commenced by Mr. Haupt [who was, by this time, Brigadier General Haupt, USA ret.], is 4 & 84/100 miles. Its base is, at the East End, 70 feet above the Deerfield River, and at the West End, 70 feet above the Hoosac River. Its grade, from the East End to the Central Shaft, is 18 & 48/100 feet per mile; from the West End to West Shaft, 26 & 4/10 feet

per mile; and from the West Shaft towards the Central Shaft, 21 & 12/100 feet per mile.

* * *

Chapin and his Western Railroad associates soon found an effective political ally in the form of an intense competitor of Crocker's, Francis William Bird (1809–1894), a paper manufacturer of Walpole, Massachusetts, who was both active in the General Court and happy with the services of the B&A, which had extended a branch line to his town in the 1840s. With Harris and Chapin's fervent encouragement, Bird worked himself into being dynamically opposed to every aspect of the tunnel project, which he trumpeted for years as an enormous waste of the public's money—a mid–19th century bridge to nowhere.

Bird is probably better remembered as the progenitor of a line of waterproof papermakers that turned his successors into the major roof shingle makers of the Northeast. But his political fulminations against the tunnel project were effective; by 1861—less than a quarter of the projected hole having been bored—he managed to end all state aid for the project (an act that ruined Haupt financially, for he had put a lot of his own resources into the bore—the principal item of which was a second, and equally unsuccessful, boring machine, designed by Charles Wilson of Springfield) and which brought things to an almost complete halt for the duration of the Civil War. It was not until the latter part of the 20th century that such a machine was to be successfully used in North America, on the Canadian Pacific's 14.5 km. Macdonald Tunnel in the Selkirk Range of western Canada, as noted in our penultimate chapter.

Bird's pamphlets, most of them printed by Wright & Potter of Boston, bore such titles as: *Facts vs. illusions: being a reply to H. Haupt's latest misinterpretations relating to the Troy and Greenfield Railroad*, 1862; *The Road to Ruin: the decline and fall of the Hoosac Tunnel*, 1862; *The Hoosac Tunnel: its condition and prospects*, 1865; *Hoosac Tunnel: our financial maelstrom*, 1866; *The Last Agony of the Great Bore*, 1868; and *The Modern Minotaur*, 1868. Haupt replied as best he could, though busily occupied elsewhere, sending an explanatory *Memorial to the Honorable Senate and House of Representatives of the Commonwealth of Massachusetts* in 1863.

Crocker, too, soldiered on, making speeches and engaging other engineers to make public their opinions on the feasibility of the whole scheme, which had advanced fitfully and dishearteningly slowly on the east. But he was no match for the vituperation emanating from Bird, who somehow got away with labeling the absent Haupt, in one of his outbursts,

> a Uriah Heep ... a Shylock and Pecksniff by turns ... squandering in wild speculations and visionary excitements, the money he made out of the Pennsylvania Railroad—the road which has had to be built over almost entirely since he left it—leaguing himself with the most unscrupulous political gamblers and profligate adventurers of the State, he has corrupted and influenced the legislature of the State, to an extent which would be impossible to one less unscrupulous and indefatigable."[8]

This contained a really cheap shot! As pointed out above, Secretary of War Stanton had ordered the cannibalization of large parts of the competing Baltimore & Ohio to repair and enhance much of the Pennsylvania during the Civil War. A beginning had been made on the western adit early in 1851, but the rock here was of a decomposed and porous nature, called saprolite (defined in our Oxford English Dictionary as "soft, clay-rich, thoroughly decomposed rock, formed *in situ* by chemical weathering of igneous and metamorphic rocks"), which drooled copious amounts of water and required continuous support of the overburden while being bored. The progress here was later expedited by virtue of a shaft which Haupt caused to be sunk in more reliable rock about a half-mile from the adit. The saprolite zone ultimately required that the first 2,600 feet (half a mile) on the west end of the tunnel be lined with five courses of brickwork — a total of 20,000,000 bricks — a contract that became a very profitable life work for Bernard N. Farren (1828–1912) of Philadelphia, who held the masonry contract. In 1887 Farren, an immigrant from Donegal, later became one of the incorporators of the Catholic University of America. The cryotechnology methods later used for excavating the muck (and rotted tea) of Boston Harbor might have been of great help in the saprolite. In an article entitled "The Story of the Hoosac Tunnel," written for the *Atlantic Monthly*, March 1882 (vol. 49, pages 289–304) one can read a further contemporary description of this substance. The author, Nathaniel Hillyer Egleston (1822–1912), was a sometime preacher and professor at Williams College, but better known as a conservationist and an early chief of what became the United States Forest Service, after implementation of the Forest Reserve Act of 1891:

> ... a silicious rock, quartzose sandstone, and some limestone, much displaced and broken up, the whole overlaid with gravel, clay and sand, and full of water accumulated from the slope of the mountain.

* * *

Though the Hoosac Tunnel was originally proposed as a portion of a canal system running from Boston to Albany, that idea was promptly shot down for being too costly and for carrying too much uncertainty — language that was already being applied to the railroad tunnel — as well as the century-later Boston Harbor project. But no other route across the northern portion of the state could be found, and there was no graceful way around the "stony" mountain. Alvah Crocker, with his residence and business in the northern tier of the state, argued (with some justice) that the Western Railroad, which went through Worcester and Springfield, left the northern towns out in the cold, and the Commonwealth owed them service equal to that which it had enabled to the southern tier of communities. Furthermore, in climbing across the Berkshires, the Western had to negotiate some very difficult grades and curvatures, reaching a summit altitude of more than 427 m. (1,400 feet) above sea level. Remarkably, the steepest eastbound grade on the entire Albany to Boston line, remains that up out of Springfield's Union Station, where the station platform is just over 100 feet above sea level.

However, when Crocker opened his Fitchburg Railroad from Boston through to Greenfield, he, and backers like Derby, clearly knew that the only way to make this route really viable would be to climb the Deerfield River valley and pierce through Hoosac Mountain, hopefully with a maximum altitude of some hundreds of meters less. On the east side, layers of gneiss and quartz in the geologically ancient Hoosac schist proved difficult to blast through. For the deeper and harder stone on the east, Haupt purchased yet another, considerably smaller, but similarly expensive and even more promptly ill-fated boring machine.

> In January 1857, a tunnel boring machine that Serrell had ordered and which Haupt inherited was delivered to North Adams [via the B&A branch line from Pittsfield]. This iron contraption, weighing over 40 t and built by the Novelty Iron Works of New York, was powered by two 40 horsepower steam engines. The Novelty Iron Works, located on the East River in New York City, was one of the country's great ship-building establishments. Four years in the future, the firm would fabricate the turret and machinery for the Union's iron-clad, Monitor. After arriving in North Adams, Serrell's machine, which was designed by Charles Wilson of Springfield, Massachusetts, had to be hauled piece by piece over the mountain to the east face of the tunnel. This labyrinth of wheels, gears and rock cutters, patented by Wilson, cost Haupt $22,272.[9]

* * *

Meanwhile, as if the tunnel protagonists did not have enough to contend with, political opposition was growing on Beacon Hill, under which a tunnel was also being planned — for what is now the Red line of the MTA. The Western Railroad had increased the effectiveness of its opposition to the Troy & Greenfield project. After the elections of 1860, Nathaniel Banks, an ally of Frank Bird's, was governor, and he sympathized deeply with the Western's spokesmen and concurred with those who worked to frustrate the tunnel's progress. Governor Andrew, who spent much of his time in office raising and supporting a regiment of Negro soldiers for the Civil War, appointed unsympathetic allies to policy positions where they could slow Haupt's progress. One such was Moses Kimball (1809–1895), an associate of the great showman, Phineas Taylor Barnum, who headed a legislative investigating committee which officially determined that Hermann Haupt had nowhere near earned the State scrip with which he had been paid.

Haupt's responses varied from the factual to the sardonic; in one of them he referred to Harris as an "ever-vigilant Cerberus [Among the other strange creatures of mythology, Cerberus was a three-headed dog that guarded the entrance to the Underworld.] ... this kind friend, whose personal attachment to me and my fortunes has made him, as he himself declares, my constant attendant for a period of five years, following my tracks incessantly." In a further response to the harassment from the Western's allies, Haupt speculated on the idea "that the most expeditious way of getting a hole through the mountain, would be to wall up a dozen lawyers at one end of the tunnel, and put a good fee at the other."

With the increasingly unfriendly political climate in Massachusetts and the onset of the Civil War, where the Union Army needed his expertise, on July 12, 1861, Haupt finally swallowed his many losses and walked away from all work on Hoosac Mountain to rebuild the railroads of Tennessee and Virginia for use by the Union Army. Frank Bird stayed on his negative campaign, however, and in 1862 he published two pamphlets excoriating Haupt and the entire project. For the public's more balanced edification, Haupt, who had suffered great personal loss in the project, retaliated in kind.

> Daniel L. Harris, president of the Connecticut River Railroad, served as hatchet man for the Western Railroad. His Connecticut River Railroad was closely connected with the Western and he was a resident of Springfield, Massachusetts, a town dependent for its prosperity on the Western Railroad. Harris was himself a railroad engineer and a member of a bridge-building firm.... Later it was noted that he was "committed to the excellencies of the Howe patent, [and] perhaps menaced by Haupt's innovation.... For Crocker and Haupt, the fight resembled that of Hercules against the 'Hydra of Lerna,' every time they answered an argument, Harris and the Western raise[d] three more claims..."
>
> Governor Henry Joseph Gardner (1819–1892) had come to power with the Know-Nothing Party's sweep of Massachusetts in the elections of 1854. That year the Know-Nothing[s] succeeded in winning all but two seats in the legislature. The following year Gardner defeated Republican Julius Rockwell, and in 1856, the Republicans even endorsed his candidacy. While campaigning in 1856, Gardner had visited North Adams and the tunnel work, declaring himself in favor of the Troy & Greenfield's tunneling of the Hoosac.
>
> Nonetheless, the political winds of 1857 were blowing in another direction and he "returned the bill to the legislature with his almighty veto." To the towns of northern Massachusetts, Governor Gardner added insult to the injury he did them by declaring that it would be "simply ridiculous for the state to embark in this preposterous scheme." The House easily overrode the governor's veto, but in the Senate, it failed to pass by a single vote. The Western railroad and the Governor had won the battle.
>
> Having been so close to victory, Haupt was devastated, but it may have been the battle that won the war for supporters of the tunnel. The towns of northern Massachusetts now realized that if they wanted to be on a mainline railroad and not be shunted off on some poorly run branch of the Western, they would have to join together. In the fall elections of 1857, those towns showed their newfound spirit, and Governor Gardner received less than 8 percent of the vote in the Franklin and Berkshire [county] towns along the path of the railroad.[10]

The Know-Nothings were an anti-foreign, anti–Roman Catholic, political organization that flourished in the United States between 1852 and 1856, members of which had been frightened by the massive immigration from Ireland and south Germany. They advocated exclusion of Catholics and foreigners from public office (but not pick-and-shovel work in a tunnel) and sought to increase the naturalization period from 5 to 21 years. The Know-Nothings won national prominence chiefly because the two major parties — Whigs and Democrats — were breaking apart over the slavery issue.

Most of its northern members soon joined the newly formed Republican party. This was also at the height of the contentious "No Irish Need Apply" (for jobs at the mills of Lowell, Holyoke and throughout the region) craze that permeates modern New England folklore, due to the uneducated condition of the great bulk of the immigrants fleeing the disastrous "potato famine" years of 1848 and 1850. Thanks to English educational policies (or lack of same) in the subject land of Eire, most of these refugees could follow oral orders but could neither read nor write.

5

Daylight at Long Last

WHEN — JUST AFTER THE CIVIL WAR WAS ENDED — the Commonwealth of Massachusetts finally decided to "get real" with what had now become a highly tense and politically controversial project, the legislature appointed a special committee to oversee it. This committee was headed, particularly in its formative period, by Tappan Wentworth (1792–1875), a scion of the famous New Hampshire family who soon went on to the 33rd United States Congress as a Whig representative from Lowell. Wentworth had been a member of the General Court for several terms, and later in the state senate, where he served with Alvah Crocker.

After talking with Alfred Nobel's North American agent, Colonel Schaffner, the state's then supervising engineer, Thomas Doane (who held that job for several years after 1863 at a salary of $3,600 per year), invited English-born chemist George Mordey Mowbray (1814–1891), who had been a pioneer in exploiting the product resulting from the world's first oil strike, of Titusville, Pennsylvania, to come for a visit to the works headquarters in North Adams. Mowbray brought his formula for an "improved" form of blasting oil (trinitroglycerine) "xylonite" into the Hoosac Mountain work. After finishing the Hoosac project, Mowbray helped develop smokeless gunpowder, but liked the hills of New England so much that he stayed on in North Adams until his death. An interesting discovery about the properties of nitroglycerine came about early in its usage at the Hoosac. Doane (1821–1897) was a native of Orleans on Cape Cod (as was Albert Rogers) and promoted most of the compressed-air methods that were finally put in use. His judgment and skill were credited by many for the completion of the enterprise.

One bitterly cold winter day when one of the state's engineers, William Granger, was moving a sleigh load of Mowbray's product across the mountain for use at the east side works, his sleigh overturned and all cartridges of the explosive were dumped in the snow, where they soon froze. It was "common knowledge" at the time that, if frozen, nitroglycerine was extremely sensitive. So Granger gathered up the wreckage of his load with great care and continued his journey in the constant fear that another upset would be his last. Upon his arrival at the Florida adit, the miners were equally cautious in placing the explosive in their drill holes, only to find that it would not detonate until it had thawed fully. Mowbray's subsequent treatise (which he kept refining over a period of several years, as patent litigation swirled around his head) on the safe use of nitroglycerine was dedicated to Walter Shanly, who was soon to appear on the job.

> To Walter Shanly, M. P.
> Indebted to you for the resources which have enabled me to investigate the properties of Nitro-Glycerin, and render its manufacture a commercial success, permit me to dedicate the following pages in token of the indomitable energy, admirable organization, integrity of purpose, and engineering talent which have rescued the Hoosac Tunnel from the mire of politics and tendered it an engineering success; notwithstanding extraordinary impediments of flood, water fissures, strikes, jealousy and indifference on the part of those chiefly interested, that must have been most disheartening to your mind, and challenged a resolution and resources seldom combined with the abilities you have shewn in this work. Our relations during the past three years having been without a ripple, render this, my simple duty, an agreeable task.
> Geo. M. Mowbray.[1]

Mowbray had arrived in late October of 1867, and because the railroads had "absolutely" refused to transport nitroglycerine from his home base in Titusville, Pennsylvania, promptly began construction of a two-story factory for making his explosive in North Adams, which was operational at the end of the year. The explosive proved highly effective when applied in 42-inch deep drill holes (as opposed to the 30-inch holes heretofore used for black powder). Safer methods for detonation were soon created, and eventually a system was in place that could detonate the explosives from the timekeeper's office, 12,000 feet back from the heading. The final detonating solution, created by a North Adams man, Charles Albert Browne (1842–1907), with the help of his brother, Isaac (and protected by U.S. Patent 128945), was a device consisting of two insulated wires held apart so a spark would cross between them, terminating in a hollowed out chamber that held fulminate of copper in a wooden plug with a pasteboard coating placed between the wires. Browne was completely blinded by a laboratory explosion on Thanksgiving Day 1869. His death, nearly forty years later, was by suicide, slitting both his wrists and throat. Though Alfred Nobel was already using fulminate of mercury in 1864, the convergence of these two technologies made the Hoosac Tunnel the first large-scale usage site of trinitroglycerin and blasting caps. The nitroglycerine was carried to the drill heading in cartridges a foot and a half or two feet in length, an inch and a half in diameter, and closed at the end with a large cork. The Rev. Gladden described the final workplace of this technology:

> Almost a mile and a half from daylight horizontally, and about a quarter of a mile vertically, a huge iron frame-work, resting on rollers, is pushed up against the face of the rock; to this the drilling machines are securely clamped, and at various angles they are pounding holes into the mountain. The clamor which they make is absolutely terrific. When the blast takes place, the carriage upon which the drilling machines are fastened is moved back a short distance, and two firm plank doors are shut before it, to protect the machinery from the flying rock...

> When a sufficient number of holes are drilled in the face of the rock, the corks are taken from these cartridges and perforated; through the holes in the cork the wires of an electrical fuse are drawn, and the cork is replaced, leaving the fuse in the cartridge, with the short ends of insulated copper wire projecting from the cork. Then the cartridges are carefully placed in the holes which have been drilled in the rock (no tamping being necessary), and the wires of the fuses are connected with longer wires attached to an electrical machine some distance toward the portal. The miners withdraw, a few turns are given to the crank of the electrical machine, the circuit is completed, and the rush of the air and the stunning reverberation proclaim that the mightiest of all the chemical forces yet discovered by man has dealt another crushing blow at this barrier of rock...
>
> One of the most serious casualties connected with it [the tunnel] took place in the autumn of 1869 at the magazine where it was stored at the east end. The magazine stood upon the hill-side, a quarter of a mile from the portal, and it contained at the time of the accident about five hundred pounds of the nitro-glycerine. Three of the miners, whose business it was, went one morning to the magazine to prepare the glycerine for the day's use; and by some unknown accident an explosion took place, killing them all. One of the men was outside the building, and he, though terribly lacerated, was identified when he was picked up; but of the other men hardly a vestige was to be found. They were literally blown to atoms. Of the building, not a plank nor timber was left in the neighborhood and nothing but an ugly fissure in the ground remained to mark the spot where it stood.[2]

A "final" version of the track was completed along the Deerfield River up to the East Portal in late summer of 1868. At the same time, miners were averaging 40 meters per month on both the working headings. On January 7, 1869, after the departure of Governor Andrew from office, who had cut off state funding for several months, the Shanly Brothers of Montreal, after much pleading on the part of state officials, bid $4,594,268 to finish what remained of the great bore, which had, nearly fifty years earlier, been estimated to cost a million dollars and then revised upward to $1,948,557 in toto.

* * *

Without Haupt on the job, progress under the mountain had stopped almost completely. When he left, the tunnel had reached 732 m. (2,400 feet) on the east end, and 186 m. (610 feet) on the west with another 158 m. (518 feet) of westward tunneling coming from the West (Haupt) Shaft. In the difficult saprolite area, he had built the first 30 meters on the west end to a 5 m. wide masonry arch, but the remaining 510 feet was still supported by timbers. This limited width posed a problem for future operation, because 5 m. of lateral arched clearance was unsuitable for the ultimate goal of a double-tracked railroad.

On August 18, 1862, the Troy & Greenfield had been forced to default on its mortgage payments to the Commonwealth, which took control of the project the very next month. On March 19, 1863, the special state commission — Storrow, Laurie and

Doane — of whom Storrow was just back from his European junket to the Frejus — submitted a feasibility report which covered several crucial points: (1) drilling should only be allowed to proceed by using compressed air and a more powerful explosive for blasting; (2) much of Haupt's work would have to be redone because he did not closely follow the engineering specifications set at the very start by the displaced Edwards; (3) a new West Portal would have to be constructed, and both ends would need to be widened; and (4) finally, the west end would need to have sturdier brick tubing installed. The State's Hoosac Tunnel Commission was taking over, and Senator Alvah Crocker was going to get it done. On the following July 1, in his capacity as acting superintendent of the work on the T&G Railroad, Crocker wrote:

> To His Excellency the Governor, and the Honorable
> The Executive Council of the Commonwealth of Massachusetts.
>
> As Commissioner acting as superintendent of work upon the Troy & Greenfield Railroad and Hoosac Tunnel, I have the honor to submit herewith my Report of the operations of the fourteen months ending December 31, 1867, and a statement of the condition of the work at that time; accompanied by reports of engineers Field and Granger, and other documents of interest as tending to show in detail the present condition of the enterprise.
>
> Prior to, contemporary with, and subsequent to the contract with Mr. B. N. Farren, I have rendered him such assistance as was in my power.
>
> I have also met with the constituted authorities of Franklin County in the matter of road crossings and the changes of common roads, to whom I desire to acknowledge my obligations for the promptitude with which they acted, and their evident and marked effort to secure for the Commonwealth a width sufficient for the railroad track in the narrow gorges of the Deerfield River.
>
> The first section of this railroad, from Greenfield to Shelburne Falls, for which twenty thousand dollars per annum is to be paid, under lease, by the Fitchburg and Vermont & Massachusetts Railroads conjointly, was opened on Jan. 1, 1868; it being understood that such portion of the same as was not quite finished, by reason of the early frost, shall be done as soon as practicable. It gives me great pleasure to state, in conclusion, that Mr. B. N. Farren has shown the same energy and skill as he has in contracts heretofore; and the Commonwealth is greatly indebted to this efficient contractor for the thorough character of the masonry, bridging, roadbed and superstructure in this work.
>
> The only work now remaining uncontracted for east of the Tunnel is the bridge and embankment over the Deerfield River, near the Tunnel. The construction of this bridge [throughout the entire project, only Howe trusses were specified for the various bridges] is rendered necessary by early spring, so that the debris from the tunnel can be used for the large embankment, of some 60,000 yards, east of the Deerfield River. Authority should be given for its construction the ensuing spring. The cost of a double-track bridge is estimated by Mr. Field, chief engineer, to be $25,000.[3]

Almost contemporaneously, Thomas Doane was named chief engineer and shortly began the sinking of the gaping central shaft 98 m. west of the tunnel's projected true center, a project enhancement which had been most wisely insisted upon by Whitwell. Teams of a dozen miners worked day and night to sink this hole to grade. These were mostly immigrant Irish laborers, whose inherited skill with pick and shovel transcended their lack of formal book learning, with a few experienced Cornish miners to direct the main work force. But though the North remained prosperous, the Civil War years had slowed the construction of the tunnel significantly. By the time of C.S.A. General Lee's surrender, in April 1865, less than 350 m. (actually 1,145 feet — mostly only as a pilot heading, as was the work on the Frejus) had been added to the work previously done under Haupt's supervision.

On the east side, Doane now finished a dam about a mile up the Deerfield River which channeled water through a 5 m. wide sluiceway into a building containing air compressors, as noted further along in Crocker's 1863 report:

> Under authority of the Commission two new turbine wheels were purchased of Messrs. Kilbourn, Lincoln & Co., at Fall River, for $1,800 each, to drive the two new compressors which were purchased of the Putnam Machine Company, of Fitchburg (the lowest bidder), for $3,000 each.... The construction of this new flume, the additional compressors, and, in case of need, the engine already referred to, will undoubtedly furnish sufficient power for running the drills continuously...
>
> In taking leave of the east end, I would add, the amount of hard rock taken out of the enlargement during the year was 4,391 cubic yards. Undoubtedly it is desirable, as soon as practicable, to bring the enlargement and heading nearer together.[4]

The use of compressed air — a finally successful idea borrowed from the Frejus project — powered the new drills by Burleigh and his associates which were mounted on movable carriages inside the tunnel and fed by rubber hoses connected to iron pipes leading from the compressor building; the compressors for the west adit and the central shaft were powered by steam engines. These were predecessor drills to those patented by Burleigh alone, and had first gone into operation on June 14, 1866. Meantime, the external line of the tunnel was resurveyed and six stone towers were erected to ensure utmost accuracy in the tunnel's alignment, which became decidedly more critical with the initiation of the Central Shaft workings. Internal alignment of the several bore segments was assured by the drilling of holes into the ceiling of the tunnel into which were driven wooden plugs. From these plugs, plumb-bobs were suspended, thus allowing surveyors to maintain close alignment. Showing, in part, the ongoing improvements in mining technology: in all of 1866 the heading of the tunnel was bored a total of 570 feet; in 1867 the rate tripled to 1,687 feet, and in only 10 months of 1871, 1,743 feet were bored.

In 1866 supervising engineer Doane had rehired Farren to create a 500-foot long, 6–8 layer thick brick tube on the west side to hold back the demoralized rock. Ultimately this tube would be 270 m. (883 feet) in length; and a further 2,300 m. (7573 feet) of the tunnel would be lined with brick, while 2,039 m. (6,690 feet) would be simple brick arching. In all, more than 20 million bricks were used in the tunnel's construction.

Initially the bricks were purchased in Springfield and shipped to the site; but in the latter stages of the process, adequate clay was found near North Adams and it became less costly to make bricks on site. By 1867 tunnel crews were averaging more than 30 m. (100 feet) of progress monthly. On July 31 the Central Shaft was found to be halfway down to grade. By August 23 more than 100 m. (450 feet) of the newly-mandated brick arching was completed and another comparable length was under way. But in August 1867 Doane quit because of political interference with what he felt to be proper engineering practice in regard to the use of Mowbray's more powerful explosive, which had come to be the main cause of the mounting death toll — ultimately 195 workmen, plus several children and assorted visitors. While Doane found employment with J. J. Hill's Chicago, Burlington & Quincy, Col. William P. Granger (1834–1903), another West Point trained civil engineer, was appointed in his place. Granger, who was born and died in Florida, Massachusetts, went on to further railroad projects, ultimately landing in the employ of the Southern Pacific. His papers are among the Special Collections of UCLA.

The Central Shaft project was left in charge of Danish-born Carl Otto Wederkinch, whose principal headache was to make sure the gaping oval (4.5 E-W by 3.5 meters N-S, 23 by 15 feet) shaft was perfectly straight and exactly in line with the tunnel — a process he did with excellence. But this shaft also became a death trap, the site of the worst single tragedy in the entire tunnel's construction. On October 17, 1867, a gasometer (a primitive form of lighting), which had been used in the hoist house basement, leaked explosive fumes which shortly thereafter contacted a candle and enveloped the whole building in flames. A crate of newly-sharpened tools dropped on those laboring below, and most of the burning hoist house crashed down into the then 177 m. deep shaft. All the workers at the bottom died from either the falling debris or asphyxiation. Two hours after the explosion, one shaft worker, a carpenter known only as Mallory, was lowered down by rope. He was pulled up gasping and could say only, "No hope!" As the shaft filled with water, some bodies surfaced. Others would not be recovered for a full year. All work ceased at the Central Shaft. But when it resumed, one of the first inventions by Elisha Graves Otis (1811–1861) was almost immediately installed and could make the 313 m. (1,028 foot) trip from top to bottom (and vice versa) in less than two minutes, as compared with the seven minutes previously required. Wederkinch (1845–1881) disappeared into the misty jungle of Honduran history after working on Adolph Sutro's tunnel that drained the mines of the Comstock Lode.

By this time everyone who mattered knew that, all told, only 2,845 m. (9,338 feet) of full dimension tunnel had actually been bored, leaving more than half again as much yet untouched. And the Greenfield *Gazette* was happy to cite the Boston *Traveller* to the effect that "the Shanlys are English engineers of excellent reputation and it is said, also, that they command unlimited means."

Water removal from the Central Shaft was a constant problem; it seeped, trickled and poured in at the rate of 15,000 gallons per hour (this is almost half the entire normal rate of flow of the nearby Cold River). In one year it was calculated to have cost $500,000 to remove 13,792 tons of rock along with 315,000 tons of water. But, on a more positive note, use of the xylonite explosive had saved almost $82,000 over the cost of black powder. As of the end of 1867, assistant engineer A. Beardsley reported to the *Scientific American* (XVII, no. 26) that "during the past year the tunnel has been advanced a total of 2,027 feet, and the new shaft has been sunk, and at its foot are the pumps which, together with those at the west shaft, are now throwing out between 900 and 1000 gallons of water per minute." No one cared to comment on Professor Hitchcock's prediction about water.

On March 5, 1869, a number of operational details were made public; including (1) the purchase of a thousand candles for use in the Central Shaft work, (2) that compressed air was now being used to work all the drills, and (3) that Professor Mowbray had purchased one mule team from the state for carrying his explosive over the mountain to the east workings. Mowbray had earlier run into one difficulty in that his manufacturing process was continuous and nitroglycerine was being produced 24-7 — even on Sunday. One weekend he ran short of the ice that was now *de rigueur* for its transport. The local ice merchant in North Adams was a strict observer of the Sabbath and refused to sell him any ice when he showed up with a cart load of TNT. Tired of wrangling, Mowbray climbed down and began to unhitch his mules so as to leave the loaded wagon in the sun in front of the ice house until the morrow. The necessary ice was promptly made available. Until the advent of commercial refrigeration in the early 20th century, well-insulated (with saw dust) ice houses were to be found adjacent to almost every major pond of New England. These were filled during the winter months with the aid of diaper-equipped horse teams. The product was then sold during the next summer, though much was also exported to places like Charleston, Havana and New Orleans.

On Patriot's Day, 1869, the Greenfield *Gazette* reported:

> Messrs. Shanly have begun work in earnest, some 200 men are at work at the east end and 150 more will be added as soon as they can be obtained. Four new compressors have been ordered with engines attached to supply power and meet any deficiencies arising from low water and accident at this point.... At the west end 75 men are now at work ... two additional boilers are being added, making six at this point.... Over 500 yards of solid rock were blasted on the 17th inst. by nitroglycerine at one discharge on the west shaft.

* * *

In a great political change after the Civil War, the Commonwealth of Massachusetts was headed for five years by Alexander Hamilton Bullock (1816–1882), a former mayor of Worcester who had been born in Royalston, a town adjacent to the line of the Fitchburg. In all, under a series of politically-appointed chief engineers and supervised by a discontinuous gaggle of politicians, the Commonwealth had managed to spend a lot more than it had made available to Haupt, and with far less progress under the mountain per dollar. On February 8, 1869, the brickwork was completed at the west adit (these crews were not affected by the previous governor's Stop Work order) and by Patriot's Day of 1869 tunneling operations were in full swing again. But 18 months later a "great flood" destroyed a large amount of the roadbed along the Deerfield River and gravel filled the west adit of the tunnel nearly to the top. Large portions of the brick arching were weakened and had to be replaced. One of the track issues — aside from its excessive curvature — was the initial quality of its ties, which were laid in poorly drained soil rather than macadam or gravel. Hemlock was cheaper ($8 per thousand feet) but spruce, at 20 percent greater cost, was more durable.

This was no mean flood; high water affected the whole of New England — perhaps another unpredicted hurricane similar to that of 1938 and which were described by some as "equinoctial storms." The Springfield *Republican* (at this writing — 2010 — a Democratic-leaning paper) reported under date of October 11, 1870:

> How the Railroads are Recuperating — Additional Reports of Monday's Havoc.
>
> The reconstructionists who have been building the trestle work at the Wilbraham break completed the structure yesterday afternoon, a half past 12 o'clock, sufficient to permit the passage of trains...
>
> Brattleboro is briskly at work removing the debris and damage of the flood, and already most of the streets and roads are passable. The total loss, as estimated by the best judges, will amount to $120,000.... The aggregate loss in Windham County, Vt. is not less than $1,500,000...
>
> The Housatonic railroad has repaired its flood losses so that trains run regularly again. The same is true of the Vermont & Massachusetts, Cheshire, Northern, Bristol, Concord & Claremont and Contoocook Valley roads. **The Troy & Greenfield is closed until further notice** [emphasis added].
>
> A correspondent says that "in Sullivan, Grafton, Merrimac, Hillsboro and Cheshire counties, N.H., the destruction of property was immense, and it was caused, for the most part, by small rivers, brooks, rills and water courses that seldom discharge but little water, and many of which are entirely dry except during showers. On the highways nearly every bridge and culvert has been washed out, taking with them in very many cases, large portions of the roadbed."

This newspaper was started in 1822 by Samuel Bowles (1797–1851) as a weekly. In 1844, under the leadership of his son, Samuel II (1826–1878), a confidant of the powerful, it became a daily with national circulation and impact. The enterprise continued under Samuel III (1851–1915) and then by his enigmatic son, Sherman (1890–1952), who consolidated three competing newspapers and various stray investments such as Atlas Tack and the Bangor & Aroostook Railroad into a convoluted empire of uncertain ownership. Throughout the controversies about the Hoosac Tunnel, the *Republican* was a consistent — if not always evenhanded — supporter of Springfield interests.

* * *

The Shanly brothers, Walter (1817–1899) and Francis (1820–1882), Irish-born civil engineers of Toronto and Montreal, when no one else would touch the job, bid

$4,594,268 in December 1868, to bore the remaining almost 2.8 km. (15,743 feet) of the tunnel to a width of 24 feet and a height of 20 feet (they did not contract to rebore the existing parts of the tunnel to those dimensions or to build a railroad, as had Haupt) before August 1, 1874. The brothers were born at Stradbally, in what was then called Queens County (now Laoighis) in Leinster and came to Canada in 1836 with their parents. The Shanly name was big in Canadian railroads and construction. Walter had been general manager of the Grand Trunk Railway and made his fame with the reconstruction of the Grand Lachine Canal along the St. Lawrence River above Montreal and then the initial Welland Canal system to connect Lake Ontario up to Lake Erie. Francis was later the chief engineer of the Intercolonial, succeeding the great Sir Sandford Fleming, who was by then working on the route for the Canadian Pacific Railway.

In May of 1870, Mowbray produced 250 pounds of nitroglycerin for daily use, and on July 4, 1871, the first train since the October flood of 1870 reached the East Portal, largely following the right* bank of the Deerfield River. On August 13 the Central Shaft finally reached grade. Late that year, the small (ten-ton) locomotive was finally in place to aid in mucking, replacing mule teams on the east. Aided by Wederkinch's sophisticated surveying techniques, work was now begun on two additional faces and a new tunneling method was developed which involved a two-level system, as had become prevalent in the Alps. On the east end tunneling was done to a height of about eight feet on the bottom portion, and 600 feet behind the heading the roof portion was stoped* out. On the west end the opposite method was applied, with the heading on top. This process was condemned by Benjamin Latrobe, who commented sourly that this procedure, though adopted as progressive by most subsequent tunneling endeavors, was done mostly to propitiate popular favor "by mere progress in running feet." Latrobe (1806–1878) was the son of an England-born engineer and architect of considerable distinction. He was closely connected with the Baltimore & Ohio and had designed its Kingwood Tunnel in Preston County, West Virginia, which ran on a 1 percent grade uphill to the east.

Two years later, westward progress from the Central Shaft was abruptly hampered by a greatly increased flow of water from newly encountered seepages, to the point that this heading had to be abandoned until December 12 when the eastern heading broke through to the Florida end of the Central Shaft bore. Then the newly encountered water could be easily pumped over the top of the grade to flow calmly out the east adit, rather than laboriously pumped up and out the Central Shaft, whence much of it had promptly seeped back down, rather than flowing to the sea via the Cold and Deerfield Rivers. Work reached its peak this year, with 900 men working three 8-hour shifts.

Professor Hitchcock to the contrary, notwithstanding, the water issue had long been bothersome, as far back as January 4, 1867. Alvah Crocker reported that he had

> made a provisional arrangement with Messrs. Knowles and Sibley, of Worcester and Warren, for a No. 9 pump to lift 250 gallons per minute, which, if it worked well and proved adequate for doing this heavy work, was to be received back by them without

> charge, and another made for the State of double capacity—No. 10. As the small pump was found to work well, the latter was ordered for the sum of $900, to be made with extra strength and care. This pump, however, did not work as well as the first, and on the 3rd of September, I ordered of Knowles and Sibley a double-acting plunger pump, to be done in six weeks, at a cost of $2,500, and to lift 1,000 gallons per minute. This pump was not delivered until the 21st of December, but I am satisfied the delay was from no fault of the makers. In the mean time the water, though not regular, had increased to a maximum of at least 1,000 gallons per minute, by the striking of pockets and otherwise. I had ordered the ditching of an adjacent swamp, which relieved us somewhat of surface water, the most persistent enemy we have had to contend with in this shaft.[5]

Only a day after Christmas 1874, the most disheartening event possible for Hoosac Tunnel advocates occurred—Alvah Crocker died. He had been attending to congressional business in Washington and left there on the 21st, intending to spend the holiday season at his home. He arrived there on the 23rd, having spent Tuesday (22nd) night with his married daughter in New York City. He had been suffering from a cold for several days, but worked on Christmas Eve at his office. On Christmas Day the cold took a turn for the worse and several physicians were called to his bedside and pronounced his illness to be acute congestion of the lungs (pneumonia). Their efforts were unavailing and the foremost citizen of Fitchburg passed away quietly at 11:00 P.M. on December 26, aged 73 years, 2 months and 12 days. Funeral services were held the following Wednesday, when "business was suspended throughout the city, and a great throng viewed the remains of him who had done so much for the place he loved"[6] Friends, political leaders and dignitaries were in attendance from all over the state and nation—including a quiet and unnoticed figure in the back of the church, retired Brigadier General Hermann Haupt, soon to be managing the Northern Pacific Railroad.

* * *

The Shanly brothers' first move had been to secure the Central Shaft from further disasters by placing platforms, each independently notched into the walls, at every 25 feet of its depth. However, before they had gotten halfway down to the bottom with this process, there was 300 feet of water newly accumulated in the hole, and heavy pumps were again required (an "extra" on their contract). But all this progress also served to reignite the opposition. Francis Bird published yet another diatribe, forty pages worth, demanding that the state annul the Shanly contract. And according to an editorial in the Springfield *Republican*, two months later, on June 14:

> The Hoosac Tunnel is quite as unsatisfactory under its new management as it ever was, but the Shanlys are so close-mouthed that we don't hear much about it. There are about 250 men at work now at the east end and the central shaft; but the progress is very slow.

The Shanlys' collective reticence to speak with the *Republican* was understandable. Other news media were considerably more informative — and generous. On that very same date, the North Adams *Transcript* told of more compressors being added at the west end and of the continuous operation of ten drills. The Greenfield *Gazette* noted — also on the same day — that the tunnel enlargements were proceeding apace, with three rotating gangs at each heading working around the clock, except on Sundays, stating: "One thing is certain, the contractors believe the work can be done ... and they mean to do it." After the Shanly contract was concluded, the state paid to have a twenty-foot masonry wall built around the top opening to prevent wandering cattle from tumbling in. As of this writing, 2010, it is still there, though somewhat weathered by time and incorporated into the large fan housing.

The Special Legislative Committee visited the workings in mid–August, and "were unanimously of the opinion that operations under the Shanlys are progressing in a most satisfactory manner." It must, therefore, have been somewhat of a disconcerting setback for the die-hard antis when the Springfield Armory Band made an excursion to visit the Hoosac Mountain headings the very next week.

The great flood of early October 1870 was a serious setback — not anticipated in the state's contract with the Shanlys, who had been told they could rely on use of the now state-owned T&G Railroad to reach the east workings. It was completely closed for several months while the contractors diverted some of their work force to its repair. The west end workings had been flooded to within "eighteen inches" of the tunnel roof. Meanwhile, the small (ten-ton) steam engine that was to replace mule teams for mucking at the east heading, had to be hauled bodily over the mountain by a ten-horse team. The first T&G train arrived at the east heading on July 4, after an absence since the previous October 2, during which the workers, who had been commuting from Greenfield by the day, had been forced to find accommodations in Florida and Shelburne. By the end of the year, the Burleigh drill carriage arrays were making an average of ten feet per day. Hoosac Mountain and its workings had now become a site for tourism. And on one weekday in late August, the public of Greenfield was informed that "the six-horse coaches of Barnes & Company took 157 passengers [over the mountain], the largest number ever taken in one day."[7]

Water inside the workings continued to plague operations, particularly in the westward heading from the Central Shaft. Walter Shanly explained the issue as follows:

> The contract prescribed certain monthly rates of progress, 385 feet [117 m.].... The first indication of wet ground west of the Central Shaft was met with in March, 1871, when the heading had been advanced less than 200 feet. It increased from 20 to 80 gallons per minute, work on both sides of the central shaft had to be suspended until very large pumping appliances could be provided in addition to such as we already had completed in October. Eastward work was resumed, but threatenings of more water on the western face were so significant that we deemed it the part of prudence not to break further into the rock on that side until by union with the heading

> advancing from the east end of the tunnel, an outlet could be gained and westward advance resumed without incurring the risk of drowning us out with its unknown quantity of water.[8]

After a bit of a hassle with the state's supervising engineer, Benjamin D. Frost (1829–1880), the Shanlys were permitted, in June, to concentrate only on the relatively dry, easterly headings, which met in mid–December 1872, thus allowing the new flow from the west to drain harmlessly out to the east adit and into the Deerfield River. One senses that the state's later minions were almost as unresponsive as the bureaucrats who had made life so miserable for Haupt, only now they were now dealing with a far tougher and politically better positioned adversary.

On Wednesday, November 25, 1874, a drill boring went through 4 m. (13 feet) of rock into empty air. And on the following morning, Thanksgiving Day in the United States,

> through this hole, electric wires were passed so that the charges of nitroglycerine on each side of the rock could be fired simultaneously with appropriate ceremony. The battery was placed 300 feet back to the east. Timber barriers were built 600 feet from the obstructing rock. The drilling machines and the workmen all moved beyond this barrier and its counterpart at the west end.
>
> Another crowd of spectators was brought in through the east end of the tunnel. The

Workmen employed by the Shanly brothers pose while completing masonry, at the west portal of the Hoosac, 1874 (Graham A.B. Vickowski at the North Adams Historical Society).

> *Boston Globe* said on the following day, "The tram car had seats; one workman propelled the car. The first impression on entering the tunnel here is that it is dismally low, as if the roof were impending for as crash. This is the heading made under State Management. Little further on, the Shanly work begins and here the height is proportional to the span. Here the imperturbable man of nitroglycerine explained how he was putting in his 75 pounds of the substance. He was not asked to dwell on the subject, but all withdrew rather quickly expressing thanks.
>
> The party from the east end included about a dozen from Boston, the party being the Hoosac Tunnel Committee, Robert Johnson, chairman. Walter Shanly, the contractor, met them at a point on the Fitchburg road, dined with them at Rice's Hotel, clad them in rubber, put them on a special train and ran 11,000 to 12,000 feet into the tunnel, and were there joined by those who had come down the central shaft.... Mr. Shanly himself fired the battery.... The east and west end workmen kept the crowds back after the blast saying Mr. Shanly should be the first to go through. He led the march, but deferred to Robert Johnson at the aperture, who was the first to pass. M. M. Gilam, Colonel Granger and Mr. Shanly followed in order. Samuel Richards, foreman of the west end blasters, charged the holes on that side; Mr. Hancock on the opposite side [Richards was later killed in a premature explosion while working with Wederkinch on Adolph Sutro's tunnel in the Comstock]. As proof of engineering, the result was admirable. The variations either of the centres or grades is but a fraction of an inch.
>
> The crowds passed through the gap and most of them went up the opposite shaft from where they had come down. After it was all over, Wheeler's Brass Band came to the west shaft and played a few jubilant notes. In the evening, the Tunnel Committee were serenaded at the Arnold House and a Grand Ball was held at the Opera House."[9]

Two months later, after a bit more tidying up in the tunnel, the first freight train followed. Finally on October 13, 1875, the first passenger train from Boston's North Station made the long-promised trip through to Troy. Farren had completed his final work on the tunnel in February, which included widening a few tight spots and building brick arching over weak spots.

Farren's first 120,000 bricks had been bought in Springfield at $9 per thousand, with freight to North Adams at $6 and cartage up to the west adit at $2, for a total of $17 per thousand, delivered. The Standing Committee estimated that, with breakage en route, these bricks cost $18, and that bricks could be made on site for half that amount. A later contractor, William Holbrook, made bricks on site for $7 per thousand. The state officially opened the tunnel on July 1, 1876, after more than two million tons of spoil had been removed, and eighteen months after Alvah Crocker's earthly remains had been consigned to his family crypt at Fitchburg's Laurel Hill Cemetery. Between August and November 1877, a stone facade was built on the East Portal. In 1881 double tracking was added so that bidirectional traffic could begin. When Haupt's claims were finally settled — at eight cents on the dollar — the final cost of the tunnel was estimated to be approximately $20,000,000 in 1880's dollars; but few people were asking for an impartial audit, most were merely happy to have the decades-long and controversial project finally completed.

The first locomotive to pass through the Hussac Tunnel emerges at the west end of the tunnel. The engine was the property of Troy and Greenfield Railroad (Graham A.B. Vickowski at the North Adams Historical Society).

On February 11, 1887, the Fitchburg Railroad purchased the 4.82-mile Hoosac Tunnel from the Commonwealth of Massachusetts for $5 million in cash and 50,000 shares of its stock (allegedly worth $20 each). The new owners decided that lighting the tunnel would make it safer and more pleasing, so they installed more than a thousand electric lights; however, continuous water leaks shorted them out so frequently they were removed within two years. Though the grade in the tunnel was relatively flat (rising only twenty feet from each portal to a center point) the coal smoke generated by the engines in traversing the tunnel was so great that gravity ventilation proved vastly insufficient and rear-end collisions occurred as a result of the murky blackness, some of which were fatal. Thanks to Whitwell's foresight, a 16-foot fan was installed at the top of the 313 m. (1,028 foot) Central Shaft, the base of which was widened and brick arching installed. A room in the center of the tunnel, irreverently known as the "Hoosac Hotel," was hollowed out for the track walkers as 85–90 trains passed through daily. Despite the big fan, ventilation remained so poor that some train crews still had to lie on the floors of their engines to find breathable air.

On July 11, 1900, the Boston & Maine bought out the Fitchburg in a massive merger; the former's shares then being then traded at $202.50, though by 1919, the B&M share price had declined to $38.50. The B&M was possessed of extensive port

Hoosac Tunnel Central Shaft fan house in 2009; entrance to which is very much frowned upon by Guilford Industries, the current owners.

facilities near Boston and the Fitchburg now had the western traffic to use them, so it was a good match — the two lines needed each other. Late the following year the B&M started replacing its wood-burning engines with oil burners, but oil smoke was no more attractive to breathe than that produced by wood or coal. In 1910 the tunnel was electrified in an effort to speed up traffic and reduce smoke. The electrification system included suspending catenary wires from the roof of the tunnel and an electrified zone that extended beyond the portals. By 1913 freight traffic was so heavy (70,000 cars monthly) that the coal-fired Zylonite power plant near Adams could not meet the demand with its 6,000 kw generator, so supplementary power had to be drawn from a hydroelectric plant on the Deerfield River three miles north of the East Portal, and not far downstream from the later Yankee Atomic power plant.

* * *

Due to the many fatalities connected with its construction and the tunnel's lingering reputation for smokiness, complicated by a necessarily tedious connection with the Delaware & Hudson or the "weary" Erie westward from Troy, through passenger traffic on this line was never very popular. By 1867, "Commodore" Cornelius Vanderbilt had managed to combine the eight independent (often with separate, across-town stations) railroads between New York City and Buffalo into one system, which — in those pre-standard time days — operated on the astronomically — determined time kept at the Albany depot. His heirs managed to acquire control of the Boston & Albany in 1900, which assured better connections for westbound travelers from Boston's South Station to places like Cleveland, Chicago and beyond, to which it ran daily "name" trains — the *Wolverine* and the *New England States*. However, its generally better gradient caused the Hoosac route to remain the preferred line for freight from the Port of Boston to the interior of the United States. In 1926, 900 m. [3,000 feet] of the west end was deepened 46 mm. (18 inches) for better clearance. In midsummer of 1946, newly arriving diesel-electric locomotives, which were far more powerful than the electric engines, eliminated the nuisance of changing motive power for the electrified zone; the wires were removed and a double motor fan was installed at the top of the Central Shaft to remove the exhaust fumes more quickly.

In 1957, with improvements in traffic control systems, the tunnel was reduced back to a single track, laid three feet north of the centerline for clearance purposes. At the end of November 1958, as all North American railroads reacted to the impact of burgeoning air travel and the growing Interstate Highway System, all passenger service west of Fitchburg was terminated. In 1973 the track was centered and replaced by the present heavy-duty continuous welded rail. Finally, in 1997, a 10-foot-wide strip of stone was removed from the tunnel's ceiling and the track was lowered to allow for ever-taller (double-stack) railcars — the rails at the East Portal were sunk below the adjacent ground level and only the northerly track on the nearby bridge over the Deerfield River continued in use.

Ultimately—with its maximum summit level of 256 m. ASL (836 feet)—the Hoosac Tunnel met Derby, Crocker, and the Commonwealth's goal of providing a more nearly competitive link from Boston to the west. A number of the non-geographical economic handicaps of Boston's port versus that of New York disappeared with the Penn/Central bankruptcy of 1970, when the ICC was now dealing with rates on a government-owned entity—Conrail. In 1975, on the centennial of its formal opening, the tunnel was declared an Historic Civil Engineering Landmark by the American Society of Civil Engineers. It remained the longest railroad tunnel in the United States until 1927 when its length was significantly exceeded by the Moffat's 6.1-mile bore (with apex at 9,239 feet ASL) through the granite under 13,259-foot James Peak for the Denver & Salt Lake Western Railroad in the Colorado Rockies. For all of its global notoriety, the Hoosac never did manage to achieve the status of being the longest tunnel in the world. That honor was denied it from the start by the Frejus, which was begun later, but holed through more than two years earlier, and was almost twice its length.

The tunnel advocates, inspired by Alvah Crocker, had achieved—finally—the lowest and easiest crossing of the Appalachian Mountains, but it was too late to be of sizeable help for its Bostonian promoters. By then the patterns of steamship lines and American shippers were thoroughly wedded to the facilities in ports like New York, Philadelphia, Baltimore, Norfolk and Charleston. Further to the Hoosac's unpopularity, the Commonwealth of Massachusetts was now forced to spend almost half the state's revenues for ten years in paying off its construction debt—a lesson not passed on to a future generation of the General Court.

* * *

Even after its completion, the Hoosac Tunnel was the subject of controversy and litigation. In the course of his rivalry "the public be damned" with Jason Gould (who frequently controlled the competitive and initially wider-gauge Erie) William Henry Vanderbilt (1821–1885) of the New York Central sought to make life difficult. Vanderbilt's father, the legendary "Commodore," had made his first fortune with ferries, tug boats and lighters servicing the oceangoing ships that called in New York, and was the personification of the problem which Elias Derby of Boston had been trying to overcome. Thus it should have come as no surprise when the name of Vanderbilt was integrally associated with issues dealing with the Hoosac Tunnel having negative impact on traffic to the port of Boston and thus to the advancement of that of New York, while that of Gould was in helpful opposition.

Ultimately the courts saw to it that the public interest prevailed, but it wasn't easy, as initially reported in the *New York Times* of May 25, 1879:

> Troy, N.Y., May 24.—The Boston, Hoosac Tunnel & Western Railway, which is Erie's connection with the tunnel, has encountered at every step the strong opposition of the Troy & Boston Road, which is one of the Vanderbilt roads. If it follows the route laid down, the Boston, Hoosac Tunnel & Western Road will cross the Troy & Boston's

> tracks at Hoosac Junction. To prevent the crossing, the latter's officers caused four tracks to be laid and placed thereon loaded freight cars.

This legal crisis was eased within months, as *Times* readers later learned:

> Troy, N.Y., Nov. 25,—The Court of Appeals today rendered a decision confirming the right of the Boston, Hoosac Tunnel & Western Railway to cross the Troy & Boston Railroad tracks whenever necessary. But the court decided that in one instance the application to cross the track was not properly made. The Troy & Bennington Road is leased by the Troy & Boston. Application for the right to cross was made to the latter, which claims it should have been made to the Troy & Bennington Company. Judge Westbrook decided that the application was properly made, and the General Term's [plenary session of the Court] sustained him.

* * *

Jason (Jay) Gould (1836–1892), of Roxbury, New York, and his son and successor, George Jay (1864–1923), were capitalists who controlled (or had their fingers into) a variety of transportation and communications enterprises from the middle of the 19th century until the latter's death. Jay's connection with railroads — as noted above — began with those in upstate New York, where he came afoul of the Vanderbilt interests early in his career. As time went on, the Goulds (largely through their insider position on the New York Stock Exchange) came to dominate quite a few American railroads, including: Texas & Pacific; Little Rock & Fort Smith; Missouri Pacific; Wabash; St. Louis, Iron Mountain & Southern; Kansas Pacific; Central Pacific and even the Western Union Telegraph Co. But their greatest construction effort went into the Western Pacific in an attempt to force rate concessions from the Harriman-controlled Union Pacific, to benefit several of the other lines in which they were interested.

This led to the construction of the "Feather River" line, mostly in California, which utilized a much lower pass (only 1,591 m. as compared with the Central Pacific's Donner Summit line some 700 m. higher) through the Sierra Nevada, which had been discovered by the half-breed trapper and explorer James Pierson Beckwourth (1798–1866) in 1850. While the construction down along the Feather River into the great Central Valley of California was regarded as quite "heavy," this line became an important segment in the *California Zephyr* route that was so well publicized in the 1930s.

The Hoosac Tunnel was a long step forward in gaining business for the port of Boston, but the historic bore never came close to making it competitive with other East Coast ports. Nevertheless, Derby and his associates — along with the taxpayers of Massachusetts — had given it their best and Alvah Crocker could at last rest in peace.

6

The Thin Air of Colorado

THE IDEA OF BORING UNDER the high mountains of Colorado — all of them — westward from Denver was proposed in 1890 by Marcus Mills (Brick) Pomeroy (1833–1898), a sometime editor, publisher and author, who might also be described as a political and social dreamer. In 1890 he announced the Denver, Apex & Western Railway, which would include a 233-mile tunnel that would dramatically cut the distance between Denver and Salt Lake City from 743 miles via the Denver & Rio Grande and 658 via the Union Pacific, utilizing the DA&W's proposed Atlantic-Pacific Railway Tunnel. This 425-mile line would have gone straight through the Rocky Mountains, passing beneath Loveland Pass, Torry's Peak, Grey's Peak (14,441 ft.) and the Mt. of the Holy Cross. Interested investors were advised to contact Mr. Pomeroy (for this purpose no longer connected with a series of fly-by-night, Midwestern publications and other lost causes) at the office of the Railway's president and general manager, Room 46 in the World Building of New York City, "for a large, illustrated, 33-page pamphlet and map of Colorado, etc., fully explaining this great work, and what small and large investors will surely receive." Besides providing such a bonanza in transportation, this tunnel (shown in cross-section in Pomeroy's brochure with a steam locomotive pulling a four-car passenger train under the mountains) was promised to "open the greatest gold and silver deposits in the world."[1]

* * *

There were only a few real transportation personalities in the thin, cold air of the Centennial State's upper reaches. (The alpinist's afflictions of HAPE [high altitude pulmonary edema] and HACE [high altitude cerebral edema] were first diagnosed in the 1960s among skiers at Aspen.) Any such list would surely include the following five.

James John Hagerman (1838–1909) was a Canadian export to American railroads — much like James Jerome Hill (see the following chapter). Of Scandinavian descent, he was born near Port Hope, Ontario, and his family moved to Newport, Michigan, in 1843. He worked his way through the University of Michigan as a sometime employee of the Milwaukee Iron Company, becoming the firm's business manager after his graduation in 1861. He invested wisely and heavily in the Norway Mine near Iron Mountain on the northern fringe of Michigan's lower peninsula. He contracted tuberculosis in 1873, and, when it worsened in 1881, moved to Switzerland, where the most effective treatments known at the time were available. Returning to the United States in 1884, the best medical advice was that the dry air of Colorado would be most healthful; so he took up residence in Colorado Springs where he became interested in the silver mining boom then beginning to flourish in southwestern Colorado. His greatest such investments were made in conjunction with Henry Gillespie (1849–1903), a native of Missouri who became known as the "father of Aspen" where he owned the Mollie Gibson mine, the single greatest silver strike in history.

William Austin Hamilton Loveland (1826–1894), a native of Chatham, at the sandy, pine tree-studded, southeast elbow of Cape Cod, participated in the Pike's Peak Gold Rush to Colorado in 1859, but thereafter stayed mostly based in Golden. He became a man of great influence in territorial affairs, including persuading his fellow politicians to convene in his building in Golden as the territorial capital, where it stayed until 1867. He was the prime mover behind the Golden, Clear Creek & Pacific Railway, which ran from Golden up toward the 3,655 m. pass that bears his name. This was via the famous Georgetown Loop — parts of whose roadbed can still be made out along the precipitous banks of that swift-flowing stream. He was also the "godfather" of the Colorado School of Mines, mayor of Golden and one-time owner of the late *Rocky Mountain News*. In 1874, along the lower part of Clear Creek in the City of Golden just after its exit from the mountains, Prussian-born Adolph Hermann Joseph Coors (1847–1929) began brewing his "Banquet Beer."

Otto Mears (1840–1931), the Russian-born friend of Uncompahgre Ute chief Ouray (1833–1859), among his many business ventures, opened a toll road across Poncha Pass, at 2,745 m. one of the lowest in the entire state. He then began providing a freighting service to the mining communities of southwestern Colorado that was finally superseded by the arrival of the Rio Grande Railroad in numerous areas. In 1880 he sold his toll road over Marshall Pass for the then very tidy sum of $13,000 so that the railroad could use his graded roadbed for its tracks to reach Gunnison and points west. Mears then went into railroading on his own, via the Rio Grande Southern and other narrow-gauge lines that operated out of Silverton. As of this writing (2010), the RGS remains a very popular tourist attraction from Durango to Silverton.

David Halliday Moffat (1839–1911) was another eastern boy, from Washingtonville in New York State's Orange County. He migrated to Denver at an early age, eventually becoming a bank president, a very well-to-do owner of mining operations in Florence and Cripple Creek, and a major civic functionary of his adopted hometown. He became such a prominent figure of Denver that when he died in New York City on March 18, 1911, the *Denver Post* of the following day, a Sunday, devoted its entire front page (with many sidebars) to his obituary. However, the railroad he strove so hard to build in aid of Denver was forced to file for bankruptcy protection soon after his death.

General William Jackson Palmer (1836–1909), a native of Kent County, Delaware, earned the Medal of Honor for his spectacular services during the Civil War and then went to work as director of surveys for the Kansas Pacific Railway. He graduated from this into the presidency of the Denver & Rio Grande and its complementary line, the Rio Grande Western, and ultimately arranged the amalgamation of the two still mostly narrow-gauge lines. The D&RGW thus became the most widespread of the several such lines serving the many silver mining camps of southwestern Colorado.

Under Palmer's stimulus and with a bit of prodding from Jason Gould, the Rio Grande redid its Tennessee Pass line in 1890 to standard gauge so that it could play a part in running through trains between New York and San Francisco Bay. They went on the B&O to St. Louis, used Missouri Pacific trackage from St. Louis to Pueblo, Palmer's line thence to Salt Lake City, and Central Pacific (later Western Pacific) tracks from there to Oakland. But the 3 percent grade up the west side of Tennessee Pass (which required massive pusher engine help from Minturn to the 3,177 m. crest) remained a downer, though the eastern approach was a far more satisfactory 1.4 percent. Thus the line became disused (though not abandoned) in 1997 when the D&RGW was merged with the Southern Pacific and thence into the Union Pacific. Had the Rio Grande formally abandoned this line, there was credible fear it would have been rapidly snapped up by its ancient enemy, the Santa Fe. So — as of this writing — this historic trackage up from Dotsero past the resort of Vail Pass and to Leadville is slowly rusting away.

During the very busy years of World War II, the D&RGW would borrow a number of 4-8-8-4* double-expansion, articulated engines from the Duluth, Mesabi & Iron Range line during the winters, when the Mesabi line was closed, but extra help was needed in Colorado. (When stationed at Pando below the west side of Tennessee Pass during the winter months of 1943 and '44, this author observed — and still recalls with clarity — the sight of 40-car freight trains puffing laboriously up the hillside above Camp Hale with one dinky little engine in front [which was all it took to pull the train down the Arkansas valley to Pueblo] and two massive 4-8-8-4s generating clouds of black smoke, one in the middle and another at the rear. Half an hour later, the big pushers would come huffing quietly back down to Minturn, to await their next job.) That was when the world's climate was such that the Great Lakes were in the habit of freezing over during the winters and the water-borne ore carriers from Duluth to Gary and Erie could not operate. However, those days are gone with the more visible onset of the global warming that mountaineers have been noticing for the last century.

Despite the skepticism of those who simply will not see the effects of global warming, the trade press (alpine journals around the world) of mountaineering has been carrying lugubrious accounts of "dirty," debris-strewn glaciers, their fronts melting steadily back; strenuous, new, rocky approaches; and unexpectedly missing snowfields for all the lifetime of this aging alpinist.

General John Quincy Adams Rollins (1816–1894) was a New Hampshire–born cattle baron and founder of the town of Rollinsville, Colorado. He ran his large herds of cattle across the range to feed hungry miners in all parts of the Centennial State in

All that's left of the original Rollinsville in 2009, the town with no bars or brothels (Graham A.B. Vickowski).

the years before and just after statehood. Among his delivery routes was a toll road he rebuilt from the first wagon train line across the Continental Divide. Rollins also became a partner with New York–born John Warren Butterfield (1801–1869) in the famous stage line predecessor to Wells Fargo, which was "guaranteed" to get to San Francisco in 22 days from St. Louis. In vivid contrast to many others, the town that bears Rollins' name was notorious for its proscribed dearth of saloons and brothels — so, given human failings, as a natural result Rollinsville has pretty much disappeared from the map. Rollins' Pass, across the Continental Divide to what is now called Winter Park, is at 3,536 m. elevation, north of James Peak, and had first been crossed by covered wagons before the Civil War.

* * *

The numerous high passes of Colorado have known an innumerable quantity of wagon roads, traces of which are still visible, if not passable. Several have been traversed by narrow-gauge (three-foot — 91.5 cm.) rail lines, the most long-lived of which was the 3,606 m. Marshall Pass crossing by the D&RGW, which was built in 1881 and not finally abandoned until 1953. This 10,846 foot pass was named for Lt. William Louis Marshall (1846–1920), a member of the 1873 "Wheeler" Survey of the Rocky Mountains, and who later became chief of the Army Corps of Engineers. The D&RGW also ran narrow-gauge tracks over Tennessee Pass in 1881 and on to Salt Lake City via Utah's 2,286 m. Soldier Summit. But when this line was changed to standard gauge in 1890, a short tunnel was bored through the rib of softer rocks found at the very crest of the pass. This crest is presently adorned with a monument honoring the nearly 1,000 members of the 10th Mountain Division who lost their lives in combat during World War II, as well as access to "Ski Cooper," which was their training slope.

Hagerman moved south to the New Mexico territory in 1892. The Sherman Silver Purchase Act was repealed in 1893, resulting in the closure of most of the mines in southwest Colorado. These had been almost unanimously exploiting the carbonate ores found in conjunction with intrusives into the widespread and massive Leadville Limestone formation. This easily recognized series is of late Mississippian Age and outcrops throughout the entire Sawatch Range in south-central Colorado and elsewhere. It is everywhere dolomitic (CaMgCO3), varying in thickness up to 60 meters and is particularly well exposed in the canyon upstream from Glenwood Springs. Nevertheless, Hagerman retained his interest in the gold properties of Cripple Creek, though he had also gone on to a variety of other projects in New Mexico.

But the name of Hagerman lives on in railroad lore primarily for his championship of the Colorado Midland Railroad, in which he had also become a major investor, in its effort to unseat the monopoly position of the Rio Grande as the transportation link for the booming town of Ute City (later Aspen). The wagon road and freighting company organized by Captain Richard Sopris (1813–1890), a sometime legislator of Kansas and mayor of Denver, to serve the Roaring Fork region was thus put out of business,

D&RGW tunnel in the Leadville limestone. Archaean granite underlies the limestone here in Glenwood Canyon (Graham A.B. Vickowski).

though the freighter/politician's name remains prominent on the westerly skyline from Aspen. Unfortunately for the Hagerman Pass route, by the time the Midland finally got its standard-gauge tracks and trains down the north fork of the Frying Pan and through to Aspen, the Rio Grande had already been running its three-foot gauge trains up the main stem of that river from Glenwood for a full year and had sewed up most of the lucrative shipping contracts. Thus, in 1890, Hagerman arranged the sale of the Midland to General Palmer's archenemy, the Atchison, Topeka & Santa Fe, and concentrated on his other ventures. In the end the Midland was never worth the massive effort put into it.

There had been a long-standing rivalry and numerous confrontations between crews working for the rival railroads, the D&RGW and the Santa Fe, the most violent of which was in June of 1879 and concerned the route from Pueblo up the narrow and scenic Royal Gorge of the Arkansas to reach the newly opened silver "hot spot" of Leadville. The Santa Fe hired the notorious Bat Masterson, then sheriff of Ford County, Kansas, to "convince" Palmer's people they should give in — for everyone knew there was room for only one set of tracks in the narrow gorge — and took over the stone roundhouse in Pueblo. But Masterson and his 30 goons were forcibly evicted by a superior armed force employed by the Rio Grande, thus setting the stage for a protracted "war." William Bartholomew Masterson (1853–1921) was a native of Iberville County, Quebec, and died at his desk as a sports writer for the *Morning Telegraph* in New York City. Ultimately, cooler heads prevailed and everyone adjourned to an arbitration imposed by the U.S. Fourth Circuit Court. The Rio Grande ended up building the line, but had to cede trackage rights to the Santa Fe. The Santa Fe had easily won the two lines' first confrontation, to gain the route over (and later under) the 2,610 m. Raton Pass into New Mexico; thus enabling that line to get to its namesake town of Santa Fe and simultaneously denying the Rio Grande convenient access to its namesake river valley.

Palmer remained fervently intent on making his line a part of something bigger. In 1909 his successors made a three-way arrangement from Chicago to the Pacific Coast, combining with the Western Pacific and the Chicago, Rock Island & Pacific for passengers to utilize the Rock Island from Chicago, the WP's easy grades of the Feather River Route through the Sierra Nevada and his line "through the Rockies and not around them." This was part of an integrated competition to the speedier "transcontinental" lines between Chicago and California such as the Atchison Topeka & Santa Fe to the south, and the Central Pacific/Union Pacific line through Wyoming.

The Western Pacific was a Gould-financed line and a latecomer. It opened in 1909

"Heavy" construction area on the WP's Feather River Route.

Close-up of Spanish Canyon bridge over Feather River.

Bridge at Spanish Canyon in Feather River.

after three years of heavy construction work, but ended up with grades of only 1 percent, in stark contrast to the Central Pacific's line which climbs to 2,175 m. and still has grades exceeding 2 percent in crossing the snowy Donner Summit. Later, the streamlined train *California Zephyr*, initiated in 1930, became very popular in the years prior to World War II, but soon utilized the Moffat Tunnel west from Denver to Glenwood Springs, via the Dotsero Cutoff, rather than the D&RGW's more scenic but older line through the Royal Gorge and over Tennessee Pass.

The major advantage of a narrower gauge is that trains can utilize a much tighter curvature and are not nearly as inhibited in acceptable gradient as the wider standard gauge. In addition, 4 percent is almost at the limit for standard gauge, whereas narrower gauge engines can easily climb at 5 percent. The major drawback to using a narrow gauge is that offbeat gauge cars and locomotives cannot operate anywhere except on their own home tracks. The DRG&W yards at Salida, where General Palmer's standard-gauge lines interfaced with both his and other narrow gauge lines, were built with an extra "third" rail and the switching engines there had a triple socket arrangement for coupling. But still, almost all of the freight that went through Salida destined to or from more distant places had to be reloaded for transhipment onward.

The acme of such incompatibility can be found in the otherwise very logical and well-synchronized railway system of Switzerland. The standard-gauge connection is at Interlaken Öst (from the station platform of which one can see the famed Jungfrau, barely 25 km. distant to the south). A narrow-gauge, sometimes cog-driven, line goes up the Lütschine valley and forks to serve both Grindelwald and Lauterbrunnen; a second but incompatible narrow-gauge Wengernalp line (completed in 1893) goes between those stations via the crest of the Kleine Scheidegg; and from that station, high on the north shoulder of the Eiger, yet a third such line will take a visitor by Adolph Guyer-Zeller's 7 km. tunnel (completed in 1912) through the Eiger and Mönch to the highest railway point of Europe, the Jungfraujoch. More than incidentally to many of the rail lines discussed herein, the Jungfraujoch, at 3,475 m., was the base from which Gerald Seligman (1886–1973), founder of the International Glaciological Society, and his fellow researchers made the first authoritative study of snow structure changes and the conditions leading to avalanche hazards.

However, this is a book on North American tunnels, and though the numerous narrow-gauge lines across the high passes of Colorado have generated a high number of historic and heroic railroad narratives, they are not really our topic. Thus, if we are to digress at all, better it should be to the South Park's Alpine Tunnel — at more than two miles above sea level, the first to penetrate the Continental Divide — en route to a discussion of that which was named for Hagerman. Like General Palmer and James Hagerman, the South Park's management also wanted to reach into the rich silver-mining country of Colorado's southwest (Aspen, Gunnison, Silverton, Telluride, etc.) and decided to try getting there by replacing the wagon road over 3,695 m. Altman Pass. But this company was burdened with the high operating costs of using Boreas Pass to reach Leadville, and its owners determined that their already questionable reputation for wintertime reliability would suffer fatally if they had more than one difficult pass to cross. A tunnel was the obvious solution, and Colorado was awash with miners who were not always fully employed.

Unfortunately, getting tracks through the Archaean crystalline rocks, some 350 m. below the crest of Altman pass was not to be a clean job of tunneling. While the aspect of the bedrock which first met the locator's eye in 1880 was of a firm and durable granite, once through this relatively thin facade, the interior turned out to be wet and crumbly for most of the more than 500 meters of tunnel — not as bad as the saprolite of the Hoosac, but still subject to countless minor cave-ins. This condition bankrupted its first contractor and forced the entire length of the tunnel roof to be supported by redwood lining, while adjacent snowsheds on the east approach accounted for an additional 250 meters of very smoky going. Despite these expensive efforts, which extended over a two-year period after 1880, there was a major cave-in in 1888 which caused the tunnel to be closed for three years. A further and larger collapse in 1910 was the end of its use by the South Park. Though, after a bit of cleaning up and a few miles of route swapping, some Rio Grande narrow-gauge trains did go that way for a couple of years.

The puffing of steam engine exhaust has been the cause of numerous minor rock falls from tunnel roofs, not merely in the now-abandoned Alpine Tunnel, but even in such grander, and still operating, locales as the Connaught.

In addition to those discussed above, narrow-gauge lines have also been pushed across other passes in Colorado: La Veta at 2,817 m.; Cumbres at 3,048 m.; and Wagon Wheel Gap (with its modern tourist train) at a comparable altitude. Unfortunately, all of the romantic narrow-gauge rail lines that once served the mineral country of Colorado have now been swallowed into larger systems and/or effectively finished their days: the D&RGW went into the UP via the SP; a few parts of the Midland into the BNSF; the Colorado Central into the UP; and the Colorado & Southern into the Chicago, Burlington & Quincy and thus to the BNSF. Those "haughty-voiced" 4-6-6-4s of the Rio Grande were all gone by 1956, replaced with diesel-electric units. By the year 2000 almost every rail in the United States west of the Mississippi had been swallowed up into one of two gigantic maws — the Union Pacific or the Burlington Northern/Santa Fe.

Boreas Pass, at a smidgen less than 3,600 m. in altitude, boasted the highest railroad in the Americas until a line was built at almost 5,000 m. to serve Peru's Cerro de Pasco copper mines in the 20th century. Boreas was traversed at Climax in 1883 by the narrow-gauge tracks of the Denver, South Park & Pacific, by then a subsidiary of the Union Pacific, in extending its line to Leadville. This also tapped the coal mines of Breckenridge and crossed 3,450 m. Fremont Pass where prospector Charles J. Senter (1845–1924), a former Indian scout for General Crook, had staked his claim to the now world-famous porphyritic molybdenum ores of Climax in 1879, though little was done by way of "improving" them until 1915.

* * *

The Colorado Midland Railroad was basically a creature of James Hagerman, who was its principal "angel." He knew, like the legendary HAW Tabor of Leadville, that there was as much money — maybe more — to be made in servicing mines (and miners) as in actually working the diggings. Hagerman's line began at Colorado Springs, where he and most of his fellow investors resided, and managed to get easily over 2,993 m. Ute Pass and 2,849 m. Trout Creek Pass to Leadville, extending a spur into the lucrative coal mines near Crested Butte, en route to the popular goal of Aspen. His locators then looked across the upper Arkansas valley to the main divide and, in 1887, completed boring their tunnel under the Continental Divide, 15 km. across the way. The hard rock going was far easier than at the almost contemporary and relatively nearby Alpine Tunnel, and the rock much more stable, so that construction costs and difficulty were far less than at Altman Pass. Furthermore, these contractors were able to import experienced tunnel laborers from Italy, some of whom had once worked on the Frejus. The result of their labors is a 654 m. (2,161 foot) bore at an altitude of 3,614 m. ASL (11,528 feet) that is now quite effectively blocked off so it cannot be entered, even by the adventurous.

Hagerman Tunnel's east portal, firmly closed in 2009 (Graham A.B. Vickowski).

The barren and windswept crest of Hagerman Pass.

Still, Hagerman Tunnel was a difficult operating push both ways. On the west much of the 30 km. from Basalt and Aspen up the north branch of the Fryingpan River as well as that on the east from Leadville up past modern Turquoise Lake at 3,008 m. ASL was at more than 3 percent — a tough slog even for the most powerful engines of that day. Furthermore, deep snow afflicted the Midland below Hagerman Pass as much as it did the nearby South Park at Altmann Pass; so the Midland was quick to abandon its Hagerman Tunnel in 1893 for the considerably longer and much lower altitude Busk/Ivanhoe Tunnel (named for the two river valleys it connects). This worked until after Hagerman had sold his controlling shares to the Santa Fe and the Midland went into bankruptcy and reorganization in 1897, two years after which its trains did not even try to get to Aspen. (In 1922 the Busk-Ivanhoe Tunnel was reworked into an automobile road as State Highway 104, which was used for several more years, until a massive cave-in forced its closure.) It had some of the most powerful steam locomotives ever built — entirely 2-8-0s with small diameter drivers and a single front truck. This design was necessary so the drivers would not readily climb out of the track on the line's tighter curves — the absence of rear truck was so the engine's wheelbase would remain short enough to negotiate those curves. A nearly fatal nail in the Midland's coffin was a massive blizzard in 1899 that closed the entire line completely for 77 days. However the Midland kept trying, it never had more than 350 miles of track, very little of which was straight or even level, and it did not reach any major exchange point with lines other than the Rio Grande.

In 1917, as a "wartime efficiency" measure, the United States Railroad Administration seized all American railroads and dictated how freight traffic would be routed. Inasmuch as the Midland was purely standard gauge, the bureaucrats under William

Charles Graham's fanciful etching of the east side of Hagerman Pass. The tunnel entrance was near the smoke stack at bottom center of this picture (© John A. Lowell & Co, 1893).

Gibbs McAdoo determined it would be more efficient for any through traffic reaching Grand Junction on the west to travel eastward on the Midland, rather than transship onto the, by then equally for all practical purposes, standard gauge Rio Grande. This apparent boon turned into a nightmare of clogged yards, for the Midland simply couldn't handle the increased traffic. It was "one Hell of a way to run a railroad." Red-faced with embarrassment over this self-inflicted disaster, the bureaucrats then completely reversed themselves and mandated that all such traffic should go via the Rio Grande, which had the switching capacity to cope. The Midland lost status as well as money in the process, and was in liquidation before the ink was dry on the Versailles Treaty. It was all gone but not completely forgotten by the time of the second World War, during which the United States government had the good sense to let railroad people, not politicians, run the railroads. McAdoo (1863–1941) did know something about railroads, having been in charge of constructing the first tunnel under the Hudson River — for the Hudson & Manhattan Railroad — but he was married to President Wilson's daughter, Eleanor, which cost him some credibility for his important office. In 1924 he sought the Democratic nomination for president, but lost out to James Middleton Cox, who, in turn, lost out to incumbent (John) Calvin Coolidge.

* * *

Among David Moffat's desires, as a strong hometown booster, was to create a more direct westerly connection from Denver to Salt Lake City, San Francisco and vicinity. The Colorado Rockies are far and away the highest part of the main North American uplift, and have been crossed by a number of its passes, of which the most easily traversed was the 3,177 m. (10,424 foot) Tennessee Pass up the Arkansas River from Pueblo. The Colorado Midland Railroad from Colorado Springs had also crossed the main divide, utilizing the Hagerman Tunnel, but both of those flat-land cities were too far south of Denver — but yet politically competitive — for Moffat's parochial taste.

Sometimes called Corona Pass, and so named for the "town" later erected at the crest of the pass, when the Moffat line's tracks actually ran over the crest of the 3,563 m. pass, this crossing was used by General Rollins' toll road over the Divide to Middle Park, at which time it also appeared on maps as Boulder Pass. As befitting for the most "direct" line west from Colorado's metropolis, the Denver, Northwestern & Pacific was located through Arvada and past the later notorious four square miles of Rocky Flats near Boulder to enter the mountains largely following the south fork of Boulder Creek to Rollinsville. There, to the west, the backbone of North America faced the railroad builders. Though Moffat had entertained the idea of a tunnel under the granitic rock of James Peak from the very start, with its promise of a no-more-than 2 percent grade, his associates and successors in the DNW&P had neither the necessary funds nor the patience to await them, while the dream of profits from a direct line to Salt Lake City and beyond remained very strong. So they began to build a grand set of curves, cuttings, trestles, and minor bores up the southeast-facing hillside north of the creek, and a comparably complex set to descend on the west. The adventurous soul can still follow this line up the hill, though the trestles are mostly collapsed and the cuts slumped in while much of its lower course has been reclaimed by the forest and the brief bore at the summit is too caved in for vehicular traffic.

Moffat's line was not the first such proposal. In 1880 a group of capitalists, including Horace Austin Warner Tabor (1830–1899), incorporated the Denver, Utah & Pacific to build a line essentially as was later taken over Rollins Pass. Some grading was done, but the line was to be of three-foot gauge and no rail was ever laid. Everything stopped the following year after unsuccessfully facing the need for several minor tunnels on the east approach. HAW Tabor, not one of the heroes of this narrative, was born in Holland, Vermont. After a series of adventures, he ultimately became a storekeeper in Leadville, where he grubstaked prospectors for a one-third interest in whatever they might locate. He thus became one of the richest men in the state. A notoriously gregarious and generous man, in time he was elected lieutenant governor of Colorado, then United States senator. But he divorced his wife (who seems to have been the one with brains) for a much younger woman (Baby Doe) and was bankrupted by the repeal of the Sherman Silver Purchase Act. His friends arranged for Tabor to spend his last years of destitution as the U.S. postmaster of Denver.

Imbued with Moffat's dream, but still lacking the necessary capital, in 1909 the

East side of abandoned Rollins Pass Route in 2009. Three switchbacks still visible on this hillside are slowly being reclaimed by the forest (Graham A.B. Vickowski).

DNW&P promoters — now reorganized under the banner of the Denver & Salt Lake Railroad — pushed their line to the highest altitude ever reached in North America by a standard gauge railroad, over the top of Rollins Pass, and utilized an expensive to operate (particularly in winter) 4 percent grade over many of those 37 km. (23 miles). But they were only able to get as far to the northwest as the town of Craig. Never getting through to the far West, almost half of the line's operating costs were incurred by snow removal. The DNW&P maintained an array of massive rotary snowplows; but sometimes even these expensive machines were unable to cope with the depth of snow, and trains would frequently become stalled while their passengers fled to safety on snowshoes. Local pride continued, however, along with increased demand for west slope water. After much politicking, in 1927 the citizens of Greater Denver passed the final massive bond issue, and Moffat's dream of a tunnel through the Archean granite of James Peak began to assume reality.

As in almost all great enterprises, the original $6.62 million estimates of construction proved far short of reality, and only the Denver area's ever-growing need for the water flowing down the rivers of the western slope prepared the citizens for the three further $6,000,000 bond issues that were necessary to ensure completion. A pioneer tunnel, 2.5 m. high by 2.5 m. wide (8 feet by 8 feet), was bored through so that crosscuts could be made to work the major bore from numerous different headings along the almost 10 km. tunnel. This pilot bore was thereafter used to carry the precious water. Much as in the case of the Hoosac and Alpine Tunnels, severely fractured ("rotten") rock — bulging in from both sides, top and bottom — was encountered near the western portal. Some 1.4 million tons of rock were finally removed, at a cost of $1,440 per meter of bore. However, though much of the tunnel had to be lined to keep its roof in place, this project was carried through for four years without interruption and with a blessedly low casualty rate of 28 persons losing their lives in the effort.

After a total construction bill that exceeded $22,000,000, the first train passed through Moffat's Tunnel in February of 1928 and went on to Craig in northcentral Colorado, the seat of what was then renamed Moffat County; but the Pacific was still a long way off. Though the tunnel — with its high point at the center and a grade of less than 1 percent on the west and half of that on the east — offered hope of shortening the trip west from Denver by nearly 300 km., there was no useful connection beyond the west portal. An otherwise assetless corporate entity called the Denver & Salt Lake Western Railroad had obtained the right to build a connection between the Rio Grande's main line (that over Tennessee Pass) at Dotsero and the western portal of the new tunnel. In 1932 — after a lengthy period of negotiation — the D&RGW began the two-year, $3,750,000, effort of building the 64 km. connection up the north fork of the Colorado River, via Kremmling and Tabernash to the west portal of the Moffat Tunnel. After 1934, trains west of Denver could travel to the coast on that vastly easier grade; though ventilation issues, despite the installation of huge fans at the east portal, still mandate that the tunnel handle no more than 25 trains per day.

Today, Amtrak runs its *California Zephyr* from places in the East to Denver and onward via the Moffat Tunnel, then over Soldier Summit to Salt Lake City and on to Oakland. The ruling* grade over Soldier Summit is 2.4 percent from Helper on the east to the crest, and 2 percent up from Provo on the west. Because the trains are scheduled to go through Glenwood Canyon and western Colorado during daylight hours, deservedly or otherwise (an assertion that would be argued strenuously by the Canadian Pacific), Amtrak advertises the route (despite the 20 minutes in the dark) as the most scenic railroad trip available in the world.

* * *

In addition to whatever complaints might emanate from the CPR, railroaders from four other continents might complain about questionable advertising, to wit:

1. Though hardly gifted with comparable scenery, Australia boasts the longest tangent track in the world: some 800 km. (500 straight miles) on the line (completed in 1912) connecting Brisbane and Sydney in the east with Perth in the west.
2. Tsar Alexander III's 10,000 km. Trans-Siberian — with its 5 foot gauge, completed in 1905 after a 14-year period of construction — is an uneventful trip for most of its traverse of seven time zones, but its recent circuit around the north of Lake Baikal (which also no longer freezes sufficiently during the winter to bear the weight of a temporary track) goes through and by some very impressive country.
3. The new (2004) 1,956 km. Chinese railroad from Quinzang to Lhasa uses three high tunnels — all of them higher than anything used in North America (Guanjiao — 4,010 m.; Fenghoosang —1,338 m.; and Yanghejing — 3,345 m.) and one-third of its length is built on permafrost. The line crosses the Tanggula Pass at 5,072 m., so the Chinese railroad authority requires a certificate of health before issuing anyone a ticket; nevertheless, each train carries supplemental oxygen.
3. Several Swiss "rack" lines over high passes, such as the Albula, 2,315 m., and the Oberalp, 2,044 m., offer excellent views (as well as a tilt-free souvenir wine glass).
4. The dual-gauge Rio Mulatos–Potosi line in the Andes of Bolivia and Peru has two stations situated above 4,775 m.; higher than any point in Colorado.

7

See America First

THE GREAT NORTHERN RAILROAD has two significant tunnels, one under the crest of the Cascade Range at Stevens Pass, west of Wenatchee, Washington, and the other in the much less challenging topographic environment of the Kootenai National Forest (formerly much of the Flathead Indian Reservation) in northwestern Montana. The one became famous on March 1, 1910, when a climax* avalanche wiped out a passenger train that was parked on a siding near its west portal. The other slipped quietly into operation many years later and has never enjoyed much notoriety.

The Great Northern Railroad, as originally laid out in 1893, crossed the Cascade Mountains via the 1238 m. (4,061 foot) Stevens Pass, which had been located by John Frank Stevens (1853–1943)—not to be confused with the surveyor and territorial governor of Washington (1849–55), Gen. Isaac Ingalls Stevens (1818–1862); nor his son, Hazard Stevens (1842–1918), who was equally distinguished in the Civil War and made the first ascent of Mt. Rainier in 1870. The pass-finding Stevens was a native of Maine who was largely self-educated in surveying and became an employee of the Great Northern in 1889. He had the almost immediate distinction of locating the Marias Pass (where his statue stands) through the Rockies and also the pass that bears his name through the Cascade Range. After serving as chief engineer for the Great Northern, in 1903 he transferred to the Chicago, Rock Island & Pacific as vice-president. In 1905, on the recommendation of his former employer, J. J. Hill, Theodore Roosevelt tapped him for the critical position of chief engineer of the Panama Canal, where he stayed for two years. He was instrumental in eliminating that project's malaria problems as well as determining the feasibility of the Gatun Lake concept, after the French (DeLesseps) fiasco of trying to construct a sea-level canal. Stevens' successor in Panama was the more famous Gen. George Washington Goethals (1858–1928), who drove the project to completion in 1914.

However, the guiding genius behind the Great Northern Railroad was always James Jerome Hill, who had been born near Guelph, Ontario, on September 18, 1838, and received a doctorate (*honoris causa*) from Yale in 1910, six years before his death. He left his father's farm in 1855 for a business career in St. Paul. There he established a fuel supply and transportation empire that came, in time, to span several of the United

States and reach as many steel tentacles into western Canada. Not for nothing was the crack express train of the Great Northern Railroad (still carried forward by Amtrak) named *The Empire Builder.*

Hill's Red River Transportation Company of St. Paul was the first enterprise (in 1875) to bring modern communications to Manitoba, the overland (largely by canoe) route from Fort William on Lake Superior falling into eclipse thereafter. Hill was also the soul and spirit of the St. Paul & Pacific Railroad, of which he acquired control in 1879 from its Dutch bondholders. He renamed the St. Paul, Minneapolis & Manitoba Railway before merging it into his later Great Northern in 1890. In 1883 Hill supplied Major Albert Rogers to help his associates in the Canadian Pacific, before obviously inevitable economic rivalries caused him to separate his equity interests from the Canadian project. Rogers — known to some of his underlings as "the Bishop," for his frequent references to and pungent (if sometimes anatomically inaccurate) recitations of Holy Scripture — was a dynamic workhorse of hard living, strong language and uncompromising diligence and loyalty — but more about him in the next chapter.

The Hills, father and son Louis Warren Hill (1872–1848), ran a congenial format for their major constructions. They never had a "Benton," as described below by Messrs. Beadle and Bowles. This condition may have some origin with the Hills, for, unlike General Rollins, they accepted human realities and allowed (even encouraged) the existence of bars and brothels in their work camps, particularly in the later and longer-lived such installations at Stevens Pass; along with resident doctors, above average wages, and separate quarters for family units.

Hill's line reached as far west as the Great Falls of the Missouri in Montana in 1887, having judiciously bypassed the earlier frontier trading location of Fort Benton. When the townsfolk there refused his request for a right-of-way, Hill simply ran his line "in a graceful arc" a mile distant, thereby setting the town on the way to oblivion — a message of response to short-sighted greed that was not lost on other settlements along the GN route. Hill maintained his fiscal equilibrium by building grain elevators and encouraging settlement as his tracks went along. He would haul a healthy immigrant (mostly from Northern Europe) halfway across the continent, if only the immigrant would agree to settle his family along the GN rails. As the CPR was begging and borrowing its way into the difficult terrain of the Rockies and Selkirks, Hill was pushing his own railroad across the plains of North Dakota and Montana toward the mountains that lay between St. Paul and his objective of Seattle (and later a fleet of Pacific steamers) without any government help and the consequent restrictions.

* * *

Samuel Bowles II (1826–1878), publisher of the influential *Springfield Republican*, in his third book, *Our New West*, 1869, discussed the wide-open temporary construction "cities" that were to be found at "the end of steel," as America's first transcontinental worked its way across the country. He described the Union Pacific's "town" of Benton, in Nebraska — which no longer exists but was named for the distinguished senator from Missouri, Thomas Hart Benton (1782–1858), the father-in-law of explorer John Charles Frémont and the first person to serve five consecutive senate terms. Publisher Bowles, a confidant of the political establishment of the day, found Benton disgusting by day and dangerous by night,

> a congregation of scum and wickedness ... almost everybody dirty, many filthy, and with the marks of lowest vice; averaging a murder a day; gambling and drinking, hurdy-gurdy dancing and the vilest of sexual commerce, the chief business and pastime of the hours. Like its predecessors, it fairly festered in corruption, disorder and death, and would have rotted, even in this dry air, had it outlasted a brief sixty-day life. But in a few weeks its tents were struck, its shanties razed, and with their dwellers moved on fifty or a hundred miles farther to repeat their life for another brief day. Where these people came from originally; where they went to when the road was finished, and their occupation over, were both puzzles too intricate for me. Hell would appear to have been raked to furnish them; and to it they must have naturally returned after graduating here, fitted for its highest seats and most diabolical service.[1]

Traveling more or less with Bowles was another journalist, John Hanson Beadle (1840–1897), a native of Indiana and later a vigorously anti–Mormon author. He wrote:

> Although the streets were filled with burning alkali dust, and water had to be hauled three miles in wagons from the North Platte River for a dollar a barrel, the lots were eagerly and quickly bought up. Two months later, Benton was a ghost town, with nothing left there but a side-track for the use and convenience of the Fort [Fred Steele].
>
> During its Hell on Wheels heyday, however, Benton had twenty-three saloons and five dance halls. Twice each day, long freight trains arrived from the East to unload tons of goods for reshipment by wagons to all points west. "For ten hours daily the streets were thronged with motley crowds of railroadmen, Mexicans and Indians, gamblers, "cappers," saloonkeepers, merchants, miners and mulewhackers.... The streets were eight inches deep in white dust as I entered the city of canvas tents and pole-houses; the suburbs appeared as banks of dirty white lime, and a new arrival with black clothes looked like nothing so much as a cockroach struggling through a flour barrel.... The great institution of Benton was the "Big Tent." This structure was a nice frame, a hundred feet long and forty feet wide, covered in canvas and conveniently floored for dancing, to which and gambling it was entirely devoted.[2]

Hill, however, differed from everyone else, including his former associates in the CPR (see next chapters), in his methods of construction. Building from his own initial capital and his line's earnings without any of the extensive federal subsidies, that made life easier for other "transcontinentals." (Easier may have been a temporary condition. The Central Pacific promoters managed to get by on a two-tier subsidy after encountering the "mountain district" just outside Sacramento; but they were called to account before the 50th Congress, in which — most fortuitously — Leland Stanford, of the Big

Four, and George Hearst (1820–1891), father of W. R. Hearst, were the two senators from California.)

Hill also decreed there would be no "momentum grading"* on his main line—though there was some minor backsliding by his subordinates on some of the line's branches in the mountains of Montana which were less rigid in their layout specifications. Nevertheless, Hill's main line ended up being built "right." Though he was able to use the very low Marias Pass, at 1,562 m. (less than a mile ASL) to cross the Continental Divide at the southeast corner of the U.S. Glacier National Park, unfortunately, things got a little hairier farther west. Hill had to do some major politicking to clear his right-of-way through the Flathead Reservation and kept at it until Glacier National Park was established in 1910. In Canada, a similarly but more accurately named park—one can actually still see some glaciers from the CPR's main line—was the political creation of the Canadian Pacific.

* * *

Albert Bowman Rogers (1829–1889) did not have the good fortune to locate Marias Pass, for when he was first on the Great Northern job, that crossing was deep inside the Flathead tribal grounds and off limits to everyone, as well as unknown to the rest of the world. When Rogers returned to Hill's employ in 1888, he was assigned to helping locate the route farther west. Before a monumentally disabling fall off his horse and subsequent death from stomach cancer, he was subordinate to Stevens in determining the route from Spokane to Wenatchee and thence westward across the crest of the Cascade Range.

Rogers, a native of Orleans, the easternmost township of Cape Cod—as was Thomas Doane—was the discoverer of two passes that now bear his name, one in the Selkirk Range of British Columbia at 1,330 m. and used by the Canadian Pacific, and another slightly higher gap in Montana, southwest of Great Falls, now used by state highway 200 and advertised as one of the continent's coldest spots.

After emerging from the hill country of northern Idaho at Spokane, the Great Northern wended its way across the generally flat, prehistorically floodswept and essentially treeless volcanic terrain of central Washington to cross the Columbia at Wenatchee, where its major difficulties really began. The GN's original line over Stevens Pass in the Cascade Range—where snowfall often aggregates more than 47 m. (140 feet) per year—ran easily up the Wenatchee River, passing Leavenworth and up along the steep-sided Tumwater Canyon. A later revision turned straight north at Leavenworth to utilize the wider and less avalanche-prone valley of Chumstick Creek rather than the continually threatening terrain of Tumwater Canyon.

In a report to Hill dated October 7, 1887, from Wenatchee, Rogers noted:

> I returned here, last night, having made the trip to the divide via the Skagit and Sauk Rivers. This route leads up to the Indian and Ward's passes [which are only two miles apart] and is the only route connecting the Skagit with the Wenatchee. Besides being

> much longer, it is not so favorable as the route via the Skykomish, [using Stevens Pass] of which I wrote in my last — greater distance, greater altitude, and snow slides on both sides of the Range, combine against it. The avalanches on the western slope are fearful — much worse than anything in the Selkirks — (on the Can Pac).

Engineer Stevens found the pass, thanks to help from a curious native, and then figured out how to get the railroad over it by a series of switchbacks — eight in all — that were very difficult both to build and then to maintain and requiring a steam engine (running half the time in reverse) on each end of every train. Coming up from the east, he used three switchbacks and a tight horseshoe curve with tunnel to gain the crest. This involved a 4 percent grade over 12 miles of track. To get down to the Skykomish River valley on the west, there were five switchbacks, all exceeding the desired 2 percent grade, and all of about 300 m. (1,000 feet) in length. The difficulty of so doing (freight trains were limited to a total of 18 cars), coupled with the high cost of snow removal, caused the Great Northern management, which was generally dominated by someone named Hill, to opt in 1897 for the creation of a 4.2 km. tunnel. First, however, and according to one of Hill's biographers,

> came one final frustration. Studying the imposing east and west faces of the pass that bore his name, John Stevens saw no alternative — until the summit tunnel could be bored — except to construct what was undeniably every railroad man's nightmare: a horribly costly series of switchbacks over the top. These would total twelve miles of track over four and one-half actual miles of terrain, with more than twenty-three hundred degrees of curvature, equal to seven full circles! Crossing this obstacle course, twenty-five unit trains would have to decouple, and engines fore and aft would have to push and pull the trains over in segments of five or six cars per train. In winter, hundreds of men would be required to shovel snow from the tracks. This one terrible bottleneck passage would, in short, drain much of the cost-efficiency from the tightly built GN system.
>
> To everyone's dread, this bit of news pushed James [Hill] over the edge. Clearing the tracks ahead, he raced full speed westward by special train and rushed up to the summit site. While colleagues stood by quaking, Stevens coolly explained his decision to his highly agitated boss. Then to the surprise and relief of the group, Hill calmly responded: "That is all right. You could have done nothing else." Without hesitation, Hill raised Steven's salary by 50 percent.[3]

Completed near the end of 1900, the first bore ran on a 1.7 percent grade (up to the east), which was close to the elsewhere ruling gradient for the entire line but was soon found difficult to ventilate. The two headings met on September 23, 1900, and disagreed by only 2 cm. over a distance of 4,210 meters. In completing this first tunnel, the GN saved 13.7 km. (8.5 mi.) of track, and 2,332 degrees of curvature. The line was soon electrified through the tunnel in order to avoid fume and smoke issues. The electricity was generated initially by a dam and powerhouse in the lower Tumwater Canyon until a favorable arrangement could be worked out with Puget Sound Power & Light to electrify everything from Skykomish to Wenatchee.

After deciding on this first Cascade Tunnel, the main line was relocated up the Chumstick Valley to a westerly crossing under a southeast shoulder of Natapoc Ridge by a short tunnel. It rejoined the existing line above the difficult Tumwater Canyon in the valley of Nason Creek until it reached an altitude of almost 1,000 m. ASL where it faced the steep ridge that marks the divide between the Wenatchee and Skykomish Rivers, which latter flows directly to Puget Sound. But there still remained some stretches on both sides of the pass where the gradient reached 4 percent, and snow depth problems persisted below both portals of the tunnel. Therefore, by 1909 the Great Northern had built miles of sturdy concrete snowsheds, mostly at and below the western portal on the "weather" side of the divide.

The GN did all it could to ease the ventilation issue in Cascade #1. The Hills bought several electric engines for exclusive tunnel use and briefly ran their own hydroelectric plant in Tumwater Canyon. Though most of the steam engines coasted through the tunnel, with the electrics doing all the work, some were equipped with streamlined appearing, elongated smoke stacks, so that such exhaust as there was came out behind the locomotive cabs. After World War II, these catenary-supplied electrics were replaced (as was all the motive power on most American railroads) with diesel-electrics.

* * *

Early in 1910, a seemingly never-ending series of moisture-laden winter storms dumped unusually deep snow across the Cascades, thus engendering avalanches that kept the GN's big, rotary snowplows busy with blockades all along the line, even between Skykomish and near sea level at the aptly named location of Startup. On the first day of March, a few major slides caused all westbound trains to be held at Leavenworth, where they were soon blocked fore and aft by another major slide at Drury (since renamed Peshastin, where the phenocryst-laden granite pinnacles are a favorite springtime Mecca for rock climbers) six miles back down toward Wenatchee. On March 2, a Wednesday, newspapers across the continent began to report a developing story datelined Everett, Washington, of a huge avalanche that had overwhelmed a whole train on the Great Northern Railroad near the town of Wellington, Washington (since then understandably renamed to Tye).

Then on March 3 a further report from Everett said that the cars of the wrecked train were not in sight, but under 40 to 50 feet of snow and trees.[4] Each day for the next week the reported body count grew higher and the stories more dramatic, ultimately reaching 86 passengers and 15 crew members. Meantime, a second avalanche story came from farther east on the GN line datelined Spokane and telling of problems at Milan, 22 miles to the east. Readers of the *New York Times* were told on page one:

> The *Oriental Limited* train eastbound, on the Great Northern Railroad, was struck by an avalanche of snow and rocks yesterday. One person was killed, and twelve others injured.... The entire train narrowly escaped plunging down a fifty-foot embankment.

Disused snowshed below Cascade Tunnel #1. The fatal avalanche at Tye was a mile to the right.

On March 8, a week after the initial reports of these avalanches, the *New York Times* mentioned the subject of such avalanches editorially, declaiming with an eye toward future preventive technology:

> It would not seem to be beyond the power of engineering skill to prevent snowslides, however it may be to landslides. Once started, the avalanche is irresistible, but obstacles that divided its material might make the start impossible.

A century later, avalanche forecasting remains an inexact science; though avalanche experts tend to agree that powder snow avalanche conditions, which generally exist only within a day or so of an actual storm, can be started by sophisticated artillery fire, thus limiting their impact to times when no personnel are in the path of danger. However, when climax conditions are imminent, the best policy is to stay away and let nature take its course, which, inconveniently, might be some time in coming.

In 19th century Switzerland, where the cheese and dairy products industry has long been important, the natives unwisely cleared most upland trees so as to increase summertime pasturage. They soon began to learn that those big, open, grassy slopes led to very unpleasant results—faster and more furious runoff in both summer and winter, and widespread avalanches that wiped out many upland settlements. After accepting the unwisdom of these clearances, the Swiss built a vast number of avalanche restraining and deflective barriers, and since then have set out to reforest their upper hillsides.

* * *

After the disaster at Wellington, the GN managers decided to get on with a lower level tunnel, which would carry the railroad through the mountains below the heavy snow altitude that was so bothersome. Initiated in 1926, a decade after the death of James Jerome Hill and after years of analyzing avalanche paths, careful planning, and geologic investigation of the complex igneous and metamorphic bedrock, Cascade #2 (shown on its east portal as Tunnel # 15) required the use of a midpoint "central" shaft. But with increasingly effective tunneling methods, it was lined throughout with concrete and opened for traffic in three years, having employed a construction crew of nearly 1,800 men, mostly in residence camps run by the railroad. The ruling grade throughout

East portal of Cascade #2 closed for ventilation, 2009.

BNSF unit coal train exiting east portal of Cascade #2. This train was returning empty from Everett.

the entire line was thereby reduced to less than 1.7 percent, making the GN the world's most efficient long-haul route.

The GN had been quick to determine that the use of electric engines would save a lot of grief in any Cascade tunnel, but there was no nearby source for such power. A generating station built in the lower Tumwater Canyon sufficed for a while, until the dam went out and Puget Sound Light & Power could tool up to handle the situation. When more powerful but square-built electric engines were purchased in the 1930s, old timers were heard to grumble to the effect that these newfangled power units, with only 60-inch driving wheels, looked like "made-over box cars."

The Cascade Pass situation was analyzed by Professor Vance:

> But the Great Northern built directly westward from Spokane to Wenatchee and then sought to find a pass across the northern Cascades that would continue the direct line as close to Seattle as possible. The pass that was located, again by John Stevens, was almost as low (at 1238 m.) [4,061 feet] as Stampede Pass, and it gave a far more direct route. But that route did bring its costs. If constructed in the open without a tunnel, the sixty miles [97 km.] of line from Wenatchee to the crest of Stevens Pass would

> have to climb some thirty-four hundred feet [1,036 m.], more than a thousand of that in the last seven or eight miles, some at severe grades. On the western side the problem was even worse, leading to grades of 4 percent in the last pitch from Scenic [Hot Springs] to the pass. As opened in 1893, this line had eight switchbacks where the train had to reverse direction as well as one horseshoe curve partly in a tunnel. The curvature was excessive, the grades brutal, and the snows very deep indeed. Probably no other stretch of railroad in the United States at this time, certainly no other transcontinental, was so taxing in its operation.
>
> Given Hill's desire for a well-engineered line, the original Steven's Pass section had to be no more than a temporary solution. The snows at the crest, if nothing else, made year-round operation extremely difficult. So, soon after the Great Northern opened from St. Paul to Seattle, construction began on a tunnel under the pass, which managed to cut out the switchbacks, though not the horseshoe curve or much of the snow. When opened in 1900 this 2.63-mile tunnel still forced 4 percent ruling grades on the Great Northern. But even worse as an operating problem was the extremely heavy snow that piled up for many months here in the North Cascades. In order to get low enough to reduce the snow problem and the costly upkeep of miles of snowsheds and heavy plows, the company undertook what was then, and remained until late 1988, the longest railroad bore in the Western Hemisphere, the Cascade Tunnel of 41,152 feet [12,542 m.], or 7.79 miles. With the [new] Cascade Tunnel, opened for service on January 12, 1929, the Great Northern finally gained the properly engineered line that Hill had always had in mind. In the fifty miles of original line over the Cascades between Peshastin and Scenic, all but seven miles were relocated, shortening the route by nearly nine miles as well as removing both the horseshoe curve and the snowsheds. "Nearly 20,000 feet of tunnels, 40,000 feet of snowsheds and the equivalent of more than five complete circles of curvature were eliminated. The grade was reduced to 1.6 percent." Thus, the ruling grade on the Great Northern was shifted back to the 1.6 percent climb up the middle fork of the Flathead River from the Rocky Mountain Trench to Marias Pass.[5]

In summing up the Great Northern Railroad, Dr. Vance opined that it seemed to him that the GN "was the first modern transcontinental to be built, showing how a railroad should be engineered and run to earn its keep rather than simply speculative profits for its promoters."

* * *

The 1961 Columbia River Treaty between the United States and Canada was aimed primarily at the idea of stabilizing the river's flow and thus electric power production at a number of downstream locations. Grand Coulee is the one most people have heard of, though there already were several more power-generating dams on the big river within the State of Washington and now two more upstream in British Columbia. As part of this treaty, an additional dam was built just above the city of Libby, Montana, on the lower Kootenay River and its construction forced the relocation of about 100 km. of the Great Northern's main line. Much to the dismay of lumber interests — the economic base of Eureka — the railroad was relocated so as to bypass their town completely and leave them on a dead-end spur. However, they remain better off than their neighbors just west, at Rexford, where the entire city was completely flooded by the resultant Lake Koocanusa.

The relocated line — the Great Northern was using international treaty money for the relocation, not its own, and could thus afford to build well, right from the get-go — turned southwest before Eureka and just west of Stryker Junction to follow an easy grade up Fortine Creek with several fine tangents. But where the grade got steeper after Twin Meadows, just below Wolf Prairie, the Great Northern's 20th century locators opted to leave the valley and continue the southbound tangent through the Salish Mountains for another 10.5 km. via the Flathead Tunnel under a shoulder of 2,007 m. Elk Mountain. The line then emerges near the upper end of Wolf Creek, down along which it goes — mostly along the right bank for some 55 km., with three bridges and two minor bores (since opened into wide cuts) — to rejoin its original route just upstream from Libby.

Wishing to avoid problems before they materialize, the Great Northern established very rigid rules for flushing the air in Flathead Tunnel, mandating that "a full flush must be completed after every train and before allowing another train to enter the tun-

A fine tangent on the Great Northern west of Flathead Tunnel.

Flathead Tunnel, exhausting fumes after passage of an eastbound freight train.

nel." Flushes are automated; with one fan in operation it takes 25 minutes for an easterly flush, which is uphill, but only 17 if both fans are used. As a further precaution, in the days when freight train business managers (conductors) rode in a caboose at the tail end of it all, not at a desk in the head end, according to the *Operating Instructions* of the Montana Division, Kootenay River Subdivision,

> if for any reason, eastward trains stop in tunnel, members of crew on both head and rear of the train must communicate with each other on the phone located in each bay of the tunnel and have a thorough understanding with entire crew whether train will be backed out of tunnel or proceed eastward to Twin Meadows.

8

Lesser Bores on the Way West

THE BUILDERS OF THE CENTRAL PACIFIC encountered their most severe problems in crossing the Sierra Nevada at 2,303 m. (7,227 foot) Donner Pass. In finding their way up and out of California — hopefully to lay track rapidly through the flats of Nevada and Utah at a rate that would pay handsomely — the Big Four's engineers had calculated that their Summit Tunnel (#6) through the tough, granite crest of the Sierra Nevada would be 506 meters long (exactly 1,659 feet). However, by New Years Day of 1867, with hand-held drills, picks, shovels, and much black powder, the mostly Chinese labor force had barely dented the headings — boring, all told, a measly nine meters (29 feet). This left a staggering amount to go. Meanwhile, construction grading crews — complete with locomotive, flat cars and 90 miles of rails — were leapfrogged across get a line built along the easier terrain in the lower Truckee Valley to the east, before that river loses itself in the dry sands of the Nevada desert. But this process was costly; those work crews were being supplied by ox and mule-drawn wagons, with everything laboriously transshipped onto ox-drawn carts for freighting from the "end of steel" over the hills to the easier terrain beyond.

The Central Pacific was the corporate creation of four men, all of whose names remain prominent in the culture of California's Bay area and elsewhere. (Amasa) Leland Stanford (1824–1893), a native of Watervliet, New York (for whose son and namesake the university is named), was the driving force behind actual construction. Legend has it that after offering a vast sum to Harvard University if only it would change its name, and being refused, Stanford decided to build its equal; the formal name of the school at Palo Alto, therefore, is Leland Stanford Junior University. Mark Hopkins (1813–1878) was the eldest of the four and treasurer of the railroad. His name is remembered in San Francisco's fanciest hotel on Nob Hill. Charles Crocker (1822–1888), no discernible relative of Alvah (the hero of chapters 4 and 5), was another enterprising merchant of Sacramento and actually in charge of the Central Pacific's construction. He later migrated into banking, where his name survived until recent years. The *eminence grise* of the Big Four was Collis Potter Huntington (1821–1900), a native of Harwinton, Connecticut, who actually stayed in the railroad business until his death and left behind one of the largest research libraries in the United States.

Though there was much subsequent second-guessing about their excessive construction costs, the Central Pacific did have certain unusual costs not borne by the Great Northern or any of the other lines progressing from the East. All its rails and rolling stock (everything except stone and sand for masonry) had to be tediously shipped from the East Coast, either around "the Horn" or across the isthmus of Panama. Hill and the others could carry their construction supplies west on their own rails for whatever price they chose to name; whereas in the year 1868 alone, the Big Four's rails cost them nearly $60 per ton, just for delivery to Sacramento.

Tunneling was another economic monster. Edwin Bryant Crocker (1818–1875), an older brother of Charles of the Big Four, a California state Supreme Court justice and legal counsel to the Central Pacific, wrote to Collis Huntington on January 7: "We are only averaging about one foot per day on each face — and Stro and I have come to the conclusion that something must be done to hasten it."[1] Even if, at best, their Chinese drillers managed one meter (3 feet) per day at the two portals and on each heading at the bottom of a central shaft, it would be close to a year before the essential tunnel would be passable for traffic. The Big Four were up against potentially crippling financial and subsidy deadlines and simply could not afford that length of time to get their rails connected down to Reno.

Crocker had read a recent issue of *Scientific American* (between 1867 and 1876 this publication carried numerous reports on the use of explosives in the Hoosac project — blasting techniques being mentioned in several) in which Mowbray's experiments (then being undertaken at the Hoosac Tunnel) were described. Drilling through the spine of the Berkshires toward North Adams in that project, engineers were starting to report dramatic results using nitroglycerine instead of black powder. There had been a serious tragedy in San Francisco within the past year, when 15 people had been killed and dozens more injured by the clumsy opening of a case of this newly discovered "blasting oil." A powerful explosion had leveled the Wells Fargo office, the Union Club and other nearby buildings near Union Square in San Francisco. On May 5, 1866, the *New York Times* headlined the event: THE PACIFIC COAST: THE NITRO-GLYCERINE EXPLOSION IN SAN FRANCISCO. Terrific Effects of the New Explosive Compound — Horrible Scene — Entire Demolition of the Building — Melancholy Loss of Life — Minute Description of the Tragic Event. Nevertheless, the *Scientific American* article pointed out a possibility that the Big Four could not afford to overlook. Anyhow, encouraged by the articles on the success of the Hoosac trials, Crocker set out to obtain all the blasting oil he could and arranged to run tests in the notoriously durable, glacially-scoured granite at Donner Summit.

Coincidentally, a Scottish inventor named James Howden (1832–1913), who was better known for his accomplishments in the field of steam engine performance, had recently appeared at the Central Pacific office in Sacramento claiming that he could manufacture the dangerously explosive compound on-site, thereby eliminating the hazard of transport. His equipment cost would not exceed $100 and he would need to be

"Chinese" wall and west portal of Donner Summit Tunnel.

paid $300 per month. Crocker took him on, but asked Huntington, who was constantly in Washington as the lobbyist and political "fixer" of the Big Four, to research manufacturing patents, explaining that there was no benefit in becoming involved in litigation — as was soon to be happening with Mowbray and Browne in Massachusetts. This decision turned out to be a Godsend saving to the Big Four, and the tracks were opened from Sacramento to Reno on June 18, 1868. The first train took eight hours to make the sinuous trip, which Amtrak promises to make, at this writing, in less than three hours.

> Mr. Howden's brew, widely feared at first by the workmen, was a yellow liquid, light and oily. He made up a fresh batch every day, and estimated that it cost only 75 cents a pound. Engineer [John R.] Gilliss reported that the new explosive was eight times as powerful as powder. By February 9 it was in use in all four headings of the Summit Tunnel. At once, though the gangs of Chinese were not increased in size, there was a notable spurt in the pace of tunneling. With gunpowder, the men had averaged only a bit more than a foot of progress a day in the headings and 2 feet in clearing out the rock that remained in the bottoms. With nitroglycerine, they speeded up to nearly 2 feet a day in the headings, and more than 4 feet in the bottoms.

East portal of Summit Tunnel at Donner Pass, 2009.

It was immediately obvious that there were other advantages to nitroglycerine. It worked best in holes only an inch and a quarter in diameter. Powder had required 2 inch holes, and more of them. After a nitroglycerine blast, a tunnel cleared of smoke faster than when powder was exploded in it. In wet rock, where gunpowder was useless, the remarkable new "blasting oil" worked like a charm. Furthermore, rock debris from its explosions was usually so fine that it didn't need further breaking up. Powder didn't do as thorough a job.

The usual blasting procedure was to drill holes 15 to 18 inches deep, and pour nitroglycerine into them until they were nearly full. If the rock was dry, each hole was plugged with a wad of hay, peppered with powder. One end of the fuse was nested in the powder and held in place with sand. In wet rock, a tin cartridge about 4 inches long, filled with powder, stoppered each holeful of nitroglycerine.[2]

Early in 1870 Central Pacific Engineer John Robert Gilliss (1842–1870) spoke to the American Society of Engineers describing the Central Pacific Tunnels, a report which was carried in full in *Van Nostrand's Eclectic Engineering Magazine*, Vol. 2, for 1870:

The tunnels of the Central Pacific are nearly all near the summit, where it crosses the western range of the Sierra Nevada. The line here lies on steep hillsides, in some cases being, for long distances, on a face of bare granite, more or less broken by projecting ledges and boulders, but with an average slope often greater than 1 to 1. In such places embankments were almost impracticable; the hills were too steep to catch the slopes, and most of the rock from cuts was thrown far down hill by heavy seam blasts. On these accounts the line, for two miles east of Donner Pass, was thrown further into the hill than on original location, thus adding to the depths of cuttings and increasing the number of tunnels, but saving retaining walls, and where tunnels were made, enabling the work to be carried on in winter. Another important object was the saving of snow-covering where tunnels were made, and giving a good foundation for it where they were not. It is within these two miles that seven tunnels are crowded.

Tunnels 1 and 2 are both west of Cisco, a small track 92 miles from Sacramento, and within 13 of the summit. They were both finished in 1866. During the fall of that year the track reached Cisco, and as fast as the gangs of Chinamen were released they were hurried to the summit to be distributed among the tunnels in its vicinity. The year before, some gangs had been sent to summit tunnel No. 6, and commenced the cuts at its extremities; winter set in before the headings were started, and the work had to be abandoned. To avoid a repetition of such delay, the approaches to all the tunnels were covered with men, and worked night and day in three shifts of eight hours each. Thus time was saved, and the tunnel organization started at once. As an illustration of the hurry, I may mention walking two miles over the hills after dark, and staking out the east end of No. 12 by the light of a bonfire; at 9 o'clock the men were at work.

In November and the early part of December there were several snow-storms, just enough to stimulate without delaying the work. The rough rocky sides of Donner Peak soon became smooth, slopes of snow and ice covering the trail that led from tunnel 8 to 9; it remained impassable until spring, and communications had to be kept up by the wagon-road, five or six hundred feet below. This, the Dutch Flat and Donner Lake wagon road, was opened soon after it was decided to adopt this route. From the Pass the descent toward the lake was over very rough ground, requiring heavy side cuts and retaining walls with numerous zigzags to gain distance. From this road the scene was strangely beautiful at night. The tall firs, though drooping under their heavy burdens, pointed to the mountains that overhung them, where the fires that lit seven tunnels shone like stars on their snowy sides. The only sound that came down to break the stillness of the winter night was the sharp ring of hammer on steel, or the heavy reports of the blasts.

Winter of 1866-7.—By the time winter had set in fairly the headings were all under ground. The work was then independent of weather, except as storms would block up tunnel entrances, or avalanches sweep over the shanties of the laborers. Before tracing the progress of the work underground, it will be well to see the character of weather out-doors...

Snow-Storms.—These storms, 44 in number, varied in length from a short snow squall to a two-week gale, and in depth from 1/4 in. to 10 ft.—none less than the former number being recorded, nor had we occasion to note any greater than the latter. This, the heaviest storm of the winter, began February 18, at 2 P.M., and snowed steadily until 10 P.M. of the 22nd, during which time 6 ft. fell. The supply of raw material was then exhausted, but the barometer kept low and the wind heavy from the

> south-west for five days more, by which time a fresh supply of damp air came up from the Pacific, and then, as the machinery was still running full speed, this was ground up with out delay. It snowed steadily until March 2nd, making loft. snow and 13 days' storm. It is true that no snow fell for 5 days, but it drifted so furiously during that time that the snow-tunnel at east end of tunnel No. 6 had to be lengthened 50 ft.

Contrary to some reports, the Chinese were paid the same as Caucasian laborers but required to furnish their own food and lodging. Their major attraction as laborers was in their stoic ability to withstand extremely perilous working conditions.

* * *

Encountering a problem with crossing the geologically younger mountains west of the Continental Divide was not a condition peculiar to the Central Pacific or the Great Northern; most other North American "transcontinentals" suffered from the same problem. As just noted, the Central Pacific/Union Pacific had its major engineering and operating problems at the 2,175 m. Donner Pass in the California Sierra Nevada, not in the relatively tranquil crossing of the Divide at 2,075 m. just west of the town that had been named for Ulysses Grant's neighbor and first Secretary of War, John Aaron Rawlins (1831–1869), in south-central Wyoming. The Canadian Pacific (the subject of our final chapters) had the multiple whammy of serious problems in building as well as operation, both at the Divide and farther west.

The Northern Pacific, sometimes controlled by Hill and much of it now part of the vast BNSF system but originally built to entirely different standards of quality than the GN, initially crossed the Continental Divide near Butte by a relatively easy line and farther west. En route to the port of Tacoma on Puget Sound it went through the granite of the Cascades via the 1,119 m. Stampede Pass, using six switchbacks and a grade of 5.6 percent, in 1884. But by 1895—with Herman Haupt as its general manager—it had bored a 3 km. tunnel to pass south of Mt. Rainier to reach Tacoma via the valley of the Snoqualmie River's South Fork. However, the NP's trains were still occasionally snowbound for a week at a time in making that crossing; though a later, lower and longer tunnel made things a lot easier and more reliable.

The Chicago, Milwaukee, St. Paul & Pacific (known as the Milwaukee line) ran its Rockefeller-financed line across central Montana. It was a competitor mostly of the Northern Pacific, and encountered most of the headaches that had come to bother Herman Haupt in his later years. As it evolved through three bankruptcies, the Milwaukee became largely electrified across much of Montana and through Snoqualmie Pass to its terminus, also at Tacoma. This pass, at 921 m. ASL, is one of the easiest Cascade passes; but unhappily for the Milwaukee, it was more roundabout than those used by its competitors and still required a two-mile tunnel (now abandoned and used as a hiking trail). Because the earlier lines had sewed up the best routes and major cities, the Milwaukee, despite its operating advantage of having locomotives feed electricity back into its catenary lines on the downgrades, was never truly able to cope. Its final bankruptcy, in 1978, resulted in the revocation of most of its "transcontinental" right-of-way; and only a few portions remain — mostly as segments of the state-owned Montana Rail Link, or its roadbed as part of a scenic hiking trail in Washington.

* * *

The more southerly "transcontinental" railroads, Southern Pacific and Santa Fe — largely unmentioned in this text due to their lack of significantly long tunnels — were also subject to interesting problems in getting through to the Pacific. The Santa Fe, having crossed through the Sangre de Cristo mountains in 1879 via a short (less than one km.) tunnel through the sandstone at the crest of 2,388 m. (7,834 foot) Raton Pass and found that to be a non-serious problem, encountered its major issue after it had absorbed the Atlantic & Pacific Railroad in 1897 and then finding a way down some 1,260 m. into the Los Angeles Basin (three lines of trackage that it now shares with the former Southern Pacific). However, the Santa Fe, in absorbing the Atlantic & Pacific, did acquire one unique tunnel, which was abandoned in 1962.

The outside edge of the steel-lined tunnel, clearly showing the rivets (Graham A.B. Vickowski).

In Arizona, west of Williams on the descent toward Ashfork, at an altitude of some 2,140 m. (6,520 feet) and only some 130 meters long, one can still find the only "steel-lined" railroad tunnel in North America. Overlain and floored by thick flows of lava, it is bored through an intermediate layer of sediments. In 1882, the A&P began closing the final gap in its "transcontinental" line — between Kingman on the west and Winslow on the east. (Lewis Kingman

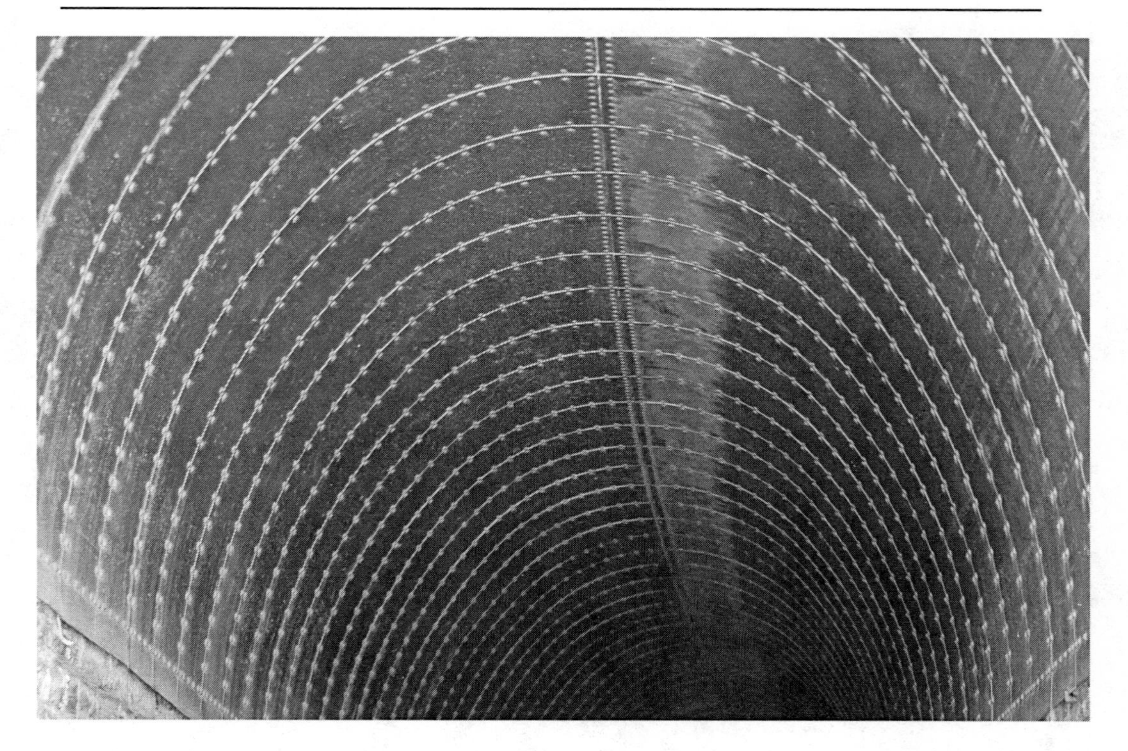

Inside the abandoned steel-lined tunnel of AT&SF in Johnson Canyon (Graham A.B. Vickowski).

was a location engineer reporting to Henry Holbrook and Edward S. Kingman was president of the AT&SF.) The only seriously steep portion of the whole route across Northern Arizona was the 40 km. stretch between Ash Fork and Williams. The critical portion was located mostly along the north side of the meandering Johnson Canyon, but required the boring of a 400 foot tunnel to circumvent one otherwise overly tight curve. In the nature of much sandstone, this tunnel soon began to suffer from degeneration of its roof and was therefore completely sheathed with wood. In 1898 sparks from the engines working hard on this upgrade set the wood afire, a tragedy in which two men died in the extinguishing effort. The Santa Fe people, who had acquired complete control of the A&P a year earlier, then opted to line the tunnel with steel boiler plate, sections of which were riveted together. This unique bore remained in use thereafter; but mostly for downhill, west-bound traffic, until a massive relocation of the Santa Fe was undertaken in connection with the construction of Interstate 40 in the years after 1956. However, the now trackless tunnel remains in very good repair.

But the SP, an outgrowth of the California Big Four's Central Pacific, found that it could go nowhere out of the great Central Valley without tackling the 1,156 m. Tehachapi Pass. By 1876, SP Chief Engineer William Hood (1846–1926) had accomplished this with a spectacular series of wide loops, short tunnels, numerous cuts and

Johnson Canyon steel-lined tunnel from upstream (east) (Graham A.B. Vickowski).

Tehachapi Loop on the Southern Pacific. The altitude difference is more than 30 m. (100 ft).

major fills in climbing up southeast of Bakersfield, but nothing nearly as impressive in descending the less precipitous terrain to the Mojave Desert on the south.

* * *

The Big Four of Central Pacific fame came to dominate California transportation, much to the highly vocal distress of many citizens of the Golden State. Thus it became politically easy for competing lines to get legislative approval, as did a variety of short lines serving the Comstock and more long lasting lines such as the Western Pacific and the Santa Fe that offered serious competition to the Big Four, which by the late 1890s had been reduced to only one, Collis Huntington. Despite his adventures into the Chesapeake & Ohio, he still retained a firm grip on the Central Pacific, which soon morphed into the Southern Pacific under his leadership.

This change of nomenclature came in a quasi-economic manner of appealing to Southern interests after the Civil War. All the existing railroads across the United States were controlled by Northern (Union) interests and the Port of New Orleans was served only by lines that ran northward to meet these other transcontinentals. Huntington, who came to control the C&O, after his stint with building the Central Pacific, was anxious to have a coast-to-coast route of his own. He led his co-owners into a name-change for the CP with the plan of extending a line from California east to New Orleans that might readily be linked from there to his C&O. The Southern Pacific Company was originally a land-holding firm, but became controlled by the Big Four in 1868. It then merged the Central Pacific into the Southern Pacific and started to expand, ultimately giving rise to the "Coastal" route described below. The inland route between California's major cities was built in the 1870s and ran from San Jose to Bakersfield and thence over Tehachapi Pass to Barstow and down into the Los Angeles basin.

By the 1890s the Southern Pacific's line gradually creeping north along the coast from Los Angeles through Santa Barbara, and that extending southward from San Jose via Salinas toward Paso Robles (Oak Pass), were within striking distance of each other. The only obstacle to a connection was a crossing of the 464 m. (1,522 foot) Cuesta Grade between San Luis Obispo (SLO) on the south and Atascadero on the north. Because of this gap, passengers and freight from the Central Coast "metropolis" of San Luis Obispo, still had to get to the rest of the world by Pacific Coast Steamship vessels into and from the Port of San Luis.

A BNSF freight crosses over itself on the Tehachapi Loop — there were six units pulling this mile-long consist.

President Huntington died on August 13 of 1900, far from the scene of his great triumphs in the West, but not before he had issued the order to complete that connection. The result was the importation of more Chinese laborers from Canton by contractor Ah Louis (whose store still stands in San Luis Obispo), that provided the nucleus of today's Chinese colony in that city. He first completed the line from the south to reach SLO in 1901, then constructed the long, sinuous grade up for 15 miles from near sea level at SLO to the final summit tunnel at nearly 400 meters ASL. Besides requiring frequent resort to pusher engines, this grade originally necessitated numerous tunnels, but the bedrock of this area — west of California's famed San Andreas Fault — is of mixed metamorphics, none of which are of a quality comparable to the granite found at Donner Summit. So these tunnels soon developed the nasty habit of piecemeal collapsing, which caused all but four of them to be opened into cuts; while, of necessity, the remaining four were ultimately lined with concrete. There was never a problem with earthquake damage for this portion of the line, which might have been expected in a region with as many minor quakes as are periodic in places like Paso Robles and to the east. These tremblers average a few dozen each year, as the North American tec-

North portal of Cuesta Grade tunnel, awaiting Amtrak's *Starlight*— the camera was actually held by a CHP officer who had been urging the author to move along.

tonic plate crunches ever so slowly, but inexorably, into and over the adjacent Pacific Plate. Since the most recent major movement along the San Andreas Fault, many of the steel girder highway bridges in this region have been retrofitted with cables to tie their I-beams more firmly to their supporting abutments; but the Cuesta Grade tunnels have — so far — been unaffected by these tremors, as they lie fully in the Pacific Plate.

The Serrano siding, halfway up the grade from SLO, is almost exactly halfway between Los Angeles and San Francisco on this "coast" line, and is a frequent passing point for trains, even unto today's Amtrak *Coast Starlight* daily which, for obvious reasons, some of the irreverent natives have rechristened to "*Starlate.*"

* * *

The task of building the second transcontinental (Los Angeles to New Orleans) was immensely eased by the work of James Gadsden (1788–1858), grandson of a signer of the Declaration of Independence, sometime military officer, Southern nationalist and friend of the influential Jefferson Davis (1808–1889). He was also involved with various railroad operations until appointed minister to Mexico by President Franklin Pierce in 1853. There he negotiated the purchase of some 45,000 square miles of land along the southern part of New Mexico and Arizona, much of it along the Gila River, which offered the easiest line between major Southern centers and the Pacific Coast.

By 1880, the Big Four had run their line past the Salton Sink (where they subsequently suffered a bit of a disaster in attempting to expand irrigation in the Imperial Valley) and across a lot of desert to reach Tucson. A year later, their tracks reached El Paso and were extended on to meet those of the Texas Pacific, thus completing the route from Long Beach, on the Pacific, to New Orleans on the Gulf of Mexico.

9

Canada's Great Project— Kicking Horse to Connaught

When, in 1871, the heretofore separate crown colony of British Columbia agreed to become part of the four-year-old Dominion of Canada, its major inducement for such an act was the promise of being linked to the new self-governing (except for foreign policy matters) part of the British Empire by a railway—within ten years. The government headed by Sir John Alexander Macdonald favored doing it as a private enterprise. But nothing came together before an election funding scandal broke about Sir John's head and his first government fell in 1873, on the eve of a world-wide economic depression. The replacement liberal regime of Sir Alexander MacKenzie (1822–1892), which lasted until 1878, sought to build the railway piecemeal as a public project. But the only contract actually completed was one given to Andrew Onderdonk (1849–1905), scion of an old Dutch family in Nieuw Amsterdam. He was a building and project engineer and contractor of considerable note, who had just completed the first seawalls near San Francisco and who died while supervising work on the East River subway tunnel. (A 2,694 m. peak in the Selkirks was belatedly named for him in 1971.) Onderdonk undertook the challenging task of building a rail line up the difficult Fraser Canyon from tidewater to Kamloops, which was finished and operating before the syndicate headed by Donald Smith (1820–1914), George Stephen (1829–1921) and James Hill undertook the bulk of Canada's great unification project in 1881. Smith, a major figure in the Hudson's Bay Company, and Stephen, president of the Bank of Montreal, were knighted in due course—Sir Donald becoming Lord Strathcona and Stephen becoming the first Baron Mount Stephen—while Hill had to be content (after 1901) with merely being a rich and influential American.

A secondary inducement for the Westerners to make a political union with the new Dominion was the support from vigorous jurist, Matthew Bailey Begbie (1819–1894), a physically imposing figure, who was Chief Justice of the Crown Colony from 1866 until his death—see the biography by David Williams, *The Man for a New Country* (Sidney, BC: Gray's, 1977). Begbie, who arrived in Victoria in 1858, was knighted in 1875. During his judicial career he traveled the length and breadth of British Columbia by foot, horse and canoe, upholding, often by the sheer strength of his physique and

Statue of Sir Matthew Bailey Begbie at the Provincial Parliament Building of British Columbia, still keeping them honest (G. Bennett).

personality, the dominance of Queen Victoria's laws in the face of hordes of fractious (mostly American) gold seekers who had flooded into this region after the rich placers of California had been largely exhausted. The most prominent peak (2,732 m.) in the view west from Revelstoke most properly bears his name.

This great railroad — the largest and longest such project thus far in the world — had encountered its first major hurdle in crossing the 1,000 km.-wide Canadian Shield area north of the Great Lakes. At that time this region's vast mineral wealth was undiscovered; the land was barren of farming potential, strewn with swampy lakes, mosquitoes and muskeg, and utterly lacking in potential traffic for any railroad. Crossing it with tracks of steel was a gigantic leap of faith; but this was necessary to avoid the perpetual bugbear of Canadian politics — dependence on going through (or in any way becoming dependent on the fickle good will of) the United States, through which all communication (other than by canoe) from eastern Canada with the area north of the 49th parallel had heretofore to pass. Heading west from these barrens, the plains of Manitoba, Saskatchewan and Alberta were a constructional cinch — a railroad locator's dream. But then came the Rocky Mountains.

Under the MacKenzie administration, Sandford Fleming, the most credible railroad man in Canada who was on the verge of seeing the Intercolonial to completion from Montreal to Halifax, had been installed as chief engineer of the Canadian Pacific project. In 1873 he undertook to find the best way through the Rocky Mountains, and over the next four years sent out numerous survey parties (the most memorable of which was that of Jarvis and Hanington, referred to earlier). The upshot of Fleming's surveys was the decision to utilize the low and gentle 1,145 m. Yellowhead Pass to cross the Continental Divide in the Rockies and then follow the easier terrain southwest from there to meet up with the Onderdonk rails at Kamloops. However, when the private consortium undertook the project with the return to power of Sir John Macdonald, they realized that with so much of the prime real estate of western Canada left unserved to the south of Yellowhead Pass, there might be cause for much of that potential business to be seduced southward into the United States. This issue was scary and had to be addressed.

One of the CPR's greatest allies in this route relocation plan was the Irish-born botanist John Macoun (1832–1920), who believed strongly in the agricultural potential of the southern plains of Alberta and Saskatchewan. His 1882 book, *Manitoba and the Great Northwest* (Guelph, ON: World), pointed out the ability of this area to become Canada's international breadbasket. In bringing his contention to fruition, he was aided by his son-in-law, Arthur Oliver Wheeler (1860–1945), the high-country surveyor of the interprovincial boundary between Alberta and the new province, who also determined the means by which irrigation helped bring Macoun's dream to reality.

* * *

Meanwhile, Albert Rogers had been granted a degree in civil engineering from Brown University and soon found employment on the Erie Canal, regular improvements to which had become a sort of graduate school for many budding civil engineers. By 1870 he had become a regular employee of James Jerome Hill, the "hero" of the previous chapter.

In 1882 the Dominion parliament officially backed off from Fleming's choice of the Yellowhead Pass at nearly 53 degrees North latitude in favor of some more southerly, but yet undiscovered, line, provided it was at least sixty miles north of the 49th parallel. This more southerly route, thus statutorily guaranteed to be far enough north to be safe from Yankee-based incursions, was deemed necessary to forestall the possibility of a lot of local traffic being siphoned off by branch lines that might be extended northward from American railroads, most ironically that which was headed by Hill, a one-time Canadian citizen. In the end, this condition came to pass mostly in the mineral-rich area of southeastern British Columbia which abutted the Idaho panhandle. But it was also Hill — a legal, voting American after 1880 — who recommended Rogers to his erstwhile associates as the man they needed to find a suitable route through the mountains. In the years just after the American Civil War, a number of disaffected Fenians, resident south of the border, had taken to making threatening demonstrations toward Canada and at least one active raid northward to demonstrate their displeasure with the way the English overlords had been and were still treating those who remained on the "old sod." This was the reverse of the procedure whereby Southern sympathizers, resident in Canada, had staged similar raids into Vermont in 1863–64.

Major Albert Bowman Rogers in formal attire (Canadian Pacific Railway; American Alpine Club).

In 1883, under the revised rules governing CPR location, construction had already gone more nearly west from Winnipeg than the line which had been projected by Fleming up the valley of the North Saskatchewan. Therefore, once accepted by Van Horne and Sir Donald Smith, Rogers hastened to determine a route westward from Calgary — perhaps via the 1,530 m. Howse Pass, or via the comparable Kootenay Pass, or up the Bow River. He passed a coal mining locality he called Padmore (Canmore) and ran a line over the Kicking Horse Pass, which had been named and traversed in 1858 by Dr. James Hector (1834–1907). A year later Rogers found a way across the more difficult Selkirk Range via a pass which Walter Moberly (1832–1915), the original surveyor of British Columbia's interior, had hinted at, and Rogers finally proved to exist. He, thus, did not have to face the more lengthy alternative, north around the Big Bend of the Columbia River, much of which is now (thanks to the same treaty that flooded Rexburg, Montana) beneath the much expanded waters of Kinbaskit Lake, and which also eliminated the fearsome Surprise Rapids.

Nearly half a century earlier, Dr. Hector, later knighted as head of the Geological Survey of New Zealand, was leading a detachment of the British-inspired Palliser Expedition to explore and define western Canada near the 49th parallel. He crossed the Kicking Horse Pass from the west, after naming the river which drained west to the Columbia because of a nearly fatal accident that befell him on its banks. Hector had determined the pass reached an altitude of 5,328 feet; a tribute to his skill with the aneroid barometer, which was remarkably close to that determined by subsequent railway surveys at 1,625 m. Rogers pondered the steep descent that faced his prospective line and determined that the only way to meet his employers' objectives regarding the preferred gradient for the route was to traverse the north slopes of Mounts Cathedral and Stephen, gradually descending on a grade of no more than 2.5 percent to reach the valley floor. When he later projected a series of short tunnels and trestles to accomplish this objective, he was told that the cost of such an idea was far beyond the CPR's almost perpetually underfunded construction budget; he would have to use a steeper line, as described below by the Rev. William Spotswood Green.

Unfortunately, today the name of the British Columbian surveyor, Walter Moberly, is known only to a few. It stands on a forgotten whistle stop of the CPR, a dozen kilometers downstream from Golden, and on a timbered pass (1,780 m.) frequented only by stray bears and errant mountaineers (as well as some lucky heli-skiers, whose tracks lie well over the dreadful alder, devils club and arbor-vitae of midsummer) some 50 km. northwest along the crest of the Selkirk Range from the pass named for Rogers. In midwinter of 1867, Moberly, obviously a man's man, went — on snowshoes and in one day — from his winter quarters cabin near the present whistle-stop, down the frozen Columbia to the Gold River. He then went up that stream to its headwaters (Moberly Pass) with a tributary of the west-flowing Goldstream (Moberly Creek) and across to Joseph LaForme's mining camp on French Creek, where he found an old friend and a warm stove. Here, he "discussed a few glasses of rum and water" before sleeping soundly on the cabin floor. The upper Columbia River — prior to the construction of Mica Creek Dam — was reasonably tranquil from its source down to that point below Golden where the Bush and Gold Rivers join the main stream, and often tended to freeze over in winter — then came the justly feared Surprise Rapids.

It was Moberly's earlier reports of a strenuous trip up the Illecillewaet River from 2nd Crossing to Tangier Summit that hinted to Rogers that the slightly larger east fork of that stream was a likely passage through the mountains. An experienced bushmaster, Moberly did not follow that fork because (1) he was then engaged in locating wagon roads to the expected mineralized areas of the Selkirks, which lay to the north; and (2) being already on the north bank of the Illecillewaet, he was wise enough not to attempt a crossing of this turbulent stream at the forks, or below. He followed up the right (west) side of Tangier Creek to its headwaters, where the Waverley Mines were later located — see his book — a rare little volume — *The Rocks and Rivers of British Columbia* (London: Blacklock, 1885).

* * *

Sir Sandford Fleming (1827–1915) was not to be taken lightly. Born in Scotland, he had come to Canada in 1845 after earning his surveying license at home in Kirkaldy, the birthplace (a century earlier) of the great economist Adam Smith. After an eventful sailing ship voyage from Glasgow, almost from the day he arrived in Quebec Fleming had been associated with railway location and operation. Finally and most notably he was with the Intercolonial, which (as mentioned earlier) ran along the south shore of the St. Lawrence estuary from Montreal and across the Shickshock Mountains to Chignecto, St. John and Halifax. By the time the Canadian Pacific was seeking a more southerly route across the Rockies, Fleming had retired from active work, devoting his expertise to national and philanthropic or scientific causes. He was a charter member of the Royal Society of Canada and stayed on, until his death, as chancellor of Queen's University in Kingston, Ontario. But prior to his formal retirement from active railway work, he was instrumental in the adoption of the concept of Standard Time, which finally came into being in 1883 on all North American Railroads, largely as a result of his efforts. Prior to the railroads' collective adoption of Standard Time in the 1880s, every community in North America had its own version of time and every railroad ran its trains on its own version of time, with little regard for what these various differences meant to the traveling public. One of the highest peaks (3,530 m.) in western Canada most fittingly bears his name — Mount Sir Sandford — as well as a 3,164 m. peak just north of Rogers Pass.

The driving force behind completion of the CPR was its president after 1882, William Cornelius Van Horne (1843–1915), an American-born railroad executive and product of the American Midwest who had served in various railroad managerial capacities there. He, too, was a product of Hill's recruitment (perhaps, in part, to eliminate such a dynamic force from the management of some of his American competition). Van Horne worked with such diligence for the CPR that he achieved knighthood in 1894. Van Horne retired from the CPR in 1910 and devoted his remaining energies to the building of railways in Cuba.

* * *

Major Rogers excited numerous comments on his manners and habits. Under date of January 20, 1883, Van Horne wrote to Jonathan Hastings, one of the CPR's financial backers in New York:

> There has been a good deal of feeling among some of the Canadian engineers, particularly those who have been accustomed to the Government Services, against Major Rogers; partly from national jealousy of one who is looked upon as an outsider, partly from his *lively* treatment of those whom he looks upon as slackers ... and partly from

> his somewhat peculiar methods of securing economy, but now also and perhaps from his daring successes ... in doing what was unsuccessfully attempted by the Government Engineers, namely, in getting through the Rocky and Selkirk Mountains by a direct line.

Typical of the complaints about Rogers was one aired in an obsequious and self-serving letter of February 23, 1885, marked private from Marcus Smith, one of those very government engineers, to one of his political patrons, Joseph Hunter. Smith (1815–1904), English-born, had worked for "the government" on the Intercolonial, and was a consultant to the second Macdonald administration from 1886 to 1892.

> I was asked by letter from Van Horne to look over the Major's work and see what he was about. He is not a man that one can discuss anything with—too egotistical but this may only be a bluff to cover his ignorance. I fear he is a thorough fraud.... It is also leaking out that the great bounce about his discovery of the pass through the Selkirk Range (which he insinuated the Gov't engineers failed to do though we never tried and would have rejected in disdain any such pass) as likely to turn out a huge blunder and a terrible loss to the country.

Another comment in the same vein appears in a book by James Henry Edward Secretan (1854–1926) entitled *Canada's Great Highway: From the First Stake to the Last Spike* (London: Lane, 1924). In the chapter headed "Major Rogers," the explorer was described on page 184 of the third volume as

> a short, sharp, snappy little chap with long dundreary whiskers. He was master of picturesque profanity, who continually chewed tobacco and was an artist at expectoration. He wore overalls with pockets behind, and had a plug of tobacco in one pocket and a sea biscuit in the other, which was his idea of a season's provisions for an engineer.

Regardless of how others felt about him, and Rogers appeared not to be affected by adverse opinions, he located a passable line down the canyon of the Kicking Horse to a location he dubbed as 1st Crossing, and which the CPR, in its desire to attract funding, would soon call Golden. Having crossed the placid Columbia River just below this place, Rogers, complete with his native retinue of three Kootenays, went south, up the valley of the Beaver River. There he saw an opening that might lead across the Selkirk Range, naming the lateral valley after one of its most prevalent locals—Bear. A year earlier Rogers had approached the same opening from the west, bushwhacking up the difficult Illecillewaet River valley to gain a crest of the 2,864 m. Avalanche Mountain above the pass that the CPR was happy to name after him. A year after that ascent, Rogers wrote to Van Horne, back in Montreal:

> On Monday, July 17, I started from the Columbia with two white men and three Indians for another trip into the Selkirks by way of Beaver River, and on the 24th I had succeeded in finding a practicable line across the summit and into the east branch of the Illecillewaet River and returned to camp on the 6 of August.

Van Horne had established a $5,000 prize for whomsoever could locate a suitable pass for the CPR, and this was soon given to Rogers. However, rather than cash the check, he carried it around for months, finally framing it so his brother's children could admire their uncle's accomplishment. However, Van Horne wanted to clear his books, so he gave Rogers a suitably engraved gold watch as an extra inducement to get the explorer to complete the transaction.

Some of the names bestowed along the way give a further hint as to the railway promoters' efforts to secure financial interest. There was the erstwhile Silver City (now Banff, where silver was never found), followed by Golden (where gold was never found). There was Field, perversely named to entice investment by a visiting American millionaire, Cyrus West Field (1819–1892), who then thought it better to build elevated railroads in New York City. Finally and most usefully, there was Revelstoke, after the titled name of Sir Evelyn Baring (1841–1917), head of the then great British investment banking firm of Baring Brothers. He bought in heavily toward the end of the CPR's cash needs, to his firm's subsequently great economic benefit.

But to ensure that the railway's adjusted line would be perceived as fiscally sensible, Van Horne needed an endorsement that would carry more weight than that of the relatively unknown Rogers or his other backers, all equally unrenowned in mountain railway location. He needed someone with the unique reputation of Fleming to give his imprimatur to the more southerly route that the CPR was now committed to taking.

* * *

Thus, in the summer of 1883, when the die was fully cast but neither route nor funding assured, Van Horne wired to Fleming, who was momentarily in London drumming up support for his newest British Imperial project — an "all red" transpacific cable. Could Canada's great surveyor come west quickly, go over the new proposed line, and make a report that would give heart to investors (and skeptical members of Parliament), thus enabling its completion? Soon after passage of the Canada Act of 1867, a financial deal had been struck with the Hudson's Bay Company, whereby that venerable firm gave up its two-century-old, poorly enforced but royally chartered monopoly to everything that was in the drainage area of the great bay.

The one event that had "sold" many members of Parliament on supporting the railway subsidy so far was the efficiency with which the CPR (then finished only across the "Shield" and part of the prairies) had moved military supplies and personnel in putting down the second rebellion against Dominion authority by supporters of Louis Riel in the summer of 1884. Riel (1844–1885) was a Metis (half-breed), a sometime seminarian, a sometime member of Parliament, for years a political refugee in the United States, and the recognized leader of his people. After a brief trial, he was found guilty of high treason and hanged at the RCMP barracks in Regina on November 16, 1885.

Anyhow, promptly cabling back his acceptance, Fleming started west once more, this time getting as far as Calgary in relative speed and comfort. From the "end of steel" at Canmore there remained about 500 km. in a direct line to Onderdonk's existing rails at Kamloops, but far more by way of an acceptable line for a railway. Fleming's task was to determine (for public consumption) that there was, indeed, a financially feasible route through the three impressive mountain ranges between Calgary and Kamloops.

Detailed layout and construction crews were already at work along the line up the Bow River as far as the Kicking Horse Pass, but none of those folk had heard of anyone making the through trip to Kamloops. As far as anyone Fleming encountered knew at this point in time, Walter Moberly was "of the opinion" that a passable line could be found utilizing the valley of the east fork of the Illecillewaet from 2nd Crossing (modern Revelstoke). Major Rogers had earlier found a route from the Columbia up the west side of the Beaver River valley to enter a pass that just might have been the one Moberly was sure existed; but no one had yet made the complete journey across this part of the Selkirk Range. To the east, the Kicking Horse line across the Rockies had been found passable a generation earlier by Dr. Hector. The Eagle Pass through the Gold Range, on the west, already possessed a wagon road, laid out by Moberly in 1869, but a reasonably direct line across the lofty and more glacier-clad Selkirks in the middle remained unknown. Some dozen years earlier, however, Moberly had made his more northerly, mid-winter crossing of the range via the Gold River and Goldstream utilizing Moberly Pass.

Fleming made the horseback trip west down to 1st Crossing without incident and came across Rogers en route. While following down the Kicking Horse River the great man found that

> we pass the second mountain lake, and about four miles from our morning camp we reach the third and largest lake [Wapta Lake], about a mile in length. We cross the path of a great snow slide, an avalanche divided into two forks, one about fifty yards and the other about one hundred and fifty yards wide. Thousands of trees, two and three feet in diameter have been broken into shreds by it, and roots, trunks and branches, in a tangled mass, have been swept away, and, with a multitude of boulders of all dimensions, hurled into the lake to form a promontory.... To the south, beyond the lake, the eye rests upon a mighty mountain [Cathedral], streaked by snow-filled crevices, and reflected in the bright, glassy lake, presenting to our eyes a most striking feature. We cross the outlet by fording a stream some forty feet wide and about sixteen inches in depth. I looked upon it with no little interest, for it is the stream we are to follow for some days.... We have to cross gorges so narrow that a biscuit might be thrown from the last horse descending, to the bell-horse six hundred feet ahead, ascending the opposite side. The fires have been running through the wood and are still burning; many of the half-burnt trees have been blown down ... obstructing the trail and making advance extremely difficult.[2]

Fleming's description of the route down the canyon of the lower Kicking Horse River shows that not much has changed, when looked at with the eye of an imaginative traveler on today's exalted Trans-Canada Highway, below which, in the very bottom of it all, the shiny, steel rails of the CPR now snake along the banks of the turbulent and silt-filled torrent.

Kicking Horse River near Field. This torrent includes the Yoho River as well as the Wapta rivers.

Soon after debouching from the canyon just above present-day Golden, Fleming met Major Rogers, who relieved his worries by assuring him that the pass across the Selkirk Range really did exist — less than two months earlier he had finished locating an acceptable route to the crest of the Selkirks from both sides. Furthermore, there was now a viable pack trail up the Beaver River and a short distance down the Illecillewaet on the west side of the range. Rogers even supplied his nephew, Albert (for whom the settlement and present resort of Albert Canyon at the junction of Tangier Creek with the Illecillewaet River was named), as a guide for Fleming's party. They relaxed in canoes as they floated down the Columbia to the mouth of the Beaver, where a pack train awaited them for the crossing of the Selkirks and for those few easy miles down the far side. Those who have bushwhacked in the mountains of British Columbia can appreciate the words Fleming's amanuensis, the Rev. George Munro Grant (1835–1902), composed on the end stage of this journey.

> Last night it rained hard, with thunder and lightning. This morning everything is wet and the trees are dripping in all directions; not a pleasant prospect for those who have to travel under them. There is, however, no halting in a journey such as ours. Our

> horses have left us. They were driven back to find pasture last night. The men must now carry on their shoulders what we require, through an untrodden forest without path or trail of any kind. Clothing, tents, food and a few cooking utensils constitute what we have to bring with us. Fortunately we can always find water.... The walking is dreadful; we climb over and creep under fallen trees of great size, and the men soon show that they feel the weight of their burdens. Their halts for rest are frequent. It is hot work for us all. The dripping rain from the bush and branches saturate us from above. Tall ferns sometimes reaching to the shoulder, and devil's clubs [echinopanax horridus] through which we had to crush our way, make us feel as if dragged through a horse-pond, and our perspiration is that of a Turkish bath.... The devil's clubs may be numbered by millions, and they are perpetually wounding us by their spikes.... We wade through alder swamps and tread down skunk cabbage and the prickly aralias, and so we continue until half-past four, when the tired men are unable to go further.... Our advance on a direct line we estimate at four miles.... So the journey goes day after day, with little relief from the interminable succession of swamps, tangled underbrush, and fallen timber.[3]

The aptly named Devil's Club is a root-propagating plant, native to the damper mountain areas west of the divide and centered in southern British Columbia. It has a

Devil's Club undergrowth in Illecillewaet Valley. Off any prepared track or trail, this is still very difficult country.

stem up to more than a meter in height, and a very few large, maple-leaf shaped leaves, almost all parts of which are covered with slender thorns that break off on contact and take about a week to fester out of the hide of any unwary passerby. At last the weary party emerged from the canyon of the Illecillewaet at 2nd Crossing (modern Revelstoke), where Moberly's wagon road through Eagle Pass beckoned to them on the far side of the Columbia River. A relief party was to have met them here with supplies, but had such a difficult time that they had cached their loads and turned back "five day's journey distant." By cutting rations in half and hurrying along, Fleming's party reached the cache, then Shuswap Lake and found a steamer to take them on to Kamloops.

* * *

Sir Sandford's final trip across the continent on railroad business started in late October of 1885, when he went all the way by CPR train. The most famous photograph in Canadian history (taken by Alexander J. Ross) shows him in early November, standing tall and dignified, complete with square, white beard and stovepipe hat, beside Sir William Van Horne and just behind Sir Donald Smith, Lord Strathcona, as the latter drives home the final spike linking Canada's new west with Canada's old east. Also in

Last Spike monument at Craigelachie, British Columbia, just off Trans-Canada Highway #1. Graham A.B. Vickowski (left) and Bern Dibner, II, are shown here.

the photograph is a boy, Edward Mallandaine (who lost his mail-delivery contract with the event), standing close behind Sir Donald. Lost elsewhere or in the crowd of onlookers at a locale named Craigellachie were those who actually found the way—Kootenay chief Kinbaskit, Major Albert Rogers and Walter Moberly—while James Hector was busy with the geology of New Zealand and Andrew Onderdonk was at work on another project back in his hometown of New York. Today one can find a suitable memorial, just off the Trans-Canada Highway west of Eagle Pass. During the darkest days of obtaining construction funding for their railway, Donald Smith and his cousin, George Stephen, exchanged telegraphic messages of encouragement using this ancient rallying cry of Clan Grant, originally applied to a location in Morayshire.

* * *

The president of the CPR welcomed all visitors—one could never tell when one of them might have access to big money—and the Rev. William Spotswood Green (1847–1919), soon to be named Inspector of the Irish Fisheries, was an early visitor to the Canadian railway's attractive mountain scenery around their about-to-be-famous Glacier House. (In 1982 The American Alpine Club published my book about this first center of North American alpinism, entitled *The Great Glacier and Its House*, from which many of the accompanying illustrations herein have been taken.) Before he could reach his destination, however, Green encountered the CPR's "temporary" 4.2 percent grade down the west side of the Kicking Horse Pass, 382 m. higher (and 6 km. away from) the elevation of the extensive gravel flats below, where the Yoho River joins the Kicking Horse. As a precaution against the possibility of runaway trains, the CPR had installed spring-loaded switches at three points on this descent. Trains on the downgrade had to stop while one brakeman got off the lead engine and held the switch open for the train to pass. In the absence of such action, the train would have been diverted onto an upgrade spur sufficient to bring it to a halt. However, during the entire two decades of operating on this steep grade, though they had other mishaps, the CPR never had one train runaway. Green described the railway's descent on pages 55–56 of his subsequent book, *Among the Selkirk Glaciers* (London: Macmillan, 1890).

> At the summit of the pass a huge locomotive with ten driving wheels, and weighing one hundred and seventeen tons, was attached to the back of the train, and trusting to its restraining power and to that of eight extra men, who came on board the train to help at screwing down the brakes attached to each car, we started at a cautiously slow pace down a gradient of one in twenty-three. The Wapta river, in whose company we had to make our way to the Columbia, on issuing from its lake at the summit of the pass, plunges down a series of cascades, descending 1,100 feet in five miles. [Some writers used the name "Wapta," Stoney Indian for "water" in place of Kicking Horse when referring to this steep downgrade.] The railway track, being unable to descend in this precipitate manner, clings to the steep precipices of the mountain side and consequently is soon left high above the valley. Across trestle bridges spanning deep ravines, and round sharp curves, we wound our way, getting views from the windows

> of the train, or better still, from the platform at the end of the car, which were sufficiently startling. Pinned on to the face of the precipice, trusting in many places to elaborate scaffoldings of pine trunks, built up from what seemed perilously insecure foundations, occasionally resting on mere notches in the rocky walls, the track winds its way downwards to Field station, and the level of the Wapta is once more reached.
>
> Here the big locomotive left us to await the arrival of the East-bound train, which with mighty puffings it had to shove up the steep incline to the summit.

This grade, very uneconomical for railroad operating purposes, was an operating nightmare for the railway, and not to be corrected until after twenty years of operation when the CPR was the most prosperous corporate entity in the country. But if Rogers' proposed route had been adopted, the initial line would have been much straighter, with an acceptable operating grade of less than 2.5 percent, and the great work of the famous Spiral Tunnels (completed in 1908, and described in the next chapter) would have been unnecessary. But, at that perilously under-financed stage of the railway's life, a 4.2 percent grade was fiscally acceptable — so as to start getting some paying traffic running — if not operationally ideal. Coal and water to feed the extra engines was not an issue, for the CPR was, then and now, copiously endowed with coal mines, and water was flowing down every mountain side.

A few pages later, Green went on to describe the CPR's initial ascent from across the Columbia at Beavermouth up to Rogers Pass:

The original Stony Creek (modified Howe truss) bridge was soon replaced with a steel arch that remains in use in 2010 (Canadian Pacific Railway; American Alpine Club).

> Higher and higher we crept along the mountain side, gradually leaving the Beaver far below. Deep ravines cleft by glacier streams, foaming down, half choked with fallen logs, were spanned by lofty trestle-bridges. One of these which we crept slowly over was Mountain Creek bridge, and we went still more slowly over those portions of the track which were laid in shallow cuttings in the loose debris which lay at a high angle on the mountain side. We could see showers of gravel shaking down as the train passed. [Most people who have never ridden in the cab of a steam locomotive do not appreciate the continual and ground-shaking shuddering that such engines exhibit when working hard on an upgrade.] Then we came to the most wonderful bridge of all, spanning Stony Creek, at the prodigious height of 205 feet [62.5 m.] above the torrent, chiefly supported by one tall pillar of trestle work, rising straight up from the bottom of the ravine, and a smaller one which is secured to the sloping side of the chasm.

Green followed this up with a dismal description of the charred ruins of the forest that had resulted from the vast fires which had raged in the area during the years of railway construction. Then, the visiting clergyman-alpinist waxed equally eloquent on the railway's numerous trestles and massive snowsheds. These feats of construction were significantly modified in later years by extensive fills, steel bridges, and two major realignments that were necessary to attain the lower (and less avalanche-prone) levels of the eight km. Connaught Tunnel (1916) and the even longer Macdonald Tunnel (1988).

> At a station called Bear Creek, where the valley forked, we left the Beaver, and following the valley of the Bear the train had to pass through a series of snowsheds. On emerging from these we found ourselves in the wonderful defile between Mounts Tupper and Macdonald, whose great precipices rose so vertically, that we could only see to the top of the precipice opposite by leaning far out of the windows. As we crept round the base of Mount Tupper and entered Rogers pass, our prospect was sadly interfered with by snow-shedding. We no sooner got out of one snowshed, and had merely got a glimpse of the magnificent scenery through which we were passing, when we went into another. These sheds are built of massive timber-work, all tongued and mortised together, and as there are many miles of them the total cost up to the present has been over 1,000,000 dollars.

Because of frequent complaints of this nature, the CPR soon laid a "summer track" outside the snowsheds, which was used from late May through October. The CPR also built some very impressive—to this day—masonry structures in the vicinity of Rogers Pass, ample evidence of their original intent that this difficult route be as permanent as they could make it. The interested person can learn more about these massive snowsheds and their place in the history of the CPR by reading the American Alpine Club's 1980 volume, *The Great Glacier and Its House*. Such a person can also still make out considerable evidence of their massiveness by "strolling" through the greenery to the south of the present highway crossing Rogers Pass. Huge balks of spruce—16" by 16"—spanning massive rock cribs, served as rafters for a roof deck of 3" thick "planks."

Snowshed (below Avalanche Crest) in early winter of 1887, looking down the tracks toward the Glacier House (Canadian Pacific Railway; American Alpine Club).

CPR train passing across Rogers Pass in winter in 1886 (Canadian Pacific Railway; American Alpine Club).

Opening the tracks at Rogers Pass railway by hand in 1886 by mostly Chinese; the CPR employed 17,000 "celestial Orientals" in construction (Canadian Pacific Railway; American Alpine Club).

Mount Macdonald is the imposing south wall of Rogers Pass, rising to 2,893 m. and named for Sir John Alexander Macdonald, the "Old Tomorrow" of Canadian politics and much beloved first prime minister of the Dominion of Canada. Non-Canadians may need to be informed that Sir John (1815–1891) stands in much the same light as George Washington, as the father of his country. With one brief absence, he held the prime ministership of his nation from the time of its founding in 1867 until his death; an event which some Canadian newspapers saw fit to announce by a headline reading simply "HE IS DEAD." Sir John had his failings, including a sustained fondness for John Barleycorn, which were well publicized by his political opponents, but he also had the love and confidence of his fellow citizens. Sir Charles Tupper (1821–1915), a physician by training, was instrumental in bringing Nova Scotia into the Dominion, and later served as prime minister.

The railway was completed through from coast to coast (Montreal to New Westminster) by the fall of 1885; but not fully opened for regular traffic until there had been time to evaluate — and partially cope with — the enormous inherent dangers from avalanche. Learning from the difficulties of the Central Pacific Railroad in maintaining its crossing of California's 2,176 m. (7,135 foot) Donner Pass, Van Horne and his key operating personnel, decided (a century before the onset of consumer safety litigation) to be more certain of the security of passengers and personnel before allowing regular operation of the entire line. That lengthy delay gave time for a few minor relocations and the construction of most of the snowsheds that constricted the subsequent view for travelers such as Green.

It was a massive one of these slides, coming down on top of a locomotive and work crew engaged in reopening the line near the crest of Rogers Pass in mid–March of 1910, resulting in more than one hundred fatalities and the widespread resultant public outcry, which forced the CPR to undertake the five-mile project of the Connaught Tunnel. It was officially opened in 1916 after six years of excavating through the tough Hammill Quartzite. The most scenic part of the whole transcontinental trip was now replaced by a ten-minute ride in the dark under Mount Macdonald.

The original Rogers Pass installation had several wide, stone-filled cribs separating the tracks at the summit of the pass, and a massive roof structure over all. Nevertheless, the well-publicized tribulations of the Central Pacific at Donner Pass paled by comparison with those the CPR endured nearly a thousand km. to the north at Rogers Pass. In 1899 an avalanche had destroyed the station built near the crest of the pass, killing all seven of its occupants. The managers of the nearby Glacier House (which was orig-

Glacier House, as the CPR hotel was known in 1910. This was the original center of mountaineering in North America, but torn down in 1927 after the Connaught Tunnel eliminated its original purpose—as a stop for feeding passengers. By 1942 the glacier had melted back to the horizon (Canadian Pacific Railway; American Alpine Club).

Loop Creek Pillar in 2008, with GABV starting up. Almost a century after the steel spans were removed, these monuments remain a rock climber's challenge.

inally established as the middle of three eatery stops when it was deemed uneconomic to haul heavy dining cars over the Mountain Division of the CPR) later found winter employment for their resident Swiss guides in routine shoveling of the roof to prevent the hotel's collapse.

This tunnel job was done in a manner similar to the Moffat, and many significant bores since that project; a small bore being driven through the mountain a few meters offset from the planned main tunnel and perpendicular to which numerous short drifts were made so that the main tunnel could be worked from a variety of headings. When finished, it was appropriately dedicated by the governor general of Canada, Patrick Albert, first Duke of Connaught (1850–1942), Queen Victoria's third son. The eight km., double-tracked tunnel shortened the line over the top of Rogers Pass by several kilometers, eliminated the need for the two-kilometer-long height-gaining loop on the west side through Loop Creek, trimmed 2,300 degrees of curvature and reduced the summit elevation by 168 meters. Not eliminated, however, was most of the upgrade from Beavermouth to the east portal. It remained necessary to station three pairs of pusher engines down by the Columbia to assist trains up the 2.1 percent grade to the tunnel, from whence they would "dead-head" back down to the bottom again.

* * *

A major effort was initiated in the 1960s to further reduce the grade at Rogers Pass. Through its subsidiary, the Fording Coal Company, since sold to a Chinese consortium, the Canadian Pacific entered into a long-term contract with a Japanese consortium to supply low-sulfur coal from the extensive CPR "captive" mines at Crowsnest Pass. This contract entailed a major upgrade for the CPR's bucolic, all but abandoned, and somewhat circuitous Kootenay Central branch along the upper Columbia River from Fort Steele to Golden and a further effort to ease the main line's grade west through the Selkirk Mountains. This branch, laid out in 1910 by a sometime president of the Alpine Club of Canada, Alexander Addison McCoubrey (1885–1942), held solely to the right bank of the slow-moving upper Columbia and was thus guided by many of the river's meanderings.

For this purpose the CPR — under considerable political pressure to keep the freight transit and associated jobs in Canada and not lose them to their historic, and threateningly nearby, American rival, the Great Northern, which also runs unit coal trains from the Flathead area, where the geology is similar to that of Crowsnest Pass, to its port of Everett — replaced all the old 85 lb. segmented rail with 136 lb. welded rail on the Kootenay Central. The company then set out to construct a new port system at Roberts Bank, some 2,260 km. distant from Crowsnest Pass, build a vast marshaling yard and repair shop at Golden, and take a good hard look at the line up to Rogers Pass.

By mid-summer of 1983, construction was well under way toward boring a second tunnel under Mount Macdonald, this one to be 91 m. lower than the Connaught, with a total length of 14.6 km. and for westbound traffic only. By the end of 1984 several construction firms were at work grading a new 1 percent line up the west side of Beaver Creek to a short (1.8 km.) tunnel under a corner of Mt. Shaughnessy (at 2,807 m. and honoring the memory of Sir Thomas George Shaughnessy (1853–1923) the third president of the CPR, who was also American-born, and followed Van Horne) northeast of Rogers Pass, while the main bore was under contract to five firms in two joint ventures. Part of the tunnel goes through the massive Hammill Quartzite, a durable formation that also makes up most of the nearby high points, while the westerly part of the bore encounters the less competent Horsethief Creek group. This part of the Macdonald Tunnel was bored with a machine somewhat similar to those ordered by Crocker and Serrell for use on the Hoosac, but with certain major differences. This one was of Swedish design, weighed in at more than 300 tons *and worked*, regularly delivering to the west adit more than 60 cubic meters of pulverized muck per day from its 6.7 m. diameter front end. This rate required the CPR to obtain 50 special dump cars of 70-ton capacity to remove this material from the portal and deposit it down the line toward Revelstoke where a concurrent double-tracking project needed the fill.

When this massive project was completed in December of 1988, the two headings

Reclaimed CPR coal property at Crowsnest Pass in 2009, where much of the present mining is underground.

Unit train yards at Golden, British Columbia, in 2009. The CPR's main line over Kicking Horse Pass, not shown, is 2 km. off to the left (north).

of this tunnel met, with an error of five cm. in the vertical and 15 in the horizontal, and the Canadian Pacific Railway again possessed the longest railroad tunnel in the Western Hemisphere,. The older Connaught Tunnel, which once held that title, was reduced to a single track centered in the tunnel and handling only eastbound traffic. Ventilation for the Macdonald Tunnel is accomplished by four 1.68 megawatt exhaust fans installed at the top of a shaft at the midpoint of the tunnel, as differentiated from the twin 500 HP diesel units that are used to suck smoke and fumes from the west end only of the Connaught. British Columbia Hydro, the distributor of power from the Revelstoke and other dams, ran a special line up to the pass for this purpose.

These unit coal trains, of which there are—at this writing—more than a dozen, consist of almost 100 "bathtub" cars hauled from Crowsnest Pass to the coast in trains of one crew, with an engine in front, a radio-controlled "slave" engine in the middle, and another at the rear. Each car carries 105 tons and they are upended while passing across a special trestle over the collier ship. The dumping operation for one train takes about two hours, with not much more time being required to load them at the multiple mining operations near Crowsnest, and an average running time of 82 hours from mine to collier.

10

Spiraling to the Top

MAJOR ROGERS DID NOT GET his way at the Kicking Horse Pass, but the issue he faced, developed a solution for, and was told to ignore remained as an operating sore spot even as the CPR was busily contending with the snowy nightmares of the Selkirks. As by then the most prosperous corporate entity in Canada, the CPR was happy running its increasingly classy hotels, both in major cities and in the scenic mountains, where the Banff Springs Hotel and the Chateau Lake Louise became its twin centerpieces after the CPR realized that mountain visitors could be a source of great profit. The original log cabin "chalet" at Lake Louise was destroyed by fire in 1892 and a much grander (but still wooden) edifice arose from the ashes. Then in 1920, a second fire took out everything except the new "concrete wing," which had been built as the first installment of its present, modern and largely fireproof emporium. In recent years, however, the CPR has sold all its famous hotels, mostly to the Fairmont Corporation.

In developing its mountain clientele, Van Horne owed much to the gratuitous advice from San Francisco–based Dr. Joshua Harrison Stallard (1821–1899), who wrote him that the CPR should import "Swiss guides" to prevent further accidents and give their hotel clients a safer experience in the mountains. Nevertheless, Glacier House (which was situated in the better climbing terrain of the Selkirks) was closed soon after the Connaught Tunnel was opened and all attention was turned to the more scenic Rockies. The historic structure at Glacier was offered to the Swiss guides for one dollar, but they refused, stating they "were guides not businessmen" so the old hotel was torn down in 1927, but its foundation piers can still be made out.

However, the issue of that 4.2 percent grade in the Rockies was of long standing, as the CPR's archivist and resident historian Omer Simon LaVallée (1925–1992) explained:

> Van Horne prepared and submitted evidence to show that the cost of maintaining special locomotives for a short, steep grade made for less expense and delay to trains, than a long, sustained climb. More particularly, construction of the temporary line would give the CPR a number of years in which to observe the climatic and geographic conditions, including the movement of glaciers and the frequency of avalanches, before deciding on the location of a more moderately graded route. Possibly Van Horne had

in mind a letter which he had recently received from an engineer, which proposed grade reductions by spiral descents, thus artificially lengthening the line in order to obtain more moderate grades. In the end, this was the solution finally selected a quarter of a century later when Charles E. Schwitzer built his well-known Spiral Tunnels.[1]

* * *

But, despite the scenery, the CPR was a transportation company at heart. CPR management (personified by Sir Thomas George Shaughnessy, CEO after Van Horne's retirement) realized it could not be idle in the face of enhanced competition for the Canadian transcontinental traffic. The Canadian Northern was evolving — the creation of William McKenzie (1849–1923) and Donald Mann (1853–1934), which utilized provincial subsidies to build countless branch lines but could never make them meet their operating costs, with which the provinces were unable to help. The Grand Trunk Pacific was also present (a subsidiary of the premier rail line of Ontario, the Grand Trunk, given a massive federal subsidy, a goodly portion of which was burned up in trying to build a line for its Central Vermont subsidiary from Palmer, Massachusetts, to Providence, Rhode Island, before the folly of such an endeavor caused it to be abandoned, uncompleted). In the early part of the 20th century, both lines were using the Yellowhead Pass, where their competing tracks ran parallel through the mountains for over 100 km. While both of those new roads were in bankruptcy by 1920, their mere potential existence stimulated the CPR into taking the long-needed steps to ease that grade at Kicking Horse Pass. After the GT and the CN were bankrupt, those roads along with numerous other short lines that were in trouble for over-expansion, were forcibly combined into the Canadian National Railways — which was a "system" in name only until its disparate parts could be rebuilt into an harmonious configuration — a five-decade-long task. While "the government" (the pejorative term used by the CPR's Swiss guides for the railway and other facilities they associated with Yellowhead Pass and Jasper) took up the duplicate track, not merely at the Continental Divide but elsewhere across the country, they also brought in resident professional guides and attempted to create attractions comparable to Lake Louise and Banff, though in far less dramatic or historical terrain. Thus the competitive stimulus continued long after the Kicking Horse grade had been taken care of. (The foregoing is a very brief explanation of a complex political and economic morass that continues to impact many operations of both the CPR and the Canadian National Railway.)

In 1905 the CPR's senior engineer in the west was John Edward Schwitzer (1870–1911), who had a distinguished record among his peer group and was assigned the task of evaluating the possibilities of lessening the Kicking Horse grade on the west side (the ruling grade on the east was already at a very satisfactory 1.4 percent). Schwitzer dusted off Major Rogers' plan of 1883, but determined there was still too much danger of land (and snow) slippage along the steep and unstable north slopes of Mounts Cathedral and Stephen. He then looked into the possibility of extending the rails in a wide loop up into the valley of the Yoho River to the north, a sweeping curve that would add several miles to the length of track, and thereby reduce the overall gradient to a satisfactory 2 percent. However, that option seemed also to be beset with numerous possibilities of rockfall and avalanche, though Van Horne had long ago professed an admiration for its scenery, particularly the spectacular Takakaw Falls.

In the end Schwitzer determined the CPR had enough problems with avalanches in the Selkirks and could lengthen the line by at least four miles through the use a method that had already been found very practical on several lines through some of the difficult passageways of the Alps — i.e., gain (or lose) altitude at an acceptable gradient by boring spiral tunnels in easier rock. The "easier rock" at Kicking Horse Pass turned out to be the thickly bedded quartzite and quartzose sandstone of the Lower Cambrian Gog Group, somewhat younger — by several hundred million years — than the Hoosac Schist.

Thus, there came into being the very visible Spiral Tunnels of Kicking Horse Pass — a two year project started in 1907. The upper bore, called #1 in the CPR records, takes about one kilometer in its $^3/_4$ circle under Cathedral Mountain. Then, the tracks emerge and descend northeastward to cross the river and make a similar loop under

Field Station in 1890, where the Rev. W. S. Green's ten-wheeler pusher engines were based (as shown in a modern exhibit at Kicking Horse Pass).

Mount Odgen, named for the auditor and vice-president of the CPR, Isaac Gouverneur Odgen (1844–1915), on the north side of the pass. Circling downward once more, the tracks recross the river, heading west again, and continue their 2.2 percent descent to the railway section point of Field. Unfortunately, the extra trackage that reduced the grade from 4.2 percent to 2.2 percent did not completely eliminate the need for pusher engines to be stationed at Field, though they are no longer of the massive nature of those described by the Rev. Green. Portions of the original 4+ percent roadbed are now used by the Trans-Canada Highway, beside which is a viewing station where automobile and tour bus passengers frequently stop to watch freight trains that are longer than the tunnels, make their passage.

* * *

The Spiral tunnels have not eliminated every hazard to the CPR at Kicking Horse Pass. Far above the railway on the east side of Cathedral Mountain there is a smallish glacier (perhaps unnoticed by Van Horne) whose lateral moraine* holds back a tiny body of water, known as Tea Cup Lake. By sad experience, the more recent CPR managers have learned that this relatively minuscule body of water deserves, and periodically has forcibly demanded, their attention. At times, glacial motions and accumulating meltwater have caused the lake level to rise sufficiently to saturate and overtop the moraine which forms its dam, thereby turning much of the calcareous moraine into mud and sweeping vast quantities of gravelly debris down the hillside and onto the tracks. This tumbling debris has also occasionally swept considerable portions of passing freight trains into the valley below.

To defend itself against the erratic foibles of this tiny pond, the CPR was forced to build a sturdy concrete tunnel so that these unwanted offerings from above could be safely swept over its tracks, and annually sends a crew up to the lake — by helicopter and with a pump — to drain its surplus waters more peacefully.

Glossary

Adit—the horizontal opening of any mine to the surface.

Alidade—a sighting device, often applied to a transit, that can be used to determine direction and level.

Climax—when applied to an avalanche, it refers to a slide of such magnitude and depth that it contains not merely the surface layers of one of more snowfalls, but everything right down to (and possibly including some of) the underlying hillside.

Cut and Cover—a method of constructing a tunnel in which all the overburden is removed and then bridged over after completion of the underlying conduit.

Dip—the angle below the horizontal shown by any linear geologic body. (See Strike.)

Drumlin—a tapered mound of subglacial morainic debris, molded in the general direction of glacial movement; generally less than 100 m. in maximum height (See Till.)

4-8-8-4—a combination of numbers indicating the wheel arrangement of a steam locomotive; the first number is the front truck (bogie), the second is the number of driving wheels, and the final is the rear truck. The largest steam locomotives often used two sets of driving wheels, with the frame under the boiler articulated so as to allow an easier curving radius, and the steam being expanded twice to attain maximum value in fuel consumption.

Friction—used to describe the typical railroad driving wheel, which depends on the adhesion by gravity of its engine weight for locomotion.

Gauge—the width between wheels of any four-wheeled vehicle. In the case of railroad wheels, it is the space normally between the inside edge of the flanges. Note that the "flat" part of a railroad wheel is actually a segment of a cone; so that as centrifugal force throws the wheels (which are rigidly attached to their axle) to the outside of any curve, the diameter of every outer wheel is thereby increased so the train can readily conform to a curve.

Grade (gradient)—the rate of ascent (or descent) expressed as a percentage of horizontal distance—i.e., one foot vertically in one hundred feet horizontally is 1 percent; two feet vertically over the same distance is 2 percent.

Hard pan (See Till.)

Heading— the actual face of any mining operation.

Momentum Grading—a means of roadbed grading whereby lengthy valleys are not filled so as to keep the roadbed on a consistent grade; but where the tracks are laid in such manner that the passing train will gain sufficient speed on the downgrade to enable it to be carried more easily up the succeeding upgrade.

Moraine (See Till.)

Muck (mucking)—the debris blasted loose in mining and the process of removing it.

Outwash— sand-, gravel-, or clay-sized fragments, carried from the meltwater streams exiting any glacier and deposited below the ice front.

Portal—the entrance to any cave, tunnel or building.

Rack— a ladder of transverse bars firmly fixed between the rails into which a sturdy, central cog wheel can mesh, thus providing a firmer grip for driving wheels than friction.

Radius—to describe the sharpness of any curve, expressed it as a segment of the circle described by a radius of X meters (or feet). (See Tangent.)

Right (or left)— as pertaining to a stream, valley (or glacier) is always as seen when looking downstream.

Ruling—this term, when applied to a gradient, refers to the irreducible limiting segment of any route.

Shaft—a vertical mine opening into the ground. (See Winze.)

Snake Rail—this term of opprobrium came about because of the occasional tendency of these malleable iron straps to come loose from their wooden underpinnings and curl upward through the cars of a passing train.

Spall— the fragmenting of a generally curved and thin segment of any rock when external heating destroys internal cohesion by differential expansion of the component minerals.

Stope— to develop the area above a drift by pulling down the roof from below.

Strike—the compass direction exhibited by the linear outcrop of any geologic formation. (See Dip.)

Tangent—any straight stretch of track (or bore) emanating from the curve of a radius. Railroads do not like curves, so tangents are desirable— the longer the better.

Till—this is the Scots term for the glacial deposit that the English call "boulder clay," Yankee farmers call "hard pan," and French alpinists call "moraine."

Trestle—often in this text of wood, latterly generally of steel; a structure for carrying any roadway over a defile, where fill or bridging is unsuitable and momentum grading unworkable.

Winze— a vertical or steeply inclined passageway between levels within a mine.

Appendix

Edward Whymper, "The Mont Cenis (Frejus) Tunnel," in *Scrambles Among the Alps: In the Years 1860–1869*, 4th ed. (London: John Murray, 1893), 52–71.

The famous Frejus Tunnel in the Western Alps — sometimes called the Mont Cenis (in Italian, Moncenisio) — was the first major railroad tunnel in the world and was done right. The geologists preceded the tunnelers, not the other way around, as was the case in the notorious bore under Hoosac Mountain. Of course, in defense of the Americans, the Mesozoic geology in the Alps is much simpler to map and predict that the homogeneous pre–Cambrian schist of Hoosac Mountain.

The author of this appendix was the famous etcher turned alpinist, Edward Whymper, who later wrote a book on his climbs among the High Andes of Peru, in which he anticipated physiologists of two generations later in describing the effects of high altitude on the respiratory systems of those who are unacclimatized to the thin air.

Whymper's *Scrambles Amongst the Alps* went through several revisions in its numerous reprint editions. He was honored by alpine societies around the world, everywhere except in his native England, where Queen Victoria's displeasure with the death of one of her favorites during the first ascent of the Matterhorn haunted Whymper's memory until his death (in Chamonix).

"When M. Medail of Bardonnêche — more than half a century ago — pointed out that a shorter tunnel could be constructed beneath the Alps between his village and Modane than at any other place in the Sardinian States having a similar elevation above the level of the sea, neither he, nor any other person, had the least idea how the project could be executed.

"The first step was taken by the geologists Sismonda and Elie de Beaumont. They predicted that calcareous schists and quartzite rocks would form a large proportion of the strata through which the tunnel would pass. It takes a miner one hour and a half to two hours to make an ordinary hole for blasting (28 inches deep) in calcareous schist, and not less than eight hours to make one 20 inches deep in quartzite. When would the tunnel have been finished if the ordinary processes had been alone employed?

"The ordinary processes were clearly unavailable. The tunnel would be of prodigious length, and would have to be constructed without shafts. At no place where a shaft would have been of any use would it have been possible to make one less than 1000 feet deep! If one had been made about midway between the two ends, it would have been no less than 5315 feet deep. 'I estimate,' says M. Conte,[1] 'that the sinking of a shaft a mile in depth would occupy not less than forty years. I do not know that a depth of 1000 feet has been hitherto passed.'[2]

"Several projects were presented to the Sardinian government, some proposing to shorten the length of the tunnel by raising its level, and others to accelerate the boring of the holes for blasting; but they were all put aside as impossible, or as having been insufficiently studied. The first one seriously considered by the government was that of M. Maus, a Belgian engineer. He proposed to construct a tunnel of 12,230 metres between Bardonnêche and Modane, with a ruling gradient of 19 in 1000. The advance of the small gallery in front was to be made by means of a machine with chisels, put in motion by springs, that would have cut the rock into blocks — leaving them attached only at the back — which were afterwards to be brought down by means of wedges.

"M. Colladon of Geneva suggested moving the tools of the machine of M. Maus by means of compressed air, but he neither pointed out the means of compressing the air, nor how it was to be applied as a motive power.

"The government had constructed the railway from Turin to Genoa, and engineers were studying how to tug the trains up the incline at Busalla, which has a gradient of 1 in 29. Mm. Grandis, Grattoni, and Sommeiller proposed to compress air by means of the '*compresseur a choc*,' and to employ it for the traction of the trains.

"Mr. Bartlett, an English engineer on the Victor Emmanuel Railway,[3] had invented a machine for making holes for blasting, which was put in motion by steam. The machine was imperfect, and while experiments were being made with it (by means of compressed air), M. Sommeiller invented the boring-machine which is now used in the tunnel.

"The problem then appeared to be solved. The inventors joined themselves to M. Ranco — who had taken part in their experiments on the Genoa Railway — and prepared a scheme, after having found out that they could compress air to a high pressure, that this air could be led from closed reservoirs and transmitted to great distances without a sensible diminution of its pressure, and that it could be employed to move the boring-machine which was intended to make the holes for blasting. A commission was appointed to examine the project, and its members satisfied themselves that the scheme was feasible. The Act of August 15, 1857, authorised the government to construct the section of the Victor Emmanuel Railway between Susa and Modane, and Mm. Grandis, Grattoni, and Sommeiller, were appointed to direct the works.

"M. Medail indicated the general direction of the tunnel between Modane and Bardonnêche. M. Maus drew his line a little more to the east, nearer to Modane. The engineers who directed the work approached the latter course, and selected that which seemed to them to be the shortest, the most easy to come out at, and, especially, the most convenient to lay out.

"It is needless to insist on the importance of the tracing of the course of the tunnel. It was necessary 1st, To establish upon the mountain a sufficient number of marks in order to determine the vertical plane passing through the axis of the gallery; 2. To measure exactly the distance between the two mouths; 3. To determine the difference of level between the two mouths, in order to arrange the gradients of the tunnel. These delicate operations were entrusted to Mm. Borelli and Copello. M. Grandis undertook the control of the work. In 1858 the triangulations and levellings were undertaken, and they were terminated at the end of the year.

"On account of the peculiar situation of the ends of the tunnel, two small, connecting, curved tunnels had to be made. At first, the construction of these terminal curves was naturally neglected for the establishment of the two false mouths in the direction of the general line.

"The length between the two false mouths is 12,220.00 metres. The entry on the side of Italy is at a height of 1335.38, France 1202.82, Difference of level 132.56. This difference of level is overcome by a gradient of 222 in 10,000, which rises from the French entry to the centre,[4] 135.64. A gradient of 1 in 2000, which rises from the Italian entry to the centre 3.06, 132.58. If a single gradient had ruled throughout, rising from the French to the Italian side, it would have been reduced to 217 in 20,000; but although this would have been of the greatest advantage in working the line, it would have added one more difficulty to the construction of the tunnel. There were enough difficulties without adding another.

"It was, besides, evident that driving the tunnel to a summit doubled the chances of the two ends meeting, and negatived to a certain extent, the possibilities of error from the two operations upon which the least dependence could be placed — the triangulation and the levelling. Provided that the two axes were in the same direction, they were obliged to meet sooner or later; whether this happened a few yards more to the north or to the south was of no importance.

"At the commencement of the tunnel, in 1857, there was no accommodation at either end for those employed on the works; and for a long time both engineers and workmen had to submit to numerous privations. Roads had to be made, and barracks to be erected. One after another, houses and shops were added, and at last the tunnel — buildings alone formed considerable villages at the two ends.

"The situations of the two mouths are essentially different from each other. That at Bardonnêche comes out at the bottom of the Valley of Rochemolles; that at Fourneaux (Modane) 300 feet above the Mont Cenis road. At the latter end the debris has been shot out from the mouth down the mountain-side; and, large as the tip (to use the language of navvies) undoubtedly is, it is difficult to believe one sees all the material that has been extracted. It is interesting as showing the greatest angle at which debris will stand. Its faces have, as nearly as possible, an angle of 45°.

"During four years the ordinary means of excavation were alone employed, and but 1300 yards were driven. In this time the machines were being constructed which were destined to supersede a large part of the manual labour. At the beginning of 1861 they were sufficiently advanced to be put to work, and in the summer of that year I went from Briançon to Bardonnêche to see them in operation.

"The clocks of Ouix had just struck twelve on the night of the 16th of August, as the diligence crawled into the village from Briançon, conveying a drunken driver, a still more intoxicated conducteur, and myself. The keeper of the inn at which we stopped declined to take me in, so I sought for repose in a neighbouring oatfield, and the next morning mightily astonished a native when I rose enveloped in my blanket bag. He looked aghast for a moment at the apparition which seemed to spring out of the ground, and then turning round in a nervous, twitching manner, dropped his spade and fairly bolted, followed by hearty shouts of laughter.

"Bardonnêche was about an hour distant. A strange banging noise could be heard a long way off, and a few minutes after my arrival, I stood in one of the shops by the side of the machine which was causing it, and by the side of M. Sommeiller, the inventor of the machine. They were experimenting with one of his '*perforatrices*,' and a new form of boring-rod, upon a huge block of rock which was already riddled by more than a hundred holes, varying from one inch to four and a half in diameter. The *perforatrice*—a simple-looking cylinder fixed in a square frame, and connected with a few pipes and stop-cocks—was placed in a fresh position in front of the rock, and, at a sign from the engineer, was set in motion. A boring-rod darted out like a flash of lightning, chipped out several fragments at a blow, and withdrew as quickly as it had advanced. Bang, bang, it went again with the noise of a gong. In ten seconds the head of the borer had eaten itself a hole; in a minute it had all but disappeared; in twelve it had drilled a hole nearly a yard deep, as cleanly as a carpenter could in a piece of wood. The rod not only moved backwards and forwards, and advanced as the hole grew deeper, but turned gently round the whole time. A jet of water, projected with great force, cooled the chisel, and washed out the chips. More air was turned on, and the sound of the blows could no longer be distinguished one from another. They made a continuous rattle, and the rate was increased from two hundred to no less than three hundred and forty strokes per minute, or about half as fast again as the motion of the piston-rod of an express locomotive when going sixty miles an hour.

"On approaching the tunnel-mouths, the pipes were seen which conducted the compressed air for the working of these boring machines. They were eight inches in diameter, supported on pillars of masonry. As these pipes, outside the tunnel, were exposed to constant variations of temperature—sometimes to as much as 54° Fahr. in a single day—it was necessary to guard against their expansion and contraction. They were fixed accordingly at stated intervals by means of iron rods, the lower ends of which were carried through the masonry and bolted to plates on the outside. The intermediate pipes were carried on rollers on the tops of the pillars, and between each of the fixed points there was one pipe having an enlarged mouth—terminated by a cheek—which received the end of the ordinary pipe. A circular pipe of leather was secured to the cheek by means of a metal washer, and, pressed down by the compressed air on the end of the ordinary pipe, made the joint sufficiently air-tight, although it did not hinder the advance or the retreat of the pipe. In the tunnel itself, where the temperature was not subject to such fluctuations, these precautions were not necessary, and the pipes were carried along the walls, supported by brackets, as far as the end of the finished work. Through these pipes highly compressed air was conducted, and was delivered at the end of the 'advanced gallery' where the boring-machines were at work, with only a slight diminution in its pressure, notwithstanding the escapes which occurred at the joints.

"On entering the tunnel one was struck by its size. The Italians, with magnificent disregard of expense, or from regard to the future, constructed it with two pairs of rails, and with a footpath on each side. From the rails to the crown of the arch its height is just 20 feet, and its width is 26 feet 6 inches. It is almost everywhere lined with masonry; a small fraction only of the rock is left unsupported. Not observed, though nevertheless existing, is a covered way about 3 feet 4 inches high, and 4 feet wide, which is made in the floor of the tunnel between the rails. It is in fact a tunnel within a tunnel. Originally its dimensions were less, and it was intended merely as a subway in which the pipes conveying the compressed air might be placed, and as a drain. It was found convenient to enlarge its size, and after that was done — on at least one occasion — it served a purpose for which it was not originally intended. On the 15th of September 1863, a sudden fall of rock occurred, which killed several miners and imprisoned about sixty others who were at work in the advanced gallery. They were greatly alarmed, and expected to be starved; but at last one of them remembered this subway, and they escaped by its means. After that occasion, the miners, knowing they had this exit, troubled themselves very little about *eboulements*.

"During its construction, the temperature of the tunnel remained tolerably uniform throughout the year, although much higher in some parts than in others. On the occasion of my visit in 1869, the exterior temperature was 63° Fahr. in the shade; a mile from the entrance it was 65°, and the mouth looked like the sun on a misty November day. At two miles the thermometer showed 70°, the atmosphere had become foul, and the mouth was invisible. In two hundred and fifty paces more, it had risen to 75°, the tunnel was filled with dense clouds of smoke, the light of an ordinary miner's lamp could not be perceived at the distance of five or six yards, and respiration was difficult, for the atmosphere was vile. This was at the end of the finished work. Hence air was drawn by pumping-engines at the mouth, for it was hereabouts that all the foul vapours naturally accumulated. The great vault was no longer overhead, and the way was reduced to a drift eight or nine feet wide and scarcely as much high, encumbered with waggons filled with debris, between which and the walls one could barely pass. In a hundred feet or so, we emerged — comparatively speaking — into a blaze of light. Two hundred greasy, smoky, but still light-giving lamps, hung from the walls.

"Drops of water flashed past them like gems. Two hundred men toiled at the enlargement of the gallery — bearded, grimy men, some on their backs, some on their sides, some working overhead, some half naked, some quite naked — all tapping laboriously at their mining-rods, and all perspiring profusely. The temperature had risen to 81.5°. The multitude of the lights, the crowd of men, and the obscurity of the smoke, helped to make the tunnel look an immense size — in fact, at this part, in its rough, unfinished condition, it was sometimes little less than 30 feet high and 35 feet wide. Not merely was rock removed at the top and sides, to be afterwards replaced by masonry, but it was occasionally excavated for an inverted arch, which was placed wherever it was necessary. The temperature was, as nearly as possible, the same at the roof of the gallery as it was on the floor; for jets of compressed air were let off above. The work of the masons would otherwise have been unendurable.

"There was a difference then of 18° Fahr. between the temperature outside the mouth and at the end of the finished work. In winter this difference was trebled or quadrupled. How much of the increase was due to the lights, men, and horses, and how much to the natural temperature of the rock? If the heat had increased in the tunnel, yard by yard, at the same rate as it does when descending into the earth, the temperature in its centre should have been about 90° higher than at its mouth. Although it was known that the rate of increase was much less than this, the actual rate was not known. I believe it is correct to say that not a single observation was made upon the natural temperature of the rock until after the advanced galleries met. Shortly after their junction was effected, at the end of 1870, Signor F. Giordano (Inspector of Italian Mines) directed his attention to the question, and found that the highest reading he could obtain (near the centre of the tunnel) was 85.1° Fahr. The temperature of the air at the same part was slightly above 86°.

"About 2000 feet on the French side of the tunnel were undergoing the processes of enlargement and completion in the summer of 1869. In some places portions of the advanced gallery remained untouched, and then one came to caverns, such as have been described above. This section was being completed faster than the gallery was being driven. It was pleasant to get away from it and farther into the bowels of the mountain; the heat became less and the atmosphere more pure. The noise of the hammers died gradually away, and at last no sound could be heard except of our own footsteps and of water running in the subway. After a time the banging of the chisels could be distinguished which were at work on the front of the attack. Five hundred paces took us to them. The ponderous frame, technically called *l'affût*, supported nine of the machines known as *perforatrices*; each *perforatrice* propelled by a long boring rod, and each boring-rod striking the rock at a rate of 200 strokes per minute, with a force of 200 pounds.[5] The terrific din that these 1800 strokes per minute, given with such force, made in as rock-chamber that was only 8 ft. 3 in. high, and 9 ft. 2 in. wide, can hardly be imagined; neither can an adequate idea be given of the admirable manner in which the machines accomplish their work. In spite of the noise and the cramped position in which the men necessarily toiled on account of the limited space, the work went steadily forward day and night. Each man knew his part. The foremen directed by signs rather than by words; the laborers guided the chisels; the workmen regulated the supply of air; the machinists were ready in case of accident; slim boys, with long-nosed cans, oiled the machinery. Order triumphed in the midst of apparent confusion. One saw the results of years of perfecting and practice. Things were very different at the beginning, when everything was new both to workmen and engineers. The best form of boring-rod for all kinds of rock, excepting such as were homogeneous, was hit upon in 1861, and it was always used afterwards. The head had the form of a Z. For homogeneous rock, the ordinary form of chisel was found best.[6] Almost all the details of the machinery, the size of the gallery, the dimensions of the holes, and the manner of firing them, were changed since the beginning; the general principles alone remain unaltered. The system latterly adopted was as follows. A hole 4¾ inches in diameter was made to a depth of about a yard, towards the centre of the drift, but rather nearer to the floor than to the roof. Fifty or sixty holes, according to the circumstances, of less diameter, but of about equal depth, were then driven into the remainder of the face. All the holes were then dried and cleaned by jets of compressed air, the *affût* was withdrawn behind strong iron-bound doors, and six of the small holes nearest to the large one were charged and fired. The force of the explosion went in the direction of least resistance, which was towards the central hole, and a breach was made such as is indicated in the longitudinal section, given below, by the thick dotted line. The remaining holes were then charged and fired in sets of six or eight at a time, those nearest to the breach being exploded first. This system was found more economical than firing a large number of shots at one time. The waggons were then advanced, and the debris was cleared away; the two pairs of rails at the sides, shown in the cross section, were for waggonets, whose contents were afterwards transferred to large waggons. The *affut* was then again advanced. These operations were repeated with unvarying regularity twice every day.

"The temperature at the working face of the advanced gallery was seldom higher than from 75° to 76°, and the atmosphere was as pure as could be desired, when the machines were at work.[7] This, notwithstanding the presence of more than thirty men,[8] and almost as many lamps, in a space about nine feet wide, eight high, and fifty long. The comparative lowness of the temperature was of course due to the expansion of the compressed air.

"At the distance of a hundred and sixty paces, the sound of the machines could not be distinguished, and the atmosphere again gradually deteriorated as we returned to the region which might, not improperly, be termed infernal. Once more we passed through the foul vapours and the army of miners, engaged on the work of enlargement. Laborious as the work of these men undoubtedly was, it was lighter and far less dangerous than that of our coal-cutters. The heat, although it seemed considerable to one coming from a lower temperature, was not excessive. The miners worked readily enough for their three francs a-day,[9] and took to their labours cheerfully; very few skulkers were seen in the Mont Cenis tunnel. The following table shows how small was the risk to life.

"Fatal accidents which occurred at the Great Tunnel of the Alps from the commencement of the works to Sept. 1871 (French side only):

Inside the Tunnel		*Outside the Tunnel*	
From falls of rock	8	Falls from heights	2
Accidents from waggons	14	From falls of rock	4
Premature explosions	3–25	Explosion of gunpowder	5–11

Total 36

"Nearly one-half of the fatal accidents arose from men being run over by waggons. This chiefly came from the impossibility of making the miners walk on the footways at the sides of the tunnel. They would walk on the rails. The result was that they were not unfrequently killed, although the greatest precautions were taken with the waggons descending with debris. The total is insignificant when one considers the number of men engaged and the length of time over which it was spread, and it compares favourably with almost any other enterprise of similar magnitude.

"The waggons laden with debris ran down, on the French side, by their own weight, on account of the gradient, and so did the truck on which I descended with my guide — the courteous engineer who directed the works. Fresh relays of miners were entering, and those whom they relieved were coming out with their arms around each others' waists 'in the manner of schoolboys and lovers.' The air seemed chilly, although it was a bright summer day; and our nostrils, for hours after leaving the tunnel, yielded such supplies of carbon as to suggest that the manufacture of compressed soot might have been profitably added to the already numerous industries of the works.

"In 1869 about four thousand men were employed on the tunnel,[10] and they completed ten to eleven feet every day. The average daily progress of the preceding five years was ten feet one inch. Each yard of progress cost latterly about £200. The total expenditure amounted to about £3,000,000 (£224 per yard). This sum, however, included the expense of the whole of the machinery and of the exterior works. The amount does not seem extravagant when we remember that for every yard of advance, never less — and frequently more — than seventy cubic yards of rock had to be excavated, and to be carried away (when the work was approaching completion) a distance of three miles; that about twenty-five cubic yards of masonry had to be built, the stone for which was conveyed twelve miles in a mountainous country; that all the machinery employed was constructed and invented expressly for the tunnel, and that the creation of two small towns was necessary.

"The strata which were pierced agreed very satisfactorily in their nature and in their thickness with the indications of the geologists.[11] Remarkably little water was met with: the miner's dreaded enemy seemed to fly before the engineer who utilised its power. I have not entered into a description of the manner in which this was accomplished, because it has been frequently done by others; but there was nothing more interesting in regard to the tunnel than the way in which the waste powers of nature were applied for the reduction of the difficulties of the undertaking. There was not a single steam-engine on the works; everything was done with compressed air, or by hydraulic power.

"Just one half of the tunnel was driven at the end of October 1866, after more than nine years of labour. The third quarter was finished by the end of 1868, and upon the 26th December 1870 the junction of the advanced galleries was successfully effected. The engineers shook hands through a hole made in the centre of the drifts, and then blew away the narrow wall which separated France from Italy.[12]

"Four weeks before this took place, the men who were employed in the advanced gallery on the French side heard distant rumbling sounds, and leaving off work, could distinctly hear their comrades firing blasts in the other gallery. At this time the two parties were about 400 feet distant from each other. As the interval which separated them lessened, so the excitement of the engineers became more and more intense. What if the two ends should not meet! At last the calculated length of the tunnel (12,220 metres) was excavated, but still the galleries did not meet! The two parties knew from the sounds of the shots that they were very close to each other, and they proceeded with the utmost caution. Several trying days of suspense passed before the happy moment arrived, and then it was discovered that there was an error of 44 feet in the calculated length. This did not, however, cause any inconvenience. The work was pressed forward with increased assiduity, and on the 1st of September 1871 the masonry was completed, the rails were laid, and the tunnel was ready for use. It was formally opened on 17th September. The inaugural train of twenty carriages, drawn by two of the largest and most powerful locomotives ever built, conveying 500 gentlemen, who had assembled together by invitation from all parts of Europe, left Turin at 6:30 A.M., and after a run of three hours and three quarters arrived at Bardonnêche. A brief halt was made here, and then the train proceeded through the tunnel to Fourneaux (Modane). The passage through occupied twenty-two minutes. At Modane, a number of distinguished persons entered the train, whose length became increased to twenty-four carriages. This monster train started from Fourneaux to return to Bardonnêche at 12:30 P.M., drawn by two locomotives, and pushed behind by a third one. The return passage of the tunnel occupied forty-two minutes. At Bardonnêche a sumptuous banquet was given, to which about 700 persons sat down; and, after it was over, the company returned to Turin.

"From the first, very little inconvenience was experienced from the imperfect ventilation of the tunnel, and the temperature at its centre was by no means oppressive. In the shade at Bardonnêche, before the first run through was made, the thermometer registered 69° Fahr. The maximum heat in my carriage when passing through was 78°, and a quick-acting mercurial maximum thermometer, which I fixed on the outside of the carriage, registered only 77.1°. The steep gradient on the French side reduced the pace of the train on the return journey, and the thermometer outside the carriage registered 82°. Inside, however, 78° was, as before, the maximum heat.

"It is difficult to apportion the credit of bringing this great work to a successful end amongst those who were engaged upon it. From the commencement to the termination

Grattoni and Sommeiller were at the head of the enterprise, and upon them its chief responsibilities rested. They designed (sometimes separately, but more usually jointly) the whole of the machinery that was employed, and they gained the chief rewards. Grattoni lived to receive the highest honours. His friend and coadjutor Germain Sommeiller, exhausted by work, retired to his birth-place, St. Jeoire en Faucigny, to obtain a little rest. It was taken too late; he succumbed to his labours, and died at the comparatively early age of fifty-six years, on the 11th of July 1871. "If we may believe the companions of his youth," said M. Conte, at the conclusion of the pamphlet from which I have already quoted, "Sommeiller cherished the idea, which we now realise, at the time he was studying at the University of Turin. This idea he never abandoned." Englishmen ought to be amongst the first to recognise his boldness and perseverance, although they played no part in the execution of the tunnel. It is the grandest conception of its kind; it must always be one of the highways of Europe and it has become an important portion of the high road to India.

Note Upon the Present Temperature of the Mont Cenis Tunnel

The lowest temperature observed at the centre of the Tunnel in 1892 was 62.6° Fahr., on February 15, at 1 P.M. At the same time, the temperature at the North (or Modane) mouth was 23° Fahr., and at the South (or Bardonneche) mouth it was 35.6° Fahr.

The highest temperature observed at the centre of the Tunnel in 1892 was 73.4° Fahr., on October 15, at 1 P.M.; and, at the same time, the temperature at the North mouth was 50°, and at the South mouth was 53.6° Fahr.

This information was supplied by Signor F. Cornetti (Strade Ferrate del Mediterraneo), who says that there is no sensible variation in temperature at the centre of the tunnel in any twenty-four hours, whatever fluctuations may occur at the mouths. Thus, on the 15th December 1892, temperature at the Bardonneche mouth ranged from 26.6° to 44.6° Fahr., and at the Modane mouth from 24.8° to 26.6° Fahr., yet in the centre of the tunnel it remained constant at 64.4° Fahr.

It would appear that the rock at the centre has cooled very considerably in the twenty-one years which have elapsed since the opening of the tunnel.

Further Reading

Beyond the several articles cited in the text, the following full-length books cited below are pertinent to the narrative.

Bain, David Haward. *Empire Express: Building the First Transcontinental Railroad.* New York: Penguin, 1999.

Brown, Dee Alexander. *Hear That Lonesome Whistle Blow: Railroads in the West.* New York: Holt, Rinehart & Winston, 1977.

Buchanan, Lamont. *Steel Rails and Iron Horses: A Pageant of American Railroading.* New York: Putnam's, 1905.

Byron, Carl R. *A Pinprick of Light: The Troy and Greenfield Railroad and Its Hoosac Tunnel.* Shelburne, VT: New England Press, 1995.

Griswold, Wesley S. *A Work of Giants; Building the First Transcontinental Railroad.* New York: McGraw-Hill, 1962.

Holbrook, Stewart H. *The Story of American Railroads.* New York: Crown, 1947.

Hunter, Robert F., and Edwin L. Dooley, Jr. *Claudius Crozet: French Engineer in America, 1790–1864.* Charlottesville: University of Virginia Press, 1989.

Kaplan, Diane E., and William E. Brown. *Guide to the Herman Haupt Papers.* New Haven: Yale University Library, 2007.

Kerr, Ronald Dale. *The Rail Lines of Southern New England: A Handbook of Railroad History.* Pepperell, MA: Branch Line Press, 1995.

Lavallée, Omer. *Van Horne's Road.* Montreal: Railfare, 1974.

Malone, Michael P. *James J. Hill: Empire Builder of the Northwest.* Norman: University of Oklahoma Press, 1996.

Martin, Albro. *James J. Hill and the Opening of the Northwest.* New York: Oxford University Press, 1976.

Roe, JoAnn. *Stevens Pass: The Story of Railroading and Recreation in the North Cascades.* Seattle: Mountaineers, 1995.

Shanly, Walter, Francis Shanly, and Frank Norman Walker. *Daylight Through the Mountain: The Life and Letters of Walter and Francis Shanly.* Montreal: Engineering Institute of Canada, 1957.

Vance, James E., Jr. *The North American Railroad: Its Origin, Evolution and Geography.* Baltimore: Johns Hopkins University Press, 1995.

Wheelwright, William B., and Sumner Kean. *The Lengthened Shadow of One Man.* Fitchburg, MA: Crocker, Burbank, 1957. (This is a sequel to and expansion of Wheelwright's *The Life and Times of Alvah Crocker.*)

The Longest Railroad Tunnels in North America

Blue Ridge	1858–1874	4,263 ft.	(1,299 m.)
Hoosac	1874–1916	25,031 ft.	(7,629 m.)
Connaught	1916–1928	26,516 ft.	(8,082 m.)
Moffat	1928–1929	32,736 ft.	(9,978 m.)
Cascade #2	1929–1988	41,184 ft.	(12,542 m.)
Macdonald	1988	48,228 ft.	(14,700 m.)

Chapter Notes

Introduction

1. Lamont Buchanan, *Steel Rails and Iron Horses: A Pageant of American Railroading* (New York: Putnam's, 1905), 76.
2. E.M. Douglas, USGS Bulletin 817, Boundaries, areas, geographic centers, and altitudes of the United States and the several states, with a brief record of important changes in their territory and government (Government Printing Office, 1930).
3. Joseph Nielson, *Memoirs of Rufus Choate: With Some Consideration of His Studies, Methods, and Opinions, and of His Style as a Speaker and Writer* (Boston: Houghton Mifflin, 1884).
4. E.M. Douglas, USGS Bulletin 817, Boundaries, areas, geographic centers, and altitudes of the United States and the several states, with a brief record of important changes in their territory and government (Government Printing Office, 1930).
5. Ibid.

Chapter 1

1. Aubrey de Sélincourt, trans., *Herodotus: The Histories* (New York: Penguin, 1972), 178.
2. Joint Special Committee on Troy and Greenfield Railroad Company, *Report on the Hoosac Tunnel and Troy and Greenfield Railroad, 1866* (Boston: Wright & Potter, 1867), 36ff.

Chapter 3

1. Colson Whitehead, *John Henry Days* (Harpswell, ME: Anchor, 2002), prologue.
2. Collection of the Albemarle County Historical Society (Albemarle, VA).
3. Ibid.
4. Ibid.

Chapter 4

1. James E. Vance, Jr., *The North American Railroad: Its Origin, Evolution and Geography* (Baltimore: Johns Hopkins University Press, 1995), 61.
2. Ibid., 62–63.
3. William Gladden, *Scribner's Magazine*, December 1870.
4. William B. Wheelwright and Sumner Kean, *The Lengthened Shadow of One Man* (Fitchburg, MA: Crocker, Burbank, 1957), 114.
5. Gladden: "Some of Crocker's associates in the Bay State Congressional delegation also acquired significant names for themselves. Benjamin F. Butler (1818–1893), a Civil War political general

who later became governor of Massachusetts, remains known in Louisiana lore as "Beast" Butler for his rigorous enforcement of occupation regulations and was one of the house managers of the impeachment proceedings against Andrew Johnson in 1868. Oakes Ames (1804–1873) remains in American history books as an ongoing symbol of the widespread corruption and looting of the federal treasury that occurred during the Grant Administrations in connection with the construction of the Union Pacific Railroad. Nathaniel Banks (1816–1894) of Waltham had already been governor of Massachusetts and then served an active role in the Civil War; he had been elected Speaker of the 34th Congress and was in and out of the congress, as well as Massachusetts, for the rest of his life. Ginery Twitchell (1811–1883), a native of Athol, migrated into railroads after he left the Congress in 1872, and served as president of the mostly New England–owned Atchison, Topeka & Santa Fe, and other lines. George Brooks (1826–1904) served another term in Congress and was then appointed to the sinecure of a judge of probate. George Hoar (1816–1903) waged a lonesome fight to bring some national standards into public education, and stayed in the Congress long enough to be named a reliably Republican member of the special Electoral Commission of 1877 that seated Rutherford Birchard Hayes as president in place of the popularly-elected Samuel Jones Tilden. Henry Laurens Dawes (1816–1903) of Pittsfield was elected to the 35th and eight succeeding Congresses, and in 1875 succeeded Washburn in the United States Senate, where he stayed until 1893."

6. Ibid.
7. Edward Rice Ardery, "Herman Haupt Tunneling the Hoosac," *Practice Periodical on Structural Design and Construction* 12, no. 2 (2007):61.
8. Edward Chase Kirkland, *Men, Cities and Transportation: A Study in New England History, 1820–1900, Volume 1* (Cambridge, MA: Harvard University Press, 1948), 407.
9. Ardery, "Herman Haupt," 64.
10. Ibid., 63.

Chapter 5

1. Walter Shanly, Francis Shanly, and Frank Norman Walker, *Daylight Through the Mountain: The Life and Letters of Walter and Francis Shanly* (Montreal: Engineering Institute of Canada, 1957).
2. Gladden, *Scribner's.*
3. William B. Wheelwright and Sumner Kean, *The Lengthened Shadow of One Man* (Fitchburg, MA: Crocker, Burbank, 1957).
4. Ibid.
5. Ibid.
6. Greenfield *Gazette*, 4 January, 1875.
7. Walter Shanly, Francis Shanly, and Frank Norman Walker, *Daylight Through the Mountain: The Life and Letters of Walter and Francis Shanly* (Montreal: Engineering Institute of Canada, 1957), 46ff.
8. Ibid.
9. Ibid., 50.

Chapter 6

1. Marcus Mills Pomeroy, *Reminiscences and Recollections of "Brick" Pomeroy: A True Story for Boys and Girls of Any Age* (New York: Advance Thought, 1890), 253–266.

Chapter 7

1. Samuel Bowles, *Our New West* (New York: Hartford Publishing, 1869), pp. 56–57.
2. Dee Alexander Brown, *Hear That Lonesome Whistle Blow: The Epic Story of the Transcontinental Railroads* (New York: Henry Holt, 2001), 111.

3. James J. Hill, *Empire Builder of the Northwest* (Norman: University of Oklahoma Press, 1996), 147.
4. Edgar A. Haine, *Railroad Wrecks* (New York: Cornwall Books, 1993), 74.
5. Vance, *North American Railroad*, 214–215.

Chapter 8

1. Stephen E. Ambrose, *Nothing Like It in the World: The Men Who Built the Transcontinental Railroad, 1863–1869* (New York: Simon & Schuster, 2000), 235.
2. Wesley S. Griswold, *A Work of Giants: Building the First Transcontinental Railroad* (New York: McGraw-Hill, 1962), 194.

Chapter 9

1. Lawrence J. Burpee, *Sandford Fleming: Empire Builder* (New York: Oxford University Press, 1915), 134.
2. Ibid.

Chapter 10

1. Omer Lavallée, *Van Horne's Road: The Building of the Canadian Pacific Railway* (Montreal: Railfare, 1974).

Appendix

1. M. Conte, a well-known French engineer, was a member of a commission appointed to examine the progress of this tunnel in 1863. His report is one of the most accurate and complete accounts of it that have been published.
2. M. Conte refers to tunnel-shafts.
3. The Victor Emmanuel Railway Company no longer exists. The section in France was joined to the Paris, Lyons, and Mediterranean Railway, and that in Italy to the Alta Italia system.
4. The summit is a few feet higher than M. Conte states, as the gradients were increased. The length of the tunnel also is slightly greater than that mentioned above. The calculated length was 13,641 yards (12,220 meters). The actual length, excluding the small curved tunnels at its ends, is 13,379 yards. Its total length, including the curved tunnels, is 14,051 yards, or 8 miles, all but 85 feet.
5. The *preforatrices* were independent machines, and one could be stopped or removed without arresting the progress of the others.
6. In 1863, on the French side, in order to advance one meter, 103 holes, 34 inches deep were bored; 125 pounds of powder and 200 meters of match were consumed; and 158 drills were used up.
7. The temperature was raised to 80° or 86° after the mines were exploded.
8. One chef; 4 machinists; 2 master miners, who determined the direction of the holes; 8 laborers, who guided the boring rods; 9 workmen, who looked after the *perforatrices;* 5 boys; 8 laborers; 2 workmen, who kept up communication with the exterior — in all, 39 persons.
9. The workmen in the advanced gallery received five francs a day and a small bonus per meter if they exceeded a certain fixed distance.
10. On the French side they were employed as follows (subdivisions are omitted for the sake of brevity):

(1) In the Advanced Gallery

Ajusteurs	13
Miners	14
Labourers	140
Boys	13
Total	**180**

(2) Enlargement by Manual Labour

Miners	510
Labourers	180
Boys	30
Total	**720**
Masonry	
Masons and Dressers of Stone	58
Labourers	170
Boys	52
Total	**280**

(3) Manufactories, Machinery, Stores (Exterior Works)

Smiths, Joiners, Fitters, etc.	120
Labourers	440
Boys	10
Total	**570**

(4) Overseers, Foremen, Clerks, etc. 60

(5) Platelayers, Transport of Materials, etc. 180

Total 1990

Horse Power of Machines

Hydraulic Wheels	480
Ventilating Machines	300
Sundry	80
Total Horse-Power of Machinery	860
Horses Employed in Clearing Away Debris	80

11. Table of the strata, commencing from the French side:

	Metres		*Thickness of the Strata in Metres*
1. Debris from	0	128	128.00
2. Anthracitic schists	128.00	2095.35	1967.35
3. Quartzite	2095.35	2476.75	381.40
4. Anhydrite	2476.75	2696.90	220.15
5. Compact calcareous rock	2696.90	2730.90	34.00
6. Talcose schists	2730.90	2780.20	49.30
7. Compact calcareous rock	2780.20	2802.02	21.82
8. Anhydrite	2802.02	2831.75	29.73
9. Calcareous schists	2831.75	2852.95	21.20
10. Anhydrite	2852.95	2867.15	14.20
11. Calcareous schists	2867.15	3264.00	396.85
12. Anhydrite	3264.00	3334.45	70.45
13. Calcareous schists	3334.45	12,233.55	8899.10

12. Table showing the annual progress of the advanced gallery on each side.

	Bardonnêche	**Modane**		
Year	*Advance Total in Metres*	*Advance Total in Metres*	*Total of the Two Sides per Annum*	*General Total*
		By Manual Labour		
1857	27.28	10.80	38.08	
1858	257.57	201.95	459.52	

Year	**Bardonnêche** *Advance Total in Metres*	**Modane** *Advance Total in Metres*	*Total of the Two Sides per Annum*	*General Total*
		By Manual Labour		
1859	236.35	132.75	362.10	
1860	203.80	139.50	343.30	
1861	193.00	193.00		
1862	243.00	243.00	1646.00	
1861	170.00	170.00		
1862	380.00	380.00		
1863	426.00	376.00	802.00	
1864	621.20	466.65	1087.85	
		By Mechanical Means		
1865	765.30	458.40	1223.70	
1866	812.70	212.29	1024.99	
1867	824.30	687.81	1512.11	
1868	638.60	681.55	1320.15	
1869	827.70	603.75	1431.45	
1870	889.45	745.85	1635.30	10,587.55

Total at Bardonnêche 7080.25
Total at Modane 5153.30
Total of tunnel 12,233.55

Bibliography

Besides consulting innumerable roadside tablets, tourism pamphlets, countless Web sites, and back issues of various newspapers (which are all appropriately cited in the text); in the course of compiling these anecdotes on railroad tunnels, the author (with occasional advice from his wife, grandson, editor and others) looked back into the following list of pertinent literature.

Abdill, George B. *This Was Railroading.* Seattle: Superior, 1957.

Athearn, Robert G. *Rebel of the Rockies.* New Haven: Yale University Press, 1962.

Bain, David Haward. *Empire Express: Building the First Transcontinental Railroad.* New York: Penguin, 1999.

Beebe, Lucius, and Charles Clegg. *Narrow Gauge in the Rockies.* Berkeley: Howell-North, 1958.

Berridge, P. S. A. *Couplings to the Khyber.* Newton Abbot, UK: David & Charles, 1969.

Best, Gerald M. *Snowplow: Clearing Mountain Rails.* Berkeley: Howell-North, 1966.

Bollinger, Edward T., and William Jones, ed. *Rails that Climb: A Narrative History of the Moffat Road.* Golden: Colorado Railroad Museum, 1979.

Borneman, Walter R. *Marshall Pass: Denver and Rio Grande Gateway to the Gunnison Country.* Colorado Springs: Century One, 1980.

Brown, Dee Alexander. *Hear That Lonesome Whistle Blow: Railroads in the West.* New York: Holt, Rinehart & Winston, 1977.

Buchanan, Lamont. *Steel Rails and Iron Horses: A Pageant of American Railroading.* New York: G. P. Putnam Sons, 1905.

Byron, *Carl R. A Pinprick of Light: The Troy and Greenfield Railroad and Its Hoosac Tunnel.* Shelburne, VT: New England Press, 1995.

Chappell, Gordon. *Scenic Line of the World.* Golden: Colorado Railroad Museum, 1970.

Cohen, Stan. *The White Pass and Yukon Route.* Missoula, MT: Pictorial Histories, 1980.

Collias, Joe G. *The Last of Steam.* Berkeley: Howell-North, 1960.

Colorado Rail Annual. Numerous years, 1963–present.

Farrington, S. Kip, Jr. *Railroading from the Head End.* Garden City, NY: Doubleday Doran, 1943.

Ferrell, Mallory Hope. *The Gilpin Gold Train.* Boulder: Pruett, 1970.

Griswold, P. R. *Colorado's Loneliest Railroad: The San Luis Southern.* Boulder: Pruett, 1980.

Griswold, Wesley S. *A Work of Giants; Building the First Transcontinental Railroad*. New York: McGraw-Hill, 1962.
Hauck, Cornelius W. "Narrow Gauge to Central and Silver Plume." *Colorado Rail Annual* 10, 1972.
Helmers, Don. *Historic Alpine Tunnel*. Denver: Sage, 1963.
Holbrook, Stewart H. *The Story of American Railroads*. New York: Crown, 1947.
Hunter, Robert F., and Edwin L. Dooley, Jr. *Claudius Crozet: French Engineer in America, 1790–1864*. Charlottesville: University of Virginia Press, 1989.
Huxtable, Nils. *Classic North American Steam*. Greenwich, CT: Brompton, 1990.
Jensen, Oliver. *Railroads in America*. New York: American Heritage, 1975.
Joint Special Committee on Troy and Greenfield Railroad Company. *Report on the Hoosac Tunnel and Troy and Greenfield Railroad, 1866*. Boston: Wright & Potter, 1867.
Jones, David Laurence. *Famous Name Trains*. Calgary: Fitzhenry & Whiteside, 2006.
Koch, Don. *The Colorado Pass Book*. Boulder: Pruett, 1980.
Lavallée, Omer. *Van Horne's Road*. Montreal: Railfare, 1974.
Malone, Michael P. *James J. Hill: Empire Builder of the Northwest*. Norman: University of Oklahoma Press, 1996.
Martin, Albro. *James J. Hill and the Opening of the Northwest*. New York: Oxford University Press, 1976.
McFarland, Edward M. *Colorado Midland Railway*. Boulder: Pruett, 1980.
Michno, Gregory F. *Encyclopedia of Indian Wars: Western Battles and Skirmishes, 1850–1890*. Missoula, MT: Mountain Press, 2003.
Middleton, William D., George M. Smerk, and Roberta L. Diehl. *Encyclopedia of North American Railroads*. Bloomington: Indiana University Press, 2007.
Miller, Charles. *Lunatic Express*. New York: Macmillan, 1971.
Putnam, William L. *The Great Glacier and its House*. New York: American Alpine Club, 1982.
Reed, Robert C. *Train Wrecks: A Pictorial History of Accidents on the Main Line*. Seattle: Superior, 1968.
Roe, JoAnn. *Stevens Pass: The Story of Railroading and Recreation in the North Cascades*. Seattle: Mountaineers, 1995
Sandström, Gösta. *Tunnels*. New York: Holt, Rinehart & Winston, 1963.
Sanford, Barrie. *Railroading in British Columbia*. Vancouver: Whitecap, 1981.
Smith, Duane A. *Horace Tabor: His Life and the Legend*. Boulder: University Press of Colorado, 1989.
Waitley, Douglas. *The Age of the Mad Dragons*. New York: Beaufort, 1981.
Walker, Frank. *Daylight Through the Mountain*. Toronto: Engineering Institute of Canada, 1957.
Whymper, Edward. *Scrambles Amongst the Alps: In the Years 1860–'69*. 4th ed. London: John Murray, 1893.
Yenne, Bill. *Atlas of North American Railroads*. St. Paul, MN: MBI, 2005.

Index